IN QUEST OF A NEW PSYCHOLOGY

Toward a Redefinition of Humanism

Richard E. Johnson, Ph.D.
Professor of Psychology
University of Regina
Canada

HUMAN SCIENCES PRESS

A Division of Behavioral Publications, Inc.
72 Fifth Avenue
New York

Library of Congress Catalog Number 74-9529

ISBN: 0-87705-212-3

Printed in the United States of America
56789 987654321

Library of Congress Cataloging in Publication Data

Johnson, Richard Eaton, 1929–
    In quest of a new psychology.

    1. Humanistic psychology. I. Title.
[DNLM: 1. Existentialism. 2. Psychology. BF121
J68i]
    BF204.J64   150'.19'2   74-9529

You must take things by storm:
you must thrust intelligence
outside itself by an act of will.

Bergson, *Creative Evolution*

CONTENTS

ACKNOWLEDGMENTS

Grateful acknowledgment is made to the following publishers for permission to reprint selections from the works listed:

Basic Books, Inc., Publishers, New York, for selections from Chapter 1, of *Being in the World: Selected Papers of Ludwig Binswanger*, by Ludwig Binswanger, translated by Jacob Needleman (c) 1963; and for selections from *Psychoanalysis and Daseinsanalysis* by Medard Boss, translated by L. B. Lefebre (c) 1963.

Victor Gollancz, Ltd., London, for selections from *The Meaning of the Creative Act* by N. Berdyaev, translated by Donald A. Lowrie (c) 1955.

Harper and Row Co., New York, for selections from *Being and Having: An Existentialist Diary* by G. Marcel, translated by K. Farrer, (c) 1965.

The Hogarth Press, Ltd., London, for selections from *New Introductory Lectures on Psychoanalysis and Other Works* by S. Freud, translated by J. Strachey (c) 1964 (world rights less U.S. and Canada); and W. W. Norton & Co., New York, for selections from *New Introductory Lectures on Psychoanalysis and Other Works* by S. Freud, translated by J. Strachey (c) 1964 (U.S. and Canada).

The Macmillan Co., London and Basingstoke, for selections from *Creative Evolution* by H. Bergson, translated by Arthur Mitchell (c) 1960; and The Macmillan Co., New York, for selections from *Walden Two* by B. F. Skinner (c) 1948.

Methuen & Co., Ltd., London, for selections from *Existentialism and Humanism* by J. P. Sartre, translated by Philip Mairet (c) 1963.

The Philosophical Library, New York, for selections from *The Creative Mind* by H. Bergson, translated by Mabelle L. Andison (c) 1946.

Princeton University Press, Princeton, N.J., for selections from *Repetition: An Essay in Experimental Psychology* by S. Kierkegaard, translated by Walter Lowrie (c) 1964.

Routledge & Kegan Paul, Ltd., London, for selections from *Phenomenology of Perception* by M. Merleau-Ponty, translated by Colin Smith (c) 1962 (world rights less U.S.); and the Humanities Press, Inc., New York, for selections from *Phenomenology of Perception* by M. Merleau-Ponty, translated by Colin Smith (c) 1962 (U.S.).

chapter 1

INTRODUCTION:
THE NEED FOR A
NEW PSYCHOLOGY OF MAN

There are six definitive volumes on the history of psychology that can be found on the shelves of almost every university library in North America. These exhaustive volumes were compiled and edited by one of the most eminent theoretical scholars in our discipline today.* And this is what he concludes about the science of psychology after a distinguished career of research into all aspects of its history: "Psychology cannot be a coherent science" for "as a 'science' or any kind of coherent discipline devoted to the empirical study of man, psychology has been misconceived"—and "this is no light matter for me to confess after a 30-year career given to exploration of the prospects and conditions for psychology becoming a significant enterprise." But his years of scholarly research convinced him that the end result of this enterprise has been nothing more than a proliferation of "pseudo-knowledge," and that "the

*Sigmund Koch is currently Vice President for Academic Affairs and University Professor, with appointments in psychology and philosophy, at Boston University. See his *Psychology: A study of a science.* New York: McGraw-Hill, 1959–63, 6 vols.

idolatry of science in our age has insured that this phony knowledge be taken seriously by people everywhere—even by sensitive, creative or sophisticated people." He further concludes that the entire "100-year course of 'scientific' psychology can now be seen to be a succession of changing doctrines about *what* to emulate in the natural sciences," and that "each such strategic doctrine was entertained not as conditional upon its cognitive fruits but functioned rather as a security fetish bringing assurance to the psychologist, and hopefully to the world, that he was a scientist."[1] Thus Koch ends his argument committed to the conclusion that after 100 years of experimentation psychology has failed and is lost. It must be discovered anew and established on more meaningful philosophical foundations if it is to survive. He points us in our search for these new human foundations toward the existential realities of "fear, trembling, loneliness, discipline, gallantry, humor . . ."[2] and it is from this perspective and on this existential ground that we begin our quest for a new psychology of man.

Now it is generally agreed that psychologists who do explore these existential dimensions of personality discover many unique and remarkable facts about the nature of man and his world. Still, these same basic existential facts are rejected by the science of psychology as distortions or even illusions because they cannot be measured by standard "scientific" methods and do not fit recognized "scientific" laws. Thus it first seems that we are confronted with a forced choice between two radical and contradictory alternatives. It first appears that we must *either* submit in the name of science *or* rebel in the name of existentialism. But on closer examination we find that the real choice is not actually between science and existentialism at all. The only real either/or that confronts us is the choice between psychology as a physical science and psychology as a human science. And we further discover, once the philosophical error that caused this initial confusion has been corrected, that our existential research does not lead us to distorted facts and false conclusions. Instead, the closer examination presented in the text demonstrates that it is those very methods and laws of psychology, which claim to measure and validate facts, that are themselves the illusions. And today these artificial "methods" and "laws" are a far greater threat to human dignity and freedom than the more widely acknowledged dangers posed by physical and medical technology. And the gravity of their threat makes it incumbent on us all to expose and challenge this academic and professional myth that psychology ever has been or ever can become a physical science.

I agree that such a direct attack on an established social institution might have seemed a vain and futile one several years ago. Yet by now the failure of psychology to provide meaningful answers to human problems has become so obvious as to make our challenge almost commonplace. But still psychology holds fast to a blind faith in its own arid dogmas and refuses to question its own sterile philosophical assumptions. And so it follows that this new controversial discipline will remain only a barren wasteland as long as those in control of our academic and professional institutions continue to insist that psychology *is* and *must be* a physical science.

My own rejection of psychology as a physical science stems from my years of professional work as a psychotherapist. I discovered from those countless hours of critical human experience that man is something much more profound than a complex animal or machine. I defended that discovery with theoretical arguments and documented excerpts in an earlier book entitled *Existential Man*. I tried in that book to relate some of the "unique and remarkable" facts which we encounter in the process of psychotherapy to a larger body of existential philosophy. Now I have tried in the present book to ground these experiences and that body of philosophy in a new heuristic model for psychology. Such a new scientific paradigm has become essential to the development of our discipline because the growing number of humanistic books, such as *Existential Man*, forces us to recognize the acute need for a scientific base that can ground and guide the development of these modern approaches. And the only meaningful base for such a new psychological paradigm is that body of insights given to us by those scientists and philosophers who fall within the historical framework now described as "existentialism." Consequently, the contrast has been made throughout the text between general psychology and this new paradigm for a human science, which we have termed *existential science*.

This need for a new theoretical paradigm in psychology has become critical to all students and practitioners who want to further their own humanistic work and to defend their own humanistic stance in academic and professional institutions. Anyone who tries to do something new in our moribund educational and psychological institutions is always under constant pressure to defend his innovative approach in formal scientific terms. And one aim of the present book is to provide a theoretical base for just such a formal defense of these new humanistic approaches. The book presents a scientific rationale for the humanistic point of view on every issue in psychology from the self to psychophysics—and in this respect it can be considered a kind of "dictionary" of humanistic terms. We also discover from these existential definitions that it is no longer necessary to view psychological events from a rational-empirical perspective in order to be "scientific" but that, conversely, we are actively engaged in the scientific process only to the extent that we view psychological events as humanistic-existential phenomena in their own right. A concrete example may make the distinction between these two scientific models and these two theoretical perspectives more succinct.

One of the unique and remarkable facts that we discover as we study the existential nature of man is the creative reality of the human will. Yet freedom and will are meaningless illusions in the rational-empirical model of psychology as a physical science. And, moreover, the model of existential science presented here does not merely recognize freedom as one isolated human construct. Instead, existential science goes much further and posits freedom and creation at the heart of life and evolution itself. Thus the introduction of this new existential model of science turns psychology upside down and, in doing that, turns humanity right side up. Existential science gives us a new definition and a new meaning for every traditional concept in psychology. The existential "revolution" thereby turns the science of psychology in a new direction and points it toward new human goals and new human horizons.

Psychology must be turned upside down and pointed in a new direction because today it is dominated by two scientific models of material determinism: psychoanalysis and behaviorism. These two theoretical models are like "palaces on a hill" alienated from the everyday reality of concrete human experience. And we quickly discover the bare fact that these academic and professional "castles" are but empty cardboard silhouettes as soon as we take a closer look and examine them in some detail. The philosophical intent of these cardboard approaches to modern psychology is best expressed in Skinner's technology of human behavior that simply pushes man "beyond freedom and dignity" in order to relieve him of his onerous struggle with existence. The same reductive formula is the essence of Freud's psychoanalytic solution since he asserts that "the moment one inquires about the sense or value of life one is sick . . . only admitting a surplus of unsatisfied libido."[3] These two scientific models of material determinism dominate contemporary academic and professional psychology, and their common motivational assumption can easily be traced in the history of philosophy back from Democritus and Epicurus, down through Bacon and Hobbes, to Darwin, Freud, and Skinner. This basic philosophical assumption is that all human experience and behavior is determined by two complementary and interdependent factors: hedonism and adaptation. The general purpose of this book is to demonstrate that neither pleasure nor adjustment are adequate motivational assumptions for psychological science, since the biological roots of man are grounded in existential freedom and creation.

Today many of us in psychology who want to study these existential roots of man have already rejected the sterile philosophies of material determinism that dominate the field. Now we are beginning to look for something more than is available within the narrow confines of our own discipline. We are beginning to break down the rigid methodological boundaries that have blocked us from research into meaningful human experience. We are even beginning to see, through the existential cracks in these walls, something of the deeper existential forces that motivate man and society. And we are even beginning to develop new methods and techniques that will enable us both to study and to activate these dynamic human potentials. The specific purpose of this book, therefore, is to present a philosophy of science which can serve as a guide in our efforts to develop and implement these new humanistic approaches to psychology.

The need for such a guide has become more and more evident as the term "humanistic psychology" has become more popular—but more ambiguous at the same time. Even psychological approaches based on philosophical positions against which existentialism first rebelled have been lumped into the same amorphous category of humanistic psychology: Skinner claims that Behavior therapy (philosophical empiricism) is a humanism, Ellis claims that Rational therapy (philosophical rationalism) is a humanism, etc.

There are also, at the other psychological extreme, some modern approaches that seem to border more on mysticism and the occult (e.g., parapsychology, psychotronics, etc.), which could not be included in any new model of psychology as a human science.* Thus it becomes obvious that there can be no meaning to the term "humanistic psychology," and consequently no method by which to defend humanism as a formal psychological discipline, so long as it continues to be distorted and perverted by professionals and laymen alike.

The technical definition of humanism is "a mode or attitude of thought or action centering upon distinctively human interests or ideals."[4] But the accumulated associations and connotations that have grown up around the word now equate it with almost any mode or attitude that could be judged, by almost any standard, to have some social merit. The confusion that now permeates the term has become so widespread that the concept can never be clarified by any simple debate between one or another of the factions who all claim to be humanists. Yet a definition of humanistic psychology must be developed, and clear distinctions and differentiations must be made, if humanism is to become a legitimate psychological enterprise. And the only decisive way to make such distinctions and differentiations is to develop a scientific model upon which the new psychological humanism can be built. So it is imperative that we ground humanism on such a model of

---

*The scientific future of the entire psychical research movement has been jeopardized by the recent resignation of Dr. Walter J. Levy, Jr., Director of Dr. Joseph B. Rhine's Institute for Parapsychology in Durham, N.C., after he was exposed and confessed to "rigging" experiments to get positive results on research into psychokinesis and extrasensory perception. Such fraud and deception by the Director of what had been, heretofore, the most scientifically respected of all the many and varied centers for psychical research supports those critics who claim that all positive results reported by parapsychologists are due to fraudulent procedures that are either blatant or subtle, intentional or accidental. (*Time*, [Science, August 26, 1974] New York: Time, Inc.)

existential science *now.* Otherwise, we run the risk that its promise will sink into the ambiguity that surrounds it and be dissolved by stronger social currents. Then humanistic psychology will be remembered only as a loose and meaningless fad that "reached its peak sometime in the sixties or seventies."

Still, I realize that those of us who find great satisfaction in our "work with people" sometimes tend to reject detailed theoretical arguments as being of little significance or interest. But it does seem clear that humanistic psychology will soon fade and dissolve unless we do take the time and effort to develop a scientific base that can sustain it. So is it also clear that humanistic psychology will continue to be excluded from academic and professional institutions until such a theoretical model has been established. And this exclusion from psychological institutions has serious practical consequences to the extent that it limits the potential impact humanism might otherwise have on the future evolution of society and man.

But the aim of a scientific rationale for humanism is not merely to defend ourselves within the politics of academic and professional institutions. We need a model of human science so that our daily efforts to provide practical social services can be grounded in a deeper and more profound concept of life. This deeper concept of life, in turn, gives us new insights into the nature of personality that can help us develop new techniques which will better facilitate human growth. Psychology as a physical science forces us out of this subjective involvement in human services in order to objectify behavior so that it can be predicted and controlled. But psychology as an existential science drives us deeper into subjective reality so that we can describe it, encompass it, and make it our own. Psychology as a human science does not ask us to cloister ourselves within the synthetic security of animal laboratories and normal distributions. It does not train us to objectify ourselves and others by an endless series of intellectual measurements and calculations. On the contrary, psychology as an existential science demands that we risk our personal being in a violent thrust down into the "flux and fire" of life. It is only at such emotional depths that we break through the intellectual symbols of scientism and grasp existence with the passion of our hearts. Psychology as an existential science demands that the methods and approaches we use to study man be as ardent and sensitive as the human subject matter which we seek to discover and understand.

I stated earlier that my specific purpose here is to present an outline for this new research model, and in so doing, to provide a theoretical rationale to help guide the future development of existential and humanistic approaches to psychology. The particular model proposed is based on a reconciliation of the metaphysics of existential philosophers such as Kierkegaard, Berdyaev, and Marcel with the metaphysics of scientific philosophers such as Bergson, Whitehead, and Teilhard de Chardin. This rapprochement between existentialism and science then leads us to a humanistic method and a humanistic model that better fits the subject matter of psychology than those traditional methods and models from the physical sciences which it has tried to emulate.

The presentation of this new scientific paradigm has been divided into five sections. The first section (History) gives the philosophical background of the perennial controversy between determinism and freedom that underlies the modern controversy between psychology as a physical science and psychology as a human science. The second section (Biology) contrasts the biological model of mechanism that is at the base of psychology as a physical science with the biological model of vitalism that is at the base of psychology as a human science. The third section (Ontology) contrasts the ontological assumption of general psychology that reduces psychological events to objects in space with the ontological premise of existential psychology that studies human events as processes in time. The fourth section (Methodology) contrasts the method of intellectual analysis used by general psychology with the method of intellectual "sympathy" or intuition used by existential science. The fifth and last section (Anthropology) contrasts pressure morality with aspiration morality and a closed society with an open society.

It is obvious just from the statement of these radical contrasts that there can be no simplistic rational or empirical solution to the perennial philosophical problem that underlies these critical alternatives. The debate about man and his nature has persisted down through the history of ideas and still the original controversy is as intractable today as when it was first formulated more than 25 centuries ago. But now this perennial philosophical debate has become a decisive "battle" in psychology which forces those of us in the discipline to make an either/or choice between psychology as a physical science and psychology as a human science. So it is incumbent on today's students and practitioners who will make tomorrow's psychology in their own image to choose between a philosophy of determinism or freedom, a biology of mechanism or vitalism, an ontology of space or time, a methodology of analysis or intuition, a morality of pressure or aspiration, and between a closed or an open society. We cannot wait for any external answer from "philosophy" or "science" because these disciplines, like psychology, are only what we ourselves decide to make them. We cannot wait for any external answer to this intractable philosophical problem because *there is none.* We are confronted with an either/or in psychology to which each of us must respond. We must each choose and create for ourselves the future nature of man and the future nature of his world.

Those of us who choose existentialism and work to

make psychology into a human science will not be disappointed. The model of existential science presented here will not lead us back to a rigid objectification of psychological theory and practice. Such a model promises, instead, to point us forward toward the development of new theoretical approaches and more effective applied methods and techniques. This heuristic paradigm that we have used to point psychology toward new goals and new horizons is based primarily on the work of a philosopher/scientist named Henri Bergson. I focused specifically on Bergson's work because his insights and his discoveries are the most original as well as the most historically significant in this new field of existential science. I have tried to make the basic tenets of his philosophy directly relevant to contemporary issues in psychology and readily available to all those persons concerned about the modern crisis in human and social evolution. The relevance and importance of Bergson's work for the future of psychology and man is embodied in the passionate tribute that *Creative Evolution* elicited from William James:

> O my Bergson, you are a magician, and your book is a marvel, a real wonder in the history of philosophy, making, if I mistake not, an entirely new era . . .
>
> As to the content of it . . . There is so much that is absolutely new that it will take a long time for your contemporaries to assimilate it . . . To me at present the vital achievement of the book is that it inflicts an irrecoverable death-wound upon Intellectualism. It can never resuscitate! But it will die hard, for all the inertia of the past is in it, and the spirit of professionalism and pedantry as well as the aesthetic-intellectual delight of dealing with categories logically distinct yet logically connected, will rally for a desperate defense. The *élan vital*, all contentless and vague as you are obliged to leave it, will be an easy substitute to make fun of. But the beast *has* its death-wound now, and the manner in which you have inflicted it is masterly in the extreme. . . . Altogether, the clash of these ideas of yours with the traditional ones will

be sure to make sparks fly that will illuminate all sorts of dark places and bring innumerable new considerations into view. . . . "I thank heaven that I have lived to this date . . . and seen Bergson's new book appear."[5]

Part I

HISTORY

chapter 2

THE EVOLUTION OF DETERMINISM FROM DEMOCRITUS TO SKINNER

It is a fact that everything began with the Greeks whether we like it or not. So it is with general psychology and existential science. All of the former can be traced back to the material determinism of Democritus: "In reality there is nothing but atoms and space." All of the latter can be traced back to the spiritual vitalism of Heraclitus: "In reality there is nothing but flux and fire." I want to begin with scant outlines of these two historical trends to provide a framework within which to discuss contemporary issues. So let us start with Democritus and follow the evolution of determinism down through the history of ideas.

Atomistic theory arose out of a logical controversy over the reality of space. Parmenides asserted that space did not exist because it could not be said that *nothing* is something. He concluded that there could be no motion because there was no space in which to move. The atomists argued that something which is not material *could* exist, and described space as a receptacle in which objects move. The latter argument led to the recognition of space and the possibility of motion. Reality could now be reduced to the motion of atoms in space. The theory constructed a mechanical model of the universe with no need for purpose or design since everything was the accidental result of atoms in motion. Nor was there any need to explain the origin of this motion because the pursuit of first causes always ends in infinite regression. They argued that it was just as reasonable to start with atoms as to start with gods.

Democritus is of particular interest to psychologists because he went beyond a description of nature into the problems of human knowledge and human conduct. He applied his mechanical model of the universe to mental processes and explained thought as a function of atoms in motion. We perceive something when the eyes absorb an image formed by atoms radiating from the object viewed. The eyes are channels through which these atomic images enter the body and make an impact on an internal cluster of atoms called the "soul." Sensation and thought are but the movement of atoms caused by these physical and mechanical processes. So did he use the same mechanical model to develop rules of conduct which one should adopt in order to attain the ideal state of "cheerfulness."*

It follows that the materialism of Democritus would directly influence a philosopher whose life was devoted to the same goal of "cheerfulness." Epicurus was a practical philosopher who believed that ideas should control life the way medicine controls the body. He began with the atomist description of reality and derived a code of human conduct from it. He argued that since man was the accidental product of the collision of atoms there could be no moral guide other than the fact that "we recognize pleasure as the first good innate in us, and from pleasure we begin every act of choice and avoidance, and to pleasure we return." Still, the modern connotation of his name is inappropriate, for he insisted that ethical hedonism be based on calculated dis-

*Democritus was known as the "laughing philosopher."

tinctions between different types of pleasure and calculated measures to ensure balanced satisfaction or "repose." He put the warning in his own words:

> When, therefore, we maintain that pleasure is the end, we do not mean the pleasures of the profligates and those that consist in sensuality, as is supposed by some who are either ignorant or disagree with us or do not understand, but freedom from pain in the body and from trouble in the mind. For it is not continuous drinking and revelings, nor the satisfaction of lusts, nor the enjoyment of fish and other luxuries of the wealthy table, which produces a pleasant life, but sober reasoning, searching out the motives for all choice and avoidance, and banishing mere opinions, to which are due the greatest disturbance of the spirit.[1]

We are forced to acknowledge the wonder of the Greeks when we realize that it is only 300 B.C. and already we have a science and an ethics for modern psychology. Today behaviorism is the dominant influence in academic-professional psychology* and it embodies both the material determinism of Democritus and the ethical hedonism of Epicurus.

The atomistic theory declined in significance after Aristotle and during the Middle Ages but the postulate of Democritus had only begun to shape the destiny of man. Its critical impact on civilization erupted with the birth of modern science in the Renaissance. Suddenly observation and mathematics began to produce dramatic results. Copernicus confronted man with a new view of the universe and Galileo confirmed it. Gilbert applied atomistic theory to magnetism and electricity. Boyle introduced the new method into chemistry. Then Harvey discovered the circu-

---

*See: American Psychological Association. *Graduate study in psychology for 1973–74.* Educational Affairs Office: Washington, D.C., 1972. Examples from behaviorism will be used at points in the text because behaviorism is the dominant trend in contemporary psychology, and because it best represents the goal of psychology to become a physical science—a goal held even by psychologists who do not consider themselves formal behaviorists.

lation of the blood. Leeuwenhoek discovered bacteria.
Newton discovered the laws of gravity. Leibnitz invented
the differential and integral calculus. All these revolutionary developments in science and mathematics forced philosophy to the conclusion that at last the basic processes of
nature could be observed and measured. Now there was
"proof" for the postulate of Democritus. Everything consists of atoms in space and everything conforms to a mechanical model. Now both the universe and man could be
explained by mechanical laws and the concept of free will
as the basis of human choice and behavior was obsolete.

The philosophical spokesman for this new scientific
attitude was Francis Bacon. He asserted that "chance" and
"fortune" in a determined universe are "names of things
that do not exist ... names which result from fantastic
suppositions and to which nothing in reality corresponds."[2] He then rejected freedom and will in man as
"things that do not exist" on the grounds that they were
analogous in the mechanics of human affairs to chance and
fortune in the mechanics of a determined universe. Bacon
considered knowledge only in terms of its practical
"power," and so he rejected all traditional philosophy as
"useless" and as nothing but superstition, speculation, and
theology. It is relevant to our presentation that he respected Democritus and adopted his materialism but rejected the work of all other philosophers as mere fantasy
and illusion. Bacon's goal was to wipe clean this slate of
"meaningless" philosophy and start over with a total reconstruction of all the sciences and arts, as well as of all
human knowledge itself. His basic contribution to this complete reorganization of knowledge was not his own scientific work but his eloquent defense of a new philosophical
attitude. Bacon is historically important because he recognized the coming of a new age and was its philosophical
champion.

Bacon communicated this modern philosophical attitude in three phases. He told us what science was not, what science was, and what we could expect from science. He first described procedural errors that had characterized traditional philosophy and that must be eliminated in order to transform philosophy into a meaningful science. He labeled these errors the idols of the mind and listed four of them. The first idols that must be destroyed were the idols of the theatre. These were the traditional systems and theories that were "but so many stage plays"[3] which had become intellectual and philosophical conventions. They distort the nature of inquiry from the beginning so that the further one goes in these misguided directions the more unrealistic and bizarre becomes the drama that he produces. The most troublesome of the idols were the idols of the marketplace. These were the distortions caused by errors in the everyday usage of commonsense language. Words are used either to describe events that have no scientific reality or to confuse and render useless the investigation of actual events. These errors of language were said to account for the endless number of pseudo problems and controversies that characterize philosophy. The other two types of errors are due to biases and prejudices of the individual or of the group. The former are termed idols of the cave and include all the subjective preferences of any particular investigator. These subjective inclinations must be discounted by the scientist and may result from specific reading materials, authority figures, personal experiences, etc. The last obstacles to science are termed the idols of the tribe and go deeper than errors of the individual, since they seem to be ingrained in human nature itself. These fallacies include the tendency to oversimplification and overgeneralization as well as the appeal to final causes.

The next phase of Bacon's contribution was his description of a method of investigation that would eliminate these errors of traditional philosophy and produce a new kind of scientific knowledge. He called the new empirical method "induction" to contrast it with the traditional method of deductive reasoning from established premises. He argued that the proper systematic arrangement of observed facts would lead to discovery of the basic laws or *forms* of nature. He proposed three inductive procedures by which these natural forms could be discovered. The first inductive procedure was to list instances of the occurrence of a quality. These were "positive instances" and the list was called the Table of Presence. The next step was to enumerate instances, as like as possible to those in the first list, in which the quality is always absent. These were "negative instances" and this list was called the Table of Absence in Proximity. The final step was to enumerate instances in which the amount of the quality varied in different objects or varied under changed conditions in the same object. This last list was called the Table of Comparative Instances. Bacon asserted that by use of these three tables he had been able to conclude that heat is present in sun rays, meteors, etc.; it is absent in the moon, northern lights, etc.; and it varies in different parts of the same animal body and in different objects such as ignited coal and wood. He further asserted that he was able to discover by the use of these tables that there is an exact correlation between heat and motion and that heat is "a species" of motion.*

The third and last phase of Bacon's contribution was his description of what man can expect from science. He defined knowledge as "power" and put no limits on the capacity of science to achieve complete control over both nature and man. He sketched this scientific utopia in a brief novel entitled *The New Atlantis*. Some consider it his most significant contribution because he introduced the model

---

*"When I say of motion that it is as the genus of which heat is a species, I would be understood to mean not that heat generates motion or that motion generates heat (though both are true in certain cases), but that heat itself, its essence and quiddity, is motion and nothing else." (Bacon, *The new organon*, p. 157.)

for a social order in which science was master of all things: A ship is lost at sea and the crew is taken ashore and nursed back to health by the people of a village on an uncharted island. The secrets of the village are gradually revealed as the men recuperate from their ordeal at sea. They are told by one of the islanders that "a King, whose memory above all others we most adore . . . was wholly bent to make his kingdom and people happy. . . . amongst the excellent acts of that King, one above all hath the pre-eminence. It was the erection and institution of the Order or Society which we call Salomon's House, the noblest foundation (as we think) that ever was upon the earth, and the lanthorn* of this kingdom."[4] Salomon's House is the equivalent of Congress or Parliament but with one exception—its members are not elected politicians who engage in debate but selected scientists who engage in research. The goal of the Order is to discover "the knowledge of Causes and secret motions of things, and the enlarging of the bounds of Human Empire, to the effecting of all things possible."[5] Some of the rulers in the House of Salomon engage in research suggestive of modern anatomy, geology, chemistry, economics, psychology, sociology, etc. Others go abroad and live for periods of time in the cultural centers of the world in order to bring back reports of new advances in science and technology to the leaders of Salomon's House. This utopia represented Bacon's ultimate tribute to the power of science and his ultimate faith in the capacity of his inductive method to solve all the problems which confront mankind.

Bacon embodied the scientific spirit of the times. So also did Thomas Hobbes. Hobbes was a contemporary of Bacon but a younger man. He served as a junior apprentice to Bacon for a number of years, taking dictation and translating Bacon's *Essays* into Latin. But Hobbes was not as devoted to induction as his master and insisted that mathe-

*lantern

matics and deduction were essential to the new development of science. Consequently, he undertook his own
reorganization of all knowledge based on observation and
on logical and mathematical deductions from axioms discovered by that observation. He argued that physical bodies were the only reality that could be directly observed and
that their principle characteristic was motion. He then followed the "atoms and space" postulate to its logical conclusion and explained all physical and mental phenomena
as nothing but "bodies in motion." Hobbes states clearly
that by motion he means movement in space: "Motion is a
continual relinquishing of one place and acquiring of another."[6] Movement is defined as a change in physical loca-
tion and occurs when a body in motion moves a body at rest
"by endeavouring to get into its place."[7]

Hobbes used the same mechanical formula to explain
all physical, mental, and social events. His specific contribution was the application of strict mechanical determinism to these latter two areas of psychology and politics. The
State was the primary mechanical system and individuals
were but components carefully controlled by the ordered
and efficient operation of the machine. Individuals did engage in higher mental processes but these were reduced to
the one common denominator of "bodies in motion." Perception is the basic mental act and all other processes "derive from that original."[8] We first see or "sense" an object
and that external object produces an image within us.
Imagination is the retention of this image within us after
the external object has been removed. Memory is the term
used to indicate the fading or decaying of an image. Thinking itself is but a mirror reflection of sensation because
ideas follow each other in the same sequence as they first
occurred in the original sensory act. Hobbes argues that
"those motions that immediately succeeded one another in
the sense, continue also together after sense" and that "the
latter followeth, by coherence of the matter moved."[9] He

explained that the mirror reflection is not always perfect because sequences are often broken by the intrusion of more dominant sensations, e.g., a particular sequence may arouse a memory that produces a temporary digression from the main theme. Thus Hobbes produced a detailed version of the "atoms and space" postulate that could account for thinking in terms of sensation, and that could reduce *all* psychological and political events to "bodies in motion."

Bacon and Hobbes had succeeded in changing the direction of philosophy and launching it upon its new scientific course. They pointed out procedural deficiencies in traditional approaches to knowledge and they proposed methodological innovations to correct them. Both were radical reformists as well as radical empiricists, and they denounced all the traditional assumptions of philosophy—except one. They did not question the implicit conviction that definite knowledge could be obtained if only the proper method of investigation was used. John Locke and David Hume pushed empiricism further and tried to determine the limits of knowledge itself.

Locke inquired into the "origin, certainty, and extent of human knowledge." He argued that we must first discern the origin of our ideas if we are to establish the nature and the limits of our knowledge. We could not question the validity of knowledge if it was taken to be based on innate principles. Therefore he rejected the philosophical assumption of *innate ideas* and developed an empirical explanation for the acquisition of knowledge. There are no innate ideas and so the mind at birth is a *tabula rasa,* or blank slate. All knowledge can be reduced to sense experiences that are inscribed upon this blank slate and then combined into more complex patterns. The original *simple ideas* can be combined into an endless variety of *complex ideas* but not one single new idea can be created by man because the origin of all knowledge is direct sense experience. Now questions of "certainty and extent" could be considered since the origin of knowledge had first been explained and located in primary sense experience.

Only simple ideas are certain and valid because they are passive imprints upon the mind and not the result of any mental activity. Complex ideas that result from mental reflection are real only to the extent that the combination of simple ideas corresponds to some actual object outside ourselves. Simple ideas are always adequate because they perfectly represent the sense experience that inscribed them on the mind. But knowledge based on complex ideas is always inadequate because complex ideas can never *exactly* reproduce the object in the external world that they try to copy. Thus our knowledge of a thing can be called true or false only to the degree that our complex ideas can be considered an adequate representation of the original object itself. We are forced to conclude that the only certain knowledge is sense experience and that all more complex forms of knowledge have only varying degrees of validity or degrees of probability. Locke warns against the search for any more absolute forms of knowledge because we are "so far from being capable of any such thing, that I conclude it lost labour to seek after it."[10]

Locke limited the extent of our knowledge but David Hume restricts it even more. He does not stop with the rejection of absolute forms of knowledge but goes on to deny even the reality of material substance and the logical necessity of causal connections. We can know only our own sense impressions and this knowledge justifies the assumption neither of substance nor of causality. Ideas are but faint and feeble copies of sense impressions that are linked together in accordance with three laws of association. We associate ideas that resemble one another (Resemblance); that occur in temporal or spatial proximity (Contiguity); or that suggest a cause or effect (Causality). Now empiricism had been pushed to its logical limit. There is no substance and no causality—only ideas in various orders of association.

Empiricism was one term that described the new scientific approach to knowledge; another was positivism. Positivism was a general attitude "of the age," but it found its most detailed and comprehensive expression in the work of Auguste Comte.* Comte divided the history of "the development of human intelligence" into three separate stages and then posited "a great fundamental law . . . that each of our leading conceptions—each branch of our knowledge—passes successively through three different theoretical conditions."[11] The first condition or stage was *theological:* all phenomena were explained in terms of divine intervention. The next stage was *metaphysical:* the same phenomena were now explained in terms of abstract processes and forces. These first two stages are considered similar, since both try to establish one basic energy source to explain nature and both seek an absolute knowledge of the innermost essence of life. The final stage in the progressive development of knowledge is *positivism,* or science. The only goal at this stage is to discover invariable relations between observable events, and all attempts to go beyond sense experience are rejected as lower forms of knowledge. The "principal aim" of positivism was to develop a "Social physics," since Comte was convinced that such a physics was "the only gap which has to be filled, to constitute, solid and entire, the Positive Philosophy."[12] And today this is the same "principal aim" of modern psychology—a "physics" of personality and society.

One more approach to knowledge within the same psychological and philosophical framework of empiricism

*"The name of M. Comte is more identified than any other with this mode of thought. He is the first who has attempted its complete systematization, and the scientific extension of it to all objects of human knowledge." (Mill, J. S. *Auguste Comte and positivism.* In *The collected works of John Stuart Mill.* J. M. Robson (Ed.), London: Routledge & Kegan Paul, 1969, p. 264.)

was the *utilitarianism* of Jeremy Bentham.[†] Bentham tried to develop a scientific and empirical foundation for moral and social justice. He concluded that all ethical judgment and all psychological motivation could be reduced to a philosophical hedonism which he called the principle of utility: "Nature has placed mankind under the governance of two sovereign masters, *pain* and *pleasure.* It is for them alone to point out what we ought to do, as well as determine what we shall do."[13] He argued that the principle of utility did not admit of direct proof. He felt it was demonstrated by the fact that all other ethical and psychological motivation from asceticism to sympathy could be dismissed as pretence and reduced to the principle of utility. This is similar to the psychoanalytic reduction of all ethical and psychological motivation to biological hedonism and the behavioristic reduction of all motivation to the principle of reinforcement. Now John Stuart Mill was a more elegant spokesman for utilitarian philosophy and he rejected the crass hedonism of Bentham for the more refined hedonism of Epicurus. He rejected Bentham's claim that "pushpin is as good as poetry," and tried to develop an ethical model based on the quality of pleasure as well as the quantity.

The historical transition from hedonistic and adaptive utility to the mechanical evolution of Darwin and Spencer was but another variation on the common theme of material determinism. Darwin was convinced early in his career that the theory of biological adaptation through natural selection would eventually "lead to a complete philosophy." And Darwin was equally convinced later in his life that the *Synthetic Philosophy* of Herbert Spencer was that complete system. He called Spencer "our philosopher," and said of him: "I suspect that hereafter he will be looked

[†]Bentham (1748–1832) was a predecessor of Comte (1798–1857) but utilitarianism is introduced in this particular sequence because of its association with and subsequent development by John Stewart Mill (1806–1873).

at as by far the greatest living philosopher in England; perhaps equal to any that have lived."[14] Only Comte's elaborate *Course of Positive Philosophy* could be considered comparable to Spencer's ambitious synthesis of all scientific knowledge. The difference between these two comprehensive systems is more a matter of emphasis than content. Comte classified the sciences according to the decreasing simplicity and generality of their subject matter: mathematics, astronomy, physics, chemistry, biology, and sociology. Each discipline depended on the one that preceded it and the progression advanced towards its apex of sociology as the final science of society.* Spencer showed the same concerns but shifted the emphasis to biology and psychology. He explained everything from the formation of nerves to the development of consciousness as the result of clashes between rival primitive impulses. The "highest manifestations" of human experience can be reduced to the "effects of a complication that has arisen by insensible steps out of the simplest elements."[15] The most complex human processes are but the adaptive resolution of impulse conflicts and the "adjustment of internal relations to external relations."[16] Thus we are brought to the threshold of modern psychology.

Psychoanalysis dominated psychology and psychiatry until recently and is still a major influence. Its reduction of all social and psychological phenomena to impulse conflict is clearly prefigured in the biological model of Darwin and Spencer. Nor can its mechanical determinism or its constricted methodological bias be seriously doubted, for Freud decisively states that

> the intellect and the mind are objects for scientific research in exactly the same way as any non-human things. Psychoanalysis has a special right to speak ... at this point, since it cannot be reproached with having neglected what is men-

*Comte is generally recognized as the "father of sociology."

tal in the picture of the universe. Its contribution to science lies precisely in having extended research to the mental field. And, incidentally, without such a psychology science would be very incomplete. If, however, the investigation of the intellectual and emotional functions of men (and of animals) is included in science, then it will be seen that nothing is altered in the attitude of science as a whole, that no new sources of knowledge or methods of research have come into being. Intuition and divination would be such, if they existed; but they may safely be reckoned as illusions, the fulfilments of wishful impulses. It is easy to see, too, that these demands . . . are only based on emotion. Science takes notice of the fact that the human mind produces these demands and is ready to examine their sources; but it has not the slightest reason to regard them as justified. On the contrary it sees this as a warning carefully to separate from knowledge everything that is illusion and an outcome of emotional demands like these.[17]

Dialogues and letters between Freud and his close personal friend, Ludwig Binswanger, state even more conclusively the *final* position of psychoanalysis, because there Freud speculates on the future of his work if he had "another lifetime" in which to advance it.

Binswanger had given the commemorative address on Freud's eightieth birthday and followed up in that address points which he had tried to make in this excerpt from an earlier private discussion with Freud:

I was about to leave and we were talking about the old days. Soon, however, the conversation turned to that which twenty years ago had brought us together and which, in spite of clear differences of opinion, had held us together, namely his life's work, his "great idea." With respect to a concrete clinical example—a serious case of compulsion neurosis— that had occupied us both a good deal, I threw out the question as to how we were to understand the failure of this patient to take the last decisive step of psychoanalytic insight and to thus continue in his misery in spite of all previous efforts and technical progress. As a contribution to the solution of the problem, I suggested that such a failure might only be understood as the result of something which could be called a deficiency of spirit (*Geistigkeit*), that is, an inability on the part of the patient to raise himself to the level of spiritual communication with the physician. Thus the patient was barred by his own lack from encompassing and overcoming his unconscious instinctual impulses at the last decisive point. I could barely believe my ears when the answer came: "Yes, spirit (*Geist*) is everything." I presumed that by spirit, Freud meant something like intelligence. But then he continued: "*Man has always known he possessed spirit: I had to show him there is such a thing as instinct.* But men are always unsatisfied, they cannot wait, they always want something whole and finished; *but one has to begin somewhere and very slowly move forward.*" Encouraged by this concession, I went a step further, explaining that I found myself forced to recognize in man something like a basic religious category; that, in any case it was impossible for me to admit that "the religious" is somehow and from somewhere a derivative phenomenon. (I was thinking, of course, not of the origin of a particular religion or even of religion in general but of something which I have since learned to call the religious I-thou relation.) But I had stretched the bow of agreement too far and began to feel its resistance. "Religion arises," so Freud declared, quickly and curtly, "out of the helplessness and anxiety of childhood and early manhood. Indisputably." With that he went to the drawer of his desk: "This is the moment for me to show you something," laid before me a finished manuscript that bore the title "The Future of an Illusion," and looked laughingly and questioningly at me. I easily guessed from the situation what the title meant. Meanwhile the moment of farewell had come. Freud accompanied me to the door. His last words, spoken with a knowing, lightly ironic smile, were: "Forgive me that I cannot satisfy your religious needs."[18]

Freud was unable to attend the commemorative ceremony itself but read a copy of the presentation. He expressed respect for the style of the address but blanket rejection of all its theoretical content in this letter to Binswanger:

Dear Friend! A sweet surprise, your lecture! Those who
heard you and reported to me were visibly untouched by it;
it must have been too difficult for them. In reading it I
rejoiced over your beautiful prose, your erudition, the scope
of your horizon, your tact in disagreement. Truly, one can
put up with infinite amounts of praise.
   But, of course, I don't believe a word of what you say. I've always
lived only in the *parterre* and basement of the building. You
claim that with a change of viewpoint one is able to see an
upper story which houses such distinguished guests as religion, art, etc. You're not the only one who thinks that, most
cultured specimens of *homo natura* believe it. In that you are
conservative, I revolutionary. If I had another lifetime of
work before me, I have no doubt that I could find room for
these noble guests in my little subterranean house. . . .[19]

Psychoanalysis has now receded in significance and
behaviorism has taken its place. Today behaviorism dominates academic and professional psychology and is rapidly
becoming a major factor in psychiatry as well. The historical antecedents of behaviorism can be traced as easily as
those of psychoanalysis, for behaviorism is but a modern
version of traditional philosophical empiricism. Skinner
says of his own work: "Much of this attitude is Baconism.
Whether my early and quite accidental contact with Bacon
is responsible or not, I have followed his principles
closely."[20] And so he has. Bacon rejected will in man as he
rejected chance in the universe. Skinner wants to abolish
"autonomous man—the inner man, the homunculus, the
possessing demon, the man defended by the literature of
freedom and dignity."[21] He insists that "his abolition is
long overdue" and we can "say good riddance," for science
must destroy this fiction if it is to analyze "the real causes
of human behavior" and turn "from the inferred to the
observed, from the miraculous to the natural, from the
inaccessible to the manipulable."[22] He even interprets the
Pavlovian emphasis on "man as a dog" to be a "step forward" because it recognizes that man "like a dog . . . is

within range of a scientific analysis."[23] Skinner concludes that freedom and dignity are now obsolete and that the only task of psychology is "to explain how the behavior of a person as a physical system is related to the conditions under which the human species evolved and the conditions under which the individual lives."[24]

Social psychology, as well as behaviorism, can be traced directly back to Francis Bacon. He "invented" it in a single sentence: "Philosophers should diligently inquire into the powers and energy of custom, exercise, habit, education, example, imitation, emulation, company, friendship, praise, reproof, exortation, reputation, laws, books, studies, etc.; for these are the things which reign in men's morals. By these agents the mind is formed and subdued."[25] Every philosopher presents either an implicit or explicit theory of social psychology when he presents his basic model of man. And today variations on the basic model of behaviorism dominate social psychology almost to the same extent that they dominate clinical and experimental psychology.

It is not our purpose to deny real controversies and distinctions between different approaches within general psychology. Rather it is our goal to show that all these different approaches fall within the same common philosophical framework of hedonism and adaptation. One example of such a controversy within general psychology itself is expressed by Skinner's statement that "Freud was a determinist—on faith," while he is a determinist on the basis of evidence.[26] These and other similar issues can be examined and debated by those who choose to do so. But such arguments are not relevant to our discussion, for it is agreed that psychoanalysis and behaviorism were *both* constructed on the same common philosophical foundation of hedonism and adaptation. "Bodies in motion" may have given way to "the behavior of organisms" in the historical development of material determinism. Yet no one can deny that general psychology is a composite of more complex and more sophisticated versions of the "atoms and space" postulate of Democritus.

Chapter 3

EXISTENTIAL FREEDOM:
ITS ROOTS IN PHILOSOPHY
AND PSYCHOLOGY

Democritus was known as the "laughing philosopher," but Heraclitus was a somber man. The former devised an efficient machine calibrated to produce harmony and "cheerfulness," but the latter probed the strife which pulses through the "flux and fire" of existence. Heraclitus was the precursor of modern existentialism in mood as well as in thought.

The early Greek philosophers had tried to determine what was permanent in nature. Thales argued that the One was water, Anaximenes that it was air, etc. Heraclitus penetrated into matter and concluded that the basic fact of nature was *change*. Fire was the one substance that changed but was at the same time the process of change itself: "The world is an ever-living fire." The crucial significance of this position lies in its further elaboration. The basic reality of fire was equated with soul or god and imbued with a wisdom which gave change an order and direction. All men share in this wisdom since fire is at the source of all our natures. Few philosophical insights have had such a profound influence on history and on civilization. It formed the basis for natural law and for political democracy, since each man was given equal access to a common truth. Heraclitus recognized the responsibility demanded from each citizen if such a philosophy was to be actualized: "Those awake have one ordered universe in common, but in sleep every man turns away to one of his own." Still it was, and continues to be, a powerful and provocative possibility for man.

The "flux and fire" of Heraclitus appears next in the person of Socrates. One might first be tempted to argue that Socrates is more the symbol of reason than of spirit. Yet I am convinced that the most authentic insight into the meaning of his life and death has been given to us by Henri Bergson:

> Socrates indeed exalts the exercise of reason, and particularly the logical function of the mind, above everything else. The irony he parades is meant to dispose of opinions which have not undergone the test of reflection, to put them to shame, so to speak, by setting them in contradiction with themselves. Dialogue, as he understands it, has given birth to the Platonic dialectics and consequently to the philosophical method, essentially rational, which we still practice. The object of such a dialogue is to arrive at concepts that may be circumscribed by definitions; these concepts will become the Platonic Ideas; and the theory of Ideas, in its turn, will serve as a model for the systems, also essentially rational, of traditional metaphysics. Socrates goes further still; virtue itself he holds to be a science, he identifies the practice of good with our knowledge of it; he thus paves the way for the doctrine which will absorb all moral life in the rational function of thought. Reason has never been set so high. At least that is what strikes us at first. But let us look closer. Socrates teaches because the oracle of Delphi has spoken. He has received a mission. He is poor, and poor he must remain. He must mix with the common folk, he must become one of them, his speech must get back to their speech. He will write nothing, so that his thoughts shall be communicated, a living thing, to minds who shall convey it to other minds. He is indifferent to cold and hunger, though in no way an ascetic;

he is merely delivered from material needs, and emancipated from his body. A "daemon" accompanies him, which makes its voice heard when a warning is necessary. He so thoroughly believes in this "daemonic voice" that he dies rather than not follow it; if he refuses to defend himself before the popular tribunal, if he goes to meet his condemnation, it is because the "daemon" has said nothing to dissuade him. In a word, his mission is of a religious and mystic order, in the present-day meaning of the word; his teaching, so perfectly rational, hinges on something that seems to transcend pure reason.[1]

Again we must pause to acknowledge the significance of early Greek thought, since it is only 400 B.C. and already we have a science and an ethics for existential approaches to modern psychology. All of these various existential approaches embody both the spiritual vitalism of Heraclitus and the ethical humanism of Socrates.

The "flux and fire" postulate continued to influence the development of philosophy and reached another historical apex at the culmination of antiquity just before the beginning of the Middle Ages. Plotinus was the most significant philosopher of this period and in many ways one of the most important of all the Greek philosophers. He provided us with a model for science and man that persisted through the Middle Ages and down to the modern existential revolution. He argued that life and the universe were intelligible only in terms of a philosophical assumption of vitalism at the core of being. He attacked the atomistic materialism of Epicurus on the grounds that such a mechanical model could not adequately account for the development of higher mental processes. He then proceeded to establish the original vitalistic model basic to the development of modern existential science. He built his existential model of science and man on the metaphor of emanation. Life pulses through the roots of a tree and flows up into the trunk and branches. A spring flows up from its own fountainhead into the rivers and oceans. The sun radiates light and warmth from the heat of its own internal energy source. Plotinus uses the metaphor of emanation merely to establish the concept of an absolute energy source or first principle from which everything in the universe emanates. He then establishes a hierarchy of nature that flows from this first principle or first cause. The model postulates a universe that evolves as a series of states which become progressively more diffuse and more meaningless as they recede in distance from the original source. Light diminishes in intensity as it radiates farther and farther from the sun and so do the stages of nature. Thus the highest form of being is that emanation closest to the original energy source, just as the brightest light is that which is closest to the sun.

Plotinus labelled this first emanation *Mind* or *Nous* which signified the sphere of ideas or the underlying order in our world. The next stage of emanation was labelled *Soul,* and was less perfect than the original Mind because it had to bridge the gap between abstract ideas and concrete reality. Concrete reality or *matter* was the final and lowest stage of emanation, because it has neither form, quality, power, nor unity. It is farthest removed from the original light and represents darkness, or the principle of evil. Thus evil is not a positive force but an absence of order or light. Moral development is a disciplined and progressive struggle up from matter through Soul, to Mind, and then to final consummation in union with the power source of the universe or the *One.* Plotinus had developed a vitalistic model of nature and man that profoundly influenced the future of religion, science and philosophy.

The emanation model of Plotinus dominated the religious controversies of the Middle Ages, but the "flux and fire" at the heart of Plotinus himself emerged out of these religious battles in the name of Blaise Pascal (1623–1662). Pascal respected the method of rational analysis which he called "the geometrical method." He was an eminent mathematician and physicist who had made distinguished use of the scientific method and considered rationality the most perfect form of knowledge. He was dedicated to the conviction that the geometrical method could do perfectly what it could do. But here Pascal stopped short. He struggled with his own awareness that the rational method could not yield the ultimate truth that our spiritual nature demands. Reason begins with primary first causes and axiomatic first principles that it can neither define nor prove. Rationality cannot penetrate to the inner meaning of existence. Pascal reluctantly and painfully recognized that intelligence was a tool made for a limited purpose and not for the discovery of absolute truth. Others had reached that conclusion and stopped there. Pascal went further. He admitted scepticism but would not accept it. He went beyond it and discovered another method of truth and knowledge. He argued that we could not write mathematical equations for this higher form of knowledge but that we could bear witness to it: "The heart has its reasons which Reason does not know; a thousand things declare it."[2]

These same words flowed in a different form from the spirit of Jean-Jacques Rousseau (1712–1778). He did not have the same scientific and scholarly background as Pascal, but they reached the same conclusion about the intuitive foundation for authentic knowledge: "Let us begin, therefore, by laying aside facts."[3]* Rousseau was rebelling against modern attempts by the sciences and the arts to answer the fundamental questions of existence. He denounced these new methods as corruptions of man's primitive integrity and rejected the civilization that they spawned as degenerate and evil. The philosophical "radicals" of his time repudiated aspects of traditional theology on rational

---

*Kierkegaard expresses the same attitude towards "data" as Pascal and Rousseau: "For if inwardness is the truth, results are only rubbish with which we should not trouble each other." (*Concluding unscientific postscript.* Trans. David Swenson & Walter Lowrie. Princeton: Princeton University Press, 1963, p. 216.)

grounds. Rousseau went further. He rejected theology altogether because it destroyed the primitive religion in man's heart. It is this total commitment to intuitive truth and knowledge that Rousseau shares with all existentialists before and after him.

Another champion of the metaphysics of nature was Frederich Schelling (1775–1854). He argued that nature tends toward spiritual realization and is only a lower form of a progressive activity which reaches its summit in spirit. He stressed the basic position of existential science that nature is a unity and continuity ever evolving toward higher and higher stages of development. These stages of development progress from sense experience to reflection, to judgment, and finally to will in which the self becomes productively active. The will is that creative process by which one attains the existential goals of self-realization and self-actualization. Schelling asserted that it is our moral responsibility to progress from habitual behavior, in which our life is only a series of states, to genuine acts that reveal dignity and respect for our own self and for the selves of others. Thus every individual has a unique and active part in the progressive development of history as the expression of human spirit and will.

The creative will emerges again as a basic philosophical theme in the work of Arthur Schopenhauer (1788–1860). Schopenhauer rejected atomistic materialism and tried to penetrate to a deeper motivational drive: "The crude materialism which even now in the middle of the nineteenth century has been served up again under the ignorant delusion that it is original . . . stupidly denies vital force, and first of all tries to explain the phenomena of life from physical and chemical forces, and those again from mechanical effects."[4] But Schopenhauer discovered below this rational-empirical model of man a deeper life force. He called it *the will to live.* Man is a "metaphysical animal" and not a rational one. Man does not reason his destiny but wills it: "Nothing is more provoking, when we are arguing against a man with reasons and explanations, and taking all pains to convince him . . . than to discover at last that he *will* not understand; that thus we had to do with his *will*."[5] Schopenhauer concludes that the will "alone is unchangeable" in nature and "has brought forth consciousness for its own ends." The will is that one force in nature that gives unity to our consciousness and "holds together all its ideas and thoughts, accompanying them like a continuous harmony."[6] Nor can we consider morality or character in terms of intellect but only in terms of will. We sense this when we prefer the "heart" to the "head," or "good will" to "shrewd cunning." Nor can we consider only the will of man, for will is the ultimate motivational force and the ultimate inner reality of life itself.

The concept of will, as developed by Schopenhauer, had a profound influence on an intense young man named Frederich Nietzsche (1844–1900). Nietzsche was deeply moved by the masterly style as well as the philosophical doctrine of Schopenhauer. Yet he rejected Schopenhauer's passive asceticism and demanded an heroic affirmation of the will. He transformed Schopenhauer's concept of "the will to live" into his own assertive doctrine of "the will to power."

Now it is obvious that we could add more names to our list and describe in detail the precise distinctions between the meaning of "will" in Nietzsche, in Schopenhauer, in Schelling, and on back to Heraclitus. But such a detailed analysis is not the intention of our brief presentation. We introduced this truncated history of will theories only to underline the common historical rebellion against atomistic materialism which is embodied in the relentless push of existential philosophy. We wanted only to underline the perennial nature of this existential drive toward something more than a rational-empirical science and knowledge of man. And this drive for something more spiritual and more metaphysical reached its zenith in the life and work of a Danish philosopher named Sören Kierkegaard.

Kierkegaard was a small and frail man who trembled under the burden of his own philosophical task. Yet he was strong enough to attack the System and its institutions while the world at large still stood in awe of them. He rebelled against all rational and empirical attempts to make "spiritual existence in virtue of thought easier and easier, yet more and more significant."[7] The tactic of his revolt was "to create difficulties everywhere!"[8] And so he did.

He argued that truth was available only to the subjective individual in his solitary encounter with it. There is no systematic, scientific, or religious authority to which one can turn. Rather, each man must turn inward and find his destiny in a personal struggle with himself. Each man must will his own truth from within for outside the self there is only "objective uncertainty." Thus "the highest truth attainable for an *existing* individual" is "*an objective uncertainty held fast in . . . the most passionate inwardness.*"[9] The heavy burden of such an existence is the unlimited responsibility forced upon us when "truth is subjectivity"[10] and "man is spirit."[11] But this burden of personal responsibility is the price we must pay for human freedom and dignity.

Kierkegaard points out the comical in any systematic or scientific attempt to "go further" than these subjective truths. He describes this comical contradiction in an analogy based on a foolish disciple of Heraclitus. Now we can first agree that Heraclitus had "gone to some effort" to prove that the eternal flux of nature makes it impossible to step into "the *same* river twice." Yet his disciple wanted to "go further" and prove that it is impossible to step into the same river even once. But this "improvement" on the argument contradicted the original assumption of Heraclitus that the essence of nature is change and mobility and it even denied the possibility of motion itself: "Poor Heraclitus, to have such a disciple!"[12] Today in psychology Skinner wants to go beyond "freedom and dignity" in order to "save mankind from itself."* Kierkegaard might remark: "Poor mankind, to have such a savior!"

There is much more that could be said about Kierkegaard and truth, but our purpose here is not to venture further into existential philosophy but rather to outline a model of science for existential psychology. And so we come to Henri Bergson.

The crucial significance of Bergson is that he gave us a detailed and sophisticated science of evolution and of man based on a metaphysical philosophy of life. He argued that the generative force of life was a psychic energy or *élan vital* that flows through matter and pushes life toward more and more complex stages of evolution. We see clearly here the overlapping and interpenetration that characterizes the history of philosophy. Bergson spoke almost lovingly of Plotinus, Nietzsche praised Heraclitus, and Kierkegaard said he became a poor man's Socrates only because no modern Socrates could be found. But the interpenetration most relevant to our discussion is the common ground between Bergson and Plotinus. They both assumed a metaphysical energy source that pushes life toward higher and higher levels of emanation and more and more complex stages of evolution. Yet Bergson's unique significance and the factor which distinguishes him from Plotinus and from his other philosophical forebears is his scientific approach to this metaphysical problem. He presents a new metaphysical science in a rationally coherent and empirically detailed model. He defends his position by examination of minute data in the biological laboratory as well as by presentation of intricate and profound philosophical arguments. He cogently defends at these diverse levels a biology of vitalism

*This is a paraphrase of Skinner's argument that only a "technology of behavior" can keep society from destroying itself. (*Beyond freedom and dignity*. New York: Alfred A. Knopf, 1971, pp. 3–5.)

against a biology of mechanism; an ontology of time against an ontology of space; and a methodology of intuition against a methodology of analysis. His scientific defense of metaphysics was loudly applauded and widely acclaimed:

> There is a thinker whose name is today on everybody's lips, who is deemed by acknowledged philosophers worthy of comparison with the greatest, and who, with his pen as well as his brain, has overleapt all technical obstacles, and won himself a reading both outside and inside the schools. Beyond any doubt, and by common consent, Mr. Henri Bergson's work will appear to future eyes among the most characteristic, fertile, and glorious of our era. It marks a never-to-be-forgotten date in history; it opens up a phase of metaphysical thought; it lays down a principle of development the limits of which are indeterminable; and it is after cool consideration, with full consciousness of the exact value of words, that we are able to pronounce the revolution which it effected equal in importance to that effected by Kant, or even by Socrates.*

And Bergson's indirect contribution to the advance of philosophy was equally significant. His widespread influence opened Europe and the world to a new view of science and of man. It was this new respect for metaphysics that prepared the way and opened the floodgates for the torrent of existentialism that was soon to come. And come it did. The names of Marcel, Sartre, Camus, Buber, Berdyaev, Merleau-Ponty, Jaspers, and Heidegger attest to the power and importance of the modern existential movement.

So do these names lead us directly back to existential psychology, for the basis of the break between Binswanger and Freud described above was this same metaphysical

---

*The tribute was paid by Edouard Le Roy. *The new philosophy of Henri Bergson*. New York: Holt, 1913, pp. 1–2. Le Roy was a contemporary of Bergson and an eminent philosopher himself. Such enthusiastic responses by philosophers were also typical of reactions by recognized psychological scholars such as William James and John Dewey.

challenge which is at the heart of modern existentialism. And the professional break between Binswanger and Freud was but one indicator of the general existential rebellion against material determinism with its systematic and scientific reduction of human experience. Even more central to the development of existential psychology were the personal as well as professional breaks from within the original psychoanalytic circle itself. Three men were excommunicated from that original group for heresy. Jung, Adler, and Rank, each in his own way and for his own reasons, rejected the biological determinism that is the basis of the psychoanalytic system. It became personally and professionally impossible for these men to work within the psychoanalytic framework and each broke away to develop his own independent theory. Jung developed a religious model, Adler a social model, and Rank an existential model. The work of Otto Rank represents the first and most important existential approach developed by a practicing psychologist and psychotherapist. Therefore let us outline the dynamics of his position in some detail.

Rank's background and training was not in medicine like the other members of the psychoanalytic group but in broad cultural areas, from engineering through history, art, psychology, and philosophy. These educational advantages placed him in a position of significance within the group and there were clear indications that Freud intended to assign the expansion of psychoanalytic theory into the area of "culture" to this brilliant and unique young man. But it did not come to pass because his uniqueness had already set the stage for the ultimate break. Rank focused from the start on the one aspect of psychoanalytic theory that best lent itself to a broader concept of man. He focused on the significance of the birth trauma. His early views on the meaning of birth were developed within the biological framework of psychoanalysis proper. He stressed the basic significance of birth but interpreted it in the language and the concepts of psychoanalytic theory. Rank presented these views in his first major work, entitled *The Trauma of Birth.* The break began with this work because it was exactly those few parts of the book that stressed Rank's uniqueness, and which were the seeds of his ultimate psychological theory, that Freud and the psychoanalytic group brutally attacked. Rank continued to function within the psychoanalytic group for a few more years but then realized that the very uniqueness which had made him an asset in the beginning had made him an enemy in the end. He broke personally, professionally, and physically with the Vienna group and spent the remainder of his life in Paris and then Philadelphia.

The need for the total break arose from the perennial conflict over the freedom and will of man. These were the issues that had been implicitly expressed in *The Trauma of Birth* and had led to the hostile reaction by the Vienna group. Now Rank devoted himself to the explicit development of this primary psychological theme. He rejected the term "psychoanalysis" and called his new method of treatment *psychotherapy.* He defined the will as the integrative power of the personality as a whole. It is not a philosophical abstraction but the concrete consequence of being born, and a necessary process for the development of the human organism. Man is not merely the product of impulses in conflict with one another and with external pressures. Man cannot be scientifically understood nor therapeutically helped by analysis of these separate biological and social forces operating within him and upon him. Man can be understood only in terms of the core of his being which is his active relationship to himself and his world. Man can be understood only in terms of his will.

The will itself must be understood in relation to natural processes of birth and growth. The will is the organic drive toward individuation and integration essential for the survival of the organism. The function of the will is best stated in terms of the organic need for autonomy and separation. Yet the inherent need to be free must not be confused with the pathology of alienation. The need for *separation* (will) must be understood in context with the equally basic need for *union* (love). These are the two existential needs of man—freedom and love. Rank's crucial importance for psychology was his recognition that man is not motivated by impulse conflicts, but by the need to reconcile these organic drives toward union and separation.

Rank described two kinds of fear that must be mastered in order to develop a creative and constructive rapprochement between freedom and love. The first fear that must be mastered is the *life fear,* or the fear of separation. The embryo in the womb functions as a symbiotic unit with its surroundings. Birth means the death of this union and consequently the fear of life. It is not just a physiological anxiety but the more general anxiety associated with the movement from one stage of integration to another. It is the anxiety inherent in any subjective crisis or encounter that makes possible the progressive transition to more and more complex levels of personality integration. It is the anxiety inherent in the process of creative risk and creative growth.

This life fear is counterbalanced by a *death fear.* The anxiety over separation tends to preserve union but the fear of passive dependence, or the death fear, tends to activate the drive of the will toward separation. Both this fear of life or separation, and this fear of death or union, must be mastered in order to develop a creative integration of these two basic life forces. Rank does not deny the significance of impulses inherent in our biological structure, such as the sexual impulses stressed in psychoanalytic theory. But he does reject the assumption that these impulses are determinants of personality. For example, hunger is the recurrent pain of separation after birth and is relieved by a new union with the breast or its equivalent. Weaning then becomes a new symbol of "birth" because it necessitates a separation from the breast, which now symbolizes the original prenatal union with the mother. The instinctual facts of hunger and oral pleasure are incidental rather than causal, as are the biological relationships to the mother and father at the oedipal stage. These instinctual facts and biological relationships are but the incidental conditions or the psychological ground for the primary metaphysical struggle toward the creative integration of separation and union, life and death, will and love.

Rank argues that this process of union and separation is essential to biological growth and is a general principle inherent in all living matter. The child must separate from the mother's breast in order to form a new and more mature relationship with her. The child must separate from the pattern and security of crawling in order to form a new and more independent relationship with the world. But the principle of union and separation goes much deeper than these biologically integrative trends of the organism. The existential process on which Rank based his theory is the psychological equivalent to this general biological principle of growth. Let us see how this psychological principle of growth develops from birth through childhood and then expresses itself in the normal man, the neurotic client, and the creative individual.

The birth trauma activates the will because the fact of separation is violently thrust upon the infant. Subsequent separations such as weaning will lead to further individuation and autonomy until the child comes to experience his own self as an existential whole and his will as an integrative reality. The will emerges first as counter-will, for the child learns that he can say "no" to adults and to his own impulses. This recognition of the autonomy of his will is a monumental step in the growth process of the child. It is the beginning of the conscious integration of the person as a unit distinct from the womb of the outer world. This recognition by the individual of his independence and autonomy is for Rank the essential human experience. The counter-will is our most valuable human discovery for it is the beginning of the development of a creative identity and of a creative self.

The counter-will develops against the parents and later representatives of external authority and is an expression of the drive toward individuation and life. It is a necessary rebellion against coercion by external authority figures in order to create a separate and independent self. It says "no" to others so that it can say "yes" to its own emergent self. The risk during these stages of rebellion is that separation will destroy the equally needed human experience of union. The anxiety associated with this effort to be an independent self and yet remain in relationship with others causes feelings of "guilt." Rank calls this almost universal and potentially creative anxiety "ethical guilt," to contrast it with "moralistic guilt" caused by violation of some social code of conduct. Ethical guilt goes much deeper into the basic process of human development and can arise either from an act of will that disrupts union or from an act of compliance that inhibits separation. Resolution of this ethical guilt is the ideal goal of the growth process and the ideal goal of psychotherapy. The person or client must discover the existential reality that union and separation are not antagonistic but complementary. He must discover that authentic interpersonal relationships are not based on control of the other but on positive respect for his unique individuality. Love and will are not in conflict because love is only *possible* when it is based on respect for the will of the other. Psychotherapy attempts to activate this process of integration by a venture of love on the part of the therapist. The therapist must respect his own personal will and at the same time love and value the counter-will of the client. Then the client no longer needs to define himself by rebellion against authority because the other in the situation supports and values the client's individual uniqueness. Now the will energy used to define what one is "not" can be redirected to discover and develop "the self that one truly is." The counter-will has been transformed by love into the creative will, and this activation of the creative will is the goal of existential psychotherapy. Rank insists that activation of the creative will is the only means to foster the development of individual man and to promote the constructive evolution of human society.

Now we can better understand the revolutionary significance of Rank's innovative approach to personality, for it turned psychoanalytic theory upside down. The neurotic client is no longer a sick individual struggling to be normal but a rebellious individual struggling to be free. The neurotic is no longer considered inferior to the normal man as in psychoanalytic theory, but superior to the normal man because he rejects the psychoanalytic goal of social and biological adaptation. He is searching for something more. The counter-will that characterizes neurosis is a rejection of stereotyped adaptation and a struggle toward creative individuality. But the normal man with no counter-will is "sick" because he has no self of his own. He has given up his will and his identity for the security of passive adjustment to the womb of his environment. He is spared the pain and anxiety inherent in the struggle to exist, but the price he pays is no less than his psychological death. Rank based his theory of man and psychotherapy on the metaphysics of will and love. This theory has served as a basic prototype for existential psychology, and many modern humanistic developments can be traced directly back to Rank.

The most important of these subsequent humanistic developments within psychology itself has been the work of Carl Rogers. Rogers' theory evolved out of his own experience and independently of Rank, but the common roots are obvious. Rogers argues that the growth process can be facilitated by a method of therapeutic intervention based on three factors. The therapist must be congruent in his relationship with the client; he must communicate unconditional positive regard or respect for the self of the client; and he must express genuine empathic concern for the feelings and struggles presented to him by the client. Rogers always kept "one foot in the scientific camp" and gathered considerable data to support his assumption that the method of "client-centered" therapy does produce constructive personality change and growth. Rogers is not an existentialist himself, but his work has served as an important "bridge" to existentialism in American psychology.* His approach to personality and psychotherapy provided the discipline with a theoretical and applied alternative to both psychoanalysis and behaviorism.

Kierkegaard and Bergson opened the floodgates of existentialism in philosophy, and Rank and Rogers have opened the floodgates of existentialism in psychology. Names like May, Bugental, Burton, Moustakas, Gendlin, Laing, and Jourard are rapidly becoming more and more recognized and more and more influential. The modern humanistic movement has even brought the "daemon" of Socrates back into psychology and so we come full circle once more. No one can be sure at this stage about the ultimate significance of this modern movement but no one can deny that these new versions of the "flux and fire" postulate of Heraclitus represent a formidable challenge to the future of psychology and of man.

---

*The work of Abraham Maslow, who coined the term "third force" to designate humanistic approaches to personality, has also served as a "bridge" to existentialism in American psychology—although Maslow was even more removed than Rogers from the basic existential position.

chapter 4

A GENERAL REVIEW
OF BASIC EXISTENTIAL
THEMES AND THEORIES

Existential psychology began with existential philosophy and the latter, in turn, began with Sören Kierkegaard (1813–1855). Kierkegaard sensed the destructive impact of modern science long before any of his contemporaries, for he noted that "the many benefactors of the age" will soon solve all our problems: "some by railways, others by omnibusses and steamboats, others by the telegraph, others by easily apprehended compendiums and short recitals of everything worth knowing." Then finally "the true benefactors of the age" will apply these same methods of science directly to human problems and make "spiritual existence in virtue of thought easier and easier, yet more and more significant."[1]* And the battle waged by Kierke-

---

*Kierkegaard warned mankind more than a century ago of the specific danger posed by modern science: "In our time it is the natural sciences which are especially dangerous. Physiology will ultimately extend itself to the point of embracing ethics. There are already sufficient clues of a new endeavor—to treat ethics as physics, whereby all of ethics becomes illusory and ethics in the race is treated statistically by averages or is calculated as one calculates vibrations in laws of nature." (*Sören Kierkegaard's journals and papers.* Trans. H. Hong and E. Hong. Bloomington, Ind.: Indiana University Press, 1975, vol. 3, no. 2807.)

gaard against this rationalization and mechanization of man was fought again half a century later from within the discipline of science itself by Henri Bergson (1859–1941). These two revolutionary thinkers changed the course of modern intellectual life; the influence of their work converged and produced a turning point in the history of philosophy and psychology. The "new direction" given by Kierkegaard and Bergson was followed up in the work of Martin Heidegger who, in turn, influenced Sartre, Camus and Merleau-Ponty. Karl Jaspers and Gabriel Marcel are two other prominent existential philosophers directly influenced by Bergson and Kierkegaard. And two more major figures who added their own perspectives to modern existentialism are Nicolas Berdyaev and Martin Buber. Now since it is upon the philosophical foundations laid by these particular men that existential psychology must be built, let us review the basic existential themes and theories that they developed in their life and work.

KIERKEGAARD (1813–1855)

Kierkegaard focused his personal attack against the objectification and rationalization of man on "Hegelianism," which was the dominant philosophy "of the age." He considered Hegel's elaborate philosophical system the "comical" culmination of a basic trend in modern science and philosophy that substituted the logical manipulation of abstractions for the concrete existence of individuals. The concrete reality of man had been replaced, in the Hegelian system, by such generalized abstractions as the "universal spirit" and the "collective consciousness." Kierkegaard lamented the fact that "our age has forsaken" the single individual "in order to take refuge in the collective idea" of Hegel.[2] Hegel's elaborate philosophical system encompassed everything but that one reality which we can all discover from within—the concrete, living, experiencing, struggling, suffering self. Kierkegaard recognized only this concrete reality of the existing individual and so he rejected the Hegelian system while the intellectual world at large rushed to "sustain" and "complete" it.* Kierkegaard rejected the Hegelian system as merely comical because it forgot "in a sort of a world-historical absent-mindedness" to consider that one concrete reality which we all experience—our own individual existence. There is no place for the individual in Hegel's "historical dialectic" or his "collective society," since the individual has a single solitary existence of his own and that unique individuality can never be appropriated nor comprehended by any rational system. It is true that mankind "in general" could be included within such a system for "this is the sort of thing that one might even induce a speculative philosopher to agree to." But "what it means to be a human being in general" is a meaningless and even comical abstraction, for only the concrete individual alone "exists."[3]

Possibly the best way to make more explicit this crucial distinction between existentialism and any collective-historical approach to man is to contrast the rational dialectic of Hegel with the existential dialectic of Kierkegaard. The rational dialectic as formulated by Hegel deals with various contradictory possibilities which, in Kierkegaard's dialectic, are labeled "stages on life's way." These two dialectics are to be contrasted not so much in their content as to the process of movement from one stage or way of life to another. Hegel conceives of these transitions from one stage to another as a "movement of reason," since the contradic-

---

*"What wonder that the System continues to sustain its life as a going concern. In general, objections are haughtily ignored; if a particular objection seems to attract a little attention, the systematic entrepreneurs engage a copyist to copy off the objection, which thereupon is incorporated in the System; and when the book is bound the System is complete." (Kierkegaard, *Concluding unscientific postscript*, pp. 111–12.)

tions can be resolved by a "rational" step that compromises the two opposing positions and leads to a "higher" stage of development. Kierkegaard agrees that such contradictions or paradoxes are a reality but he founds his whole philosophy on the argument that these paradoxes cannot be resolved by any method of rational intervention. His argument is based on the assertion that these contradictions, or alternate ways of life, are not "relative" paradoxes but "absolute" paradoxes. Consequently, they cannot be resolved by reason for there is no intelligible starting point for the rational compromise of an absolute paradox; i.e., there is no such thing as a logical starting point for the reconciliation of an absolute contradiction. Therefore, the promise of the Hegelian system and the system itself are nothing but illusions because there is no rational means by which the best of both possible worlds can be abstracted and integrated at a "higher" level of development. Man is confronted, instead, with the anxiety and dread of an irrational choice between one *or* the other of two absolutely irreconcilable alternatives.*

Now the choice must be an irrational one because absolute paradoxes are not the "errors" or "problems" of reason but are the basic "results" or "contributions" of reason. The exhaustion of rational defenses for each alternative way always leads to an irreconcilable contradiction. So it is reason itself that always forces us to choose beyond reason. And this is true exactly because it is the very nature and function of reason to always exhaust itself in just such an irreconcilable contradiction.† Thus, creative movement

*And Kierkegaard pushes his position to its ultimate limit for he insists that "personality will for all eternity protest against the idea that absolute contrasts can be mediated." (*Sören Kierkegaards journals and papers*, vol. 2 [date of entry, 1839], p. 210.)

†The Sophists capitalized on this fact 2500 years ago. They were willing to take either side of any argument, since on rational grounds alone either side could be equally well defended.

beyond the stagnant impasse of reason is possible for the existing individual only by a "leap of faith" grounded in the passion of subjective truth and personal commitment. No one way of life or no one system of values can be defended as more *rational* than any other. Consequently, the existing individual cannot wait for reason to give him an answer to the question of his own fate and his own identity because it has none to offer. Nor can he hope to avoid the anxiety and dread of choice by a *both/and* neutralization of the alternatives because the paradox is never a relative one but always an absolute one. And so the illusion which underlies the assumption fostered by physical science and speculative philosophy that "reason answers all" impales itself on the horns of these absolute rational paradoxes.

It was necessary for Kierkegaard to expose and destroy this illusion of rationalism and to challenge the Hegelian dialectic, because morality and responsibility can have no existential meaning except in an irrational world. Choice and commitment, rather than rationalism, would be the comical illusions if reason itself were demonstrated to be the ultimate reality. The existential imperative that an individual confront the anxiety and dread of his own freedom and make a subjective commitment to life would be only comical if the same answers could be found simply by rational manipulation of the objective system itself. It was therefore necessary for Kierkegaard to attack the "system" which represented the ultimate rationalization and objectification of existence in order to force man to a crucial awareness of the fact that reality begins *beyond* reason on the existential ground of subjectivity, choice, freedom, and individuality.

HEIDEGGER (1889–   )

Martin Heidegger is by far the most significant philosopher in contemporary existential and phenomenological thought. He not only links Kierkegaard and Bergson to modern philosophers such as Sartre, Camus, and Merleau-Ponty; he also links Kierkegaard and Bergson to the most prominent figures in modern existential psychology: Binswanger and Boss. Heidegger is so central to the development of modern existential philosophy and psychology that we must sketch his theory in some detail.

Heidegger is a profound scholar who has immersed himself in the history of philosophy and integrated its diverse and complex trends into a coherent and revolutionary new approach. He is that rare example of a philosopher who combines theoretical speculation concerning abstract principles with concrete insights into basic problems that concern the existing individual in the real world. His primary philosophical task is to examine the nature of Being, but he approaches this traditional philosophical problem in new and innovative ways. He asks three questions in his attempt to fathom the meaning of Being. The first one is a technical question that asks only, "What is the meaning of the term 'Being'?" The second and third questions are much more complex, for he now asks "What is Being itself?" and "Why is there Being?" Heidegger is convinced that the answers we give to these fundamental questions about the nature of Being are crucial not only for the future of philosophy but also for the future of man. And he further argues that the failure of modern philosophy is due precisely to the fact that philosophers have abandoned the study of Being as if they already understood it. Thus they continue to develop philosophical systems without an adequate conception of Being—which is the necessary foundation for all knowledge.

Heidegger's own attempt to understand Being as the ground of knowledge begins with the study of one specific type of Being—the human Being, or Dasein. The unique feature of Dasein is that it is not like an object among other objects because "it is distinguished by the fact that, in its very Being, that Being is an *issue* for it."[4] This unique feature of Dasein makes it the one being in nature that can serve as a starting point for an inquiry into the nature of Being, since it is the only primal entity "which already comports itself, in its Being, toward what we are asking about when we ask this question."[5] And it is because of this unique and distinct relationship of the human being, as Dasein, to Being itself, that an answer to our inquiry concerning the nature of Being "must be sought in the *existential analytic of Dasein.*"[6] Consequently, Heidegger begins his phenomenological investigation of Being, and his attack on the "whole history of philosophy," from the perspective of this one basic concept of the human being as Dasein. We must therefore try to understand this new concept of man for it is not only the point of departure for Heidegger's phenomenology of Being but the crucial cornerstone of modern existential philosophy and psychology as well.

Now the remarkable characteristic of Dasein that distinguishes it from other beings is that it can question the nature of its own Being. It is concerned about itself and this fundamental concern of man for himself is called "care." Man as Dasein, or "care," is essentially concerned about himself in the sense of a preoccupation with the meaning of his own existence. Man is not merely motivated to satisfy basic physical needs but is structurally motivated to discover and understand the meaning of his own life. Care is the concern of man to discover himself and to establish his own personal identity. Dasein as care is a unique type of being that seeks to encounter and create its own personal self and its own personal destiny. The identity and fate of an object or "tool" is established by its intended function within a social system and is always referred beyond itself, e.g., a hammer is defined in terms of its intended function to "pound" or "nail" something. But Dasein is that one Being in nature that "in its very Being" is concerned about the identity and fate of its own existence. It is the one entity in all of nature that has been "delivered over" to the power and choice of its own will.[7] Dasein thereby occupies a unique position in our natural world. It is the one Being that is destined for and referred to *itself only* and nothing beyond itself. Thus Heidegger's conception of man is that he is essentially and structurally motivated toward the discovery and creation of his own self. The basic motivation of man is neither biological satisfaction nor psychological adjustment but the philosophical creation and expression of the self. Heidegger also warns us that this human quest for self-discovery and self-actualization is not an elite philosophical project but is the project of *every* existing human being. Professional philosophers do not have a privileged position in relation to this task, and their "professionalism" can often block them from an authentic encounter and struggle with the problem itself. Each man expresses this essential structure of Dasein when he separates himself from his socialized and objectified condition and asks himself the meaning of his own *life* and the meaning of his own ultimate and inescapable *death.*

It is obvious that Heidegger describes the essential structure of Dasein as the "search for self-discovery and self-actualization" only in terms of an inherent potential of man and not as a determined necessity. Only a cursory glance at our contemporary world is required to discern that the objectification and socialization of man has tended to destroy this essential structural component of Dasein and to provide "ready-made" artifical answers to the basic questions asked by man of himself. The nature of Dasein as described by Heidegger only points to a basic *structural potential* of man and not, of course, to any psychic or causal necessity. Those who freely choose to activate this human potential and to create and express their own individual being are said to exist *authentically,* while those who submit to social and intellectual objectification are said to be inauthentic in their lives. The authentic individual thinks and acts from the "mineness" of his own chosen identity while the inauthentic individual is determined by the "other-ness" of the "they" or *"das Man."* *

The potential for authenticity and the potential for inauthenticity are both basic structures in the Dasein of each individual and are not determined by genetic or environmental causes. The authentic individual recognizes the "facticity" of his "thrown" condition, i.e., that he has been thrust into a particular situation with particular parents and with particular social forces pressing upon him. He also recognizes that he can live inauthentically in this "fallen" state and be determined by it—or live authentically and choose to create his own relationship to himself and to his situation by activation of his unique human potentials. Authentic man is forever oriented toward these unique human potentials and toward the actualization of them. He is not simply his past but his present and his projected future as well. Nor is this concept of life as a process in time merely an abstraction "lost in the infinite," for it is a concrete reality bounded by the inescapable limits of human finitude. Heidegger stresses that human anxiety is rooted in this recognition of man's bounded finitude, and that the most concrete manifestation of this inescapable finitude arises when each of us encounters and confronts the reality of his own ultimate death. Anxiety, loneliness, and despair do not accompany speculation about the general nature of death as a social topic for the "they" or *"das Man,"* but such feelings do accompany the authentic recognition by each individual alone of the inescapable fact of his own personal and impending death. And the inescapable death of each Dasein is but a concrete expression of the Nothingness that is an essential structural aspect of Being itself. The finitude of each Dasein and the anxiety it provokes is not a mistake

*"The Self of everyday Dasein is the *they-self*, which we distinguish from the *authentic Self*—that is, from the Self which has been taken hold of in its own way. As they-self, the particular Dasein has been *dispersed* into the 'they' [*das Man*]." (Heidegger, *Being and time*, p. 167.)

that can be "explained" or "corrected"; it is a stark dimension of the basic nature of our being-in-the-world. It cannot be eliminated or escaped—it must be encountered and mastered. Such mastery is possible if one chooses freedom and authenticity and wills his own relationship to the reality of his own facticity and his own finitude.

SARTRE (1905–   )

Sartre was directly influenced by Heidegger but he reversed Heidegger's philosophical goal. Heidegger attempted to understand Being in the abstract by a study of the individual person, or Dasein. He studied the psychological existence of the concrete individual only as a means of understanding the philosophical basis of Being in general. Sartre, on the other hand, is concerned almost exclusively with the existence of the concrete individual, and is only indirectly concerned with the traditional philosophical problem of the nature of Being. Therefore, his classical statement that "existence precedes essence"[8] places the priority of his philosophical concerns in their proper perspective.

Sartre uses the analogy of the manufacture of an instrument or a tool to state his basic position. He argues that the creation of man by God is generally considered analogous to the manufacture of a tool by a skilled craftsman or artisan. And it is further assumed that this creation of man by God is the result of a definite plan and is directed toward a definite purpose. Therefore, the conception or essence of man resided in the mind of God before God created man, just as the conception or essence of the tool resided in the mind of the craftsman before he manufactured it. Now it is true that many philosophers in history have rejected the notion of a God; but Sartre uses atheism as an argument for rejecting not only God but human nature itself. Other philosophers have rejected God but still maintained that there is a nature of man or an essence of man that precedes his existence. Sartre, however, argues that if there is no God then there is no such thing as human nature, because there is no one to have a conception of it in the first place. Human nature cannot be defined before it is actually lived, because it cannot be thought out and conceptualized in advance of the fact of its existence. Man must therefore exist first for only in the concrete act of existence itself can he discover and create his essence. Man must first accept his thrown condition and out of his existence in it choose and become the self or "essence" that he will be:

> We mean that man first of all exists, encounters himself, surges up in the world—and defines himself afterwards. If man as the existentialist sees him is not definable, it is because to begin with he is nothing. He will not be anything until later, and then he will be what he makes of himself. Thus, there is no human nature, because there is no God to have a conception of it. Man simply is. Not that he is simply what he conceives himself to be, but he is what he wills, and as he conceives himself after already existing—as he wills to be after that leap towards existence. Man is nothing else but that which he makes of himself. That is the first principle of existentialism.[9]

Now it is easy to understand that part of Sartre's argument which states that God does not exist. The concept of a being who is complete within himself and at the same time is his own cause is a contradiction. But the second part of his argument is more difficult to follow because human nature could still be created by the concrete biological and psychological processes of evolution as readily as by the hand of an omnipotent God. The analogy of the craftsman and the tool, therefore, does not seem to hold. But its logical validity is not a significant issue, since the metaphor is used only as a devise to stress that man is totally free to make himself and totally responsible for the self that he does make. Sartre's atheism is an integral and necessary part of his revolt against any authoritarian restriction on the freedom of man to choose and will his own values and his own life.

Intrinsic to this insistence on man's unlimited freedom and unlimited responsibility is the dignity that existentialism gives to Dasein. The source of that dignity lies in our human consciousness and subjectivity. These attributes are unique to Dasein and are not structural characteristics of other objects in the natural world. Only man moves toward a future that he himself has chosen and created, while other natural objects cannot master their thrown condition and are determined by it. Sartre calls this latter mode of determined existence, "being-in-itself" ("en-soi"), and the former creative mode of existence which is unique to man, "being-for-itself" ("pour-soi").* The contrast between these two modes of being stresses the dignity of man as Dasein that is basic to all existentialism and makes it an "optimistic" theory in spite of the heavy burden of responsibility that it imposes upon us. The optimism and dignity lie in the recognition that man is not a determined object but a conscious subject who can freely choose and will his own relationship to himself and to his world. The challenge inherent in Sartre's assertion that "existence precedes essence" makes each man create himself in his own image and makes each man responsible for what he does become. A rock is not responsible for its existence, and Sartre argues that man could not be held responsible for his own life if his essential nature was already a given and fixed condition.

---

*"The for-itself does not arise with a *wholly given* end ... the for-itself 'makes itself' ". (*Being and nothingness: An essay on phenomenological ontology.* Trans. H. Barnes. New York: Washington Square Press, 1972, p. 704.) Sartre argues that the attempt to reduce existential freedom to psychological determinism is merely the contradiction of "an attempt to apprehend oneself [being-for-itself] as being-in-itself." (*Ibid.*, pp. 567–8.)

The basis of Sartre's ethical position is exactly this unlimited freedom and unlimited responsibility that is imposed upon each of us. The unlimited freedom does not lead to an amoral relativism, since the unlimited responsibility forces us back to a strict moral accountability. Each man must choose his own existence and there is no escape from complete responsibility for that choice. The unlimited nature of this responsibility also forces each man to choose not only for himself, but for all men. He is not responsible simply for his own individuality but he is responsible for the individual, social, and political condition of all other men as well. Thus Sartre does acknowledge one concept of "human nature". He agrees that when we create our own individual self with its own particular values, we create at the same time an "image" or "ideal" of human nature. And each action by which we affirm that chosen self and its values must be judged by us as right not just for our own self but right for all other men as well:

> When we say that man chooses himself, we do mean that every one of us must choose himself; but by that we also mean that in choosing for himself he chooses for all men. For in effect, of all the actions a man may take in order to create himself as he wills to be, there is not one which is not creative, at the same time, of an image of man such as he believes he ought to be. To choose between this or that is at the same time to affirm the value of that which is chosen; for we are unable ever to choose the worse. What we choose is always the better; and nothing can be better for us unless it is better for all. If, moreover, existence precedes essence and we will to exist at the same time as we fashion our image, that image is valid for all and for the entire epoch in which we find ourselves. Our responsibility is thus much greater than we had supposed, for it concerns mankind as a whole.[10]

There is no universal law by which to judge the moral content of our choices but there is this one moral imperative of unlimited accountability and responsibility. Sartre's morality demands that each of us be committed to his own free choice of action and be willing for others to choose that same action. Those who avoid the responsibility of freedom are said to be in "bad faith," and those who avoid the responsibility to choose for all men on the grounds that other men will not make the same choices are guilty of "self deception." Those who avoid existential responsibility for their choices either through "bad faith" or "self deception" fragment their own self and their own conscience, and so they are said to exist inauthentically. But man can never really escape this existential responsibility for he can never really convince himself that he is determined by his history, by his organism, by his environment, by his fate, or by anything. Man recognizes at some level of his awareness that he alone creates his own self and his own destiny by his own free choices and by his own free actions. Nor can man argue that he is responsible in those choices and those actions only to himself and not to others since man is a "being-for-others" as well as a "being-for-himself."

MERLEAU-PONTY (1908–1961)

The work of Merleau-Ponty is of particular interest to psychologists because he approached the problem of Being from a phenomenological study of perception and focused considerable attention on a phenomenological critique of behaviorism. The basic aim of his philosophy was "to understand the relations of consciousness and nature,"[11] and he took the study of perception as his point of departure for that project. He insisted that the first step in any phenomenological investigation must always be "the rejection of science." The scientific method provides us with a "rationale or explanation" of the world that becomes a substitute for and an obstacle to authentic perception of that world:

I am not the outcome or the meeting-point of numerous causal agencies which determine my bodily or psychological make-up. I cannot conceive myself as nothing but a bit of the world, a mere object of biological, psychological or sociological investigation. I cannot shut myself up within the realm of science. All my knowledge of the world, even my scientific knowledge, is gained from my own particular point of view, or from some experience of the world without which the symbols of science would be meaningless. The whole universe of science is built upon the world as directly experienced, and if we want to subject science itself to rigorous scrutiny and arrive at a precise assessment of its meaning and scope, we must begin by reawakening the basic experience of the world of which science is the second-order expression. Science has not and never will have, by its nature, the same significance *qua* form of being as the world which we perceive, for the simple reason that it is a rationale or explanation of that world.[12]

But phenomenology aims to return to the concrete reality of "the things themselves," and to investigate the factual nature of those events which science can examine only as abstractions and generalizations. It was for this reason that Merleau-Ponty rejected science and attempted to discover the basic nature of man's relation to himself and to his world by a careful and detailed phenomenological investigation of the process of perception.

Merleau-Ponty began his investigation of perception with "the rejection of science" in order to penetrate deeper into the dynamics of the process of perception itself. He could not find the answers he sought in the scientific methods and formulas that reduce man to a determined object. He declared

I am the absolute source, my existence does not stem from my antecedents, from my physical and social environment; instead it moves outward towards them and sustains them, for I alone bring into being for myself (and therefore into being in the only sense the word can have for me) the tradi-

tion which I elect to carry on, or the horizon whose distance
from me would be abolished—since that distance is not one
of its properties—if I were not there to scan it with my
gaze.[13]

It is this "I am the absolute source" that is the unique
existential thrust of Merleau-Ponty's investigation of perception. And, consistent with this point of view, he concludes that man can perceive something only if it is
presented to him, but that he is always free to impose his
own intentions and interpretations upon that which is presented. Man is never determined or "bound" in his perceptual acts to any one particular attitude or any one particular
response to a given stimulus. There is always a range of
ambiguity in perception to the point that one can even to
some extent construct his own world, since it is never completely determined by physiological or psychological factors. It is on this ground that Merleau-Ponty rejected the
behaviorist assumption of a one-to-one correlation between stimulus and response. He recognized that it was
possible to establish in special laboratory situations a fixed
stimulus-response pattern; but he argued that in the real
world the body is not a passive object merely reacting to
external pressures. Rather, man is a subjective agent who
organizes his relationship to himself and to his world
through the active and creative process of perception.

Merleau-Ponty further argued that behaviorists, because of their constricted view of science, did not even
properly understand the concept of behavior itself. He defined behavior as "a significative whole or a structure which
properly belongs neither to the external world nor to internal life."[14] He agreed that objects in the natural world
could manifest this general type of behavior but he insisted
that only humans could engage in conceptual and symbolic
modes of action. And it is these conceptual and symbolic
forms of behavior that permit the response to any given

stimulus to be mediated by subjective values and attitudes that can be freely chosen by a conscious and creative self. Therefore, the definition of behavior as "a significative whole or a structure" of our being-in-the-world forces us to recognize that any authentic science of behavior must take into account man's unique capacity to attribute meaning to his acts and to respond in terms of that meaning.

The phenomenological study of perception must also consider the implications of the fact that perception is always and necessarily a perception at a particular point in time that includes within it a relation to the past as well as to the future. The perceiving subject can make sense of his observed world only if it includes this possibility to experience time as a process and as a continuity. But Merleau-Ponty argues that science must exclude the process and continuity of time because it can only observe objective facts at a particular point in time—a point in time that has no past and no future because it has already been "abstracted from" the reality of experienced time. Thus the only way for us to make existential sense of observed facts is to "reject science" and examine these facts within the reality of experienced time as continuity and process. But this, in turn, leads to the introduction of subjectivity as a real phenomenon and forces psychology to reject the "scientific" method in favor of the phenomenological method. Thus the consciousness of time as well as the consciousness of self are both essential factors in any meaningful act of perception or behavior.

Merleau-Ponty defends the reality of existential freedom on this same ground. He argues that because of the subjective consciousness of self and time there is no one-to-one correspondence between stimulus and response. Consequently, there is no fixed and determined causal connection between the individual and his world. He also defends existential freedom on the ground that for one thing to cause another they must be two totally separate and independent things or events. For example, a tree will fall if it is cut down with an axe or a window will break if it is smashed with a rock. The determined causal connection is easily established in these examples because the two factors in each case are totally separate and independent. But the actions of an individual cannot be simply explained as being caused by his physical world since the relationship between the individual and his world is not that of two totally separate and independent objects. Rather, the relationship between the individual and his world is that of an active subject who is himself a part of that world, for Dasein is structurally a being-in-the-world. Thus man is free because he cannot be totally separated from the world and reduced to an object in it. He is free because his perceptual and behavioral acts are always mediated by the values and the attitudes of the self that he has chosen and created.

Marcel (1889–1973)

The primary philosophical goal of Gabriel Marcel was to transform empiricism from a rigid "positivistic" method to a meaningful "existential" process—and that goal demanded a new starting point. Now it is of the very nature of traditional rational and empirical methods that they deal only with abstractions and generalizations, but Marcel chose his own concrete human experiences as the starting point for his own existential empiricism. He introduced into empiricism the priority of the existing individual that abstract science and philosophy had tended either to neglect or to destroy. He wanted to develop a new method of empirical inquiry and description that could provide an adequate account of the existence of the concrete individual that always "slipped through" the abstractions and generalizations of traditional empirical science. He rejected the concept of "experience" as presented in these traditional systems since experience is not an accumulation of isolated sensations, perceptions, and emotions but is a process centered and focused in the experiencing subject himself. And the new empirical method of "reflection" that Marcel introduced enabled him to participate in this process of subjective experiencing as he investigated the reality of the concrete person and his being-in-the-world. He did not try to construct an arbitrary and artificial separation of the self of the investigator from the reality of his being-in-the-world and then claim that he had made independent and "scientific" judgments about isolated objects. Instead, the empirical method of reflection transforms this abstract and artificial empiricism into a concrete process of intuitive encounters in the real world. Reflection in Marcel's method simply means that we turn our attention back upon itself so that we can examine the dynamics of our own concrete acts and experiences. The first phase of his reflective method or "primary reflection" is analytical because it requires that we suspend our judgment in order to make a detailed analysis of the causes or elements of the particular act or experience that we intend to study. The second phase of his reflective method or "secondary reflection" is synthetic and integrative because it establishes the unity of those same acts and experiences that had already been investigated at a different level by the first analytic phase of the method.*   Secondary reflection is considered the basic model for this new method because it demonstrates that empiricism is a concrete life process and not just an abstract and detached laboratory "science." Marcel wanted to make empiricism a reflective process of living and growing so that it could give meaning to the existence of the concrete individual rather than merely "crank out" more

---

*It is for this reason that Marcel refers to secondary reflection as a "recuperative" process. (*Reflection and mystery*. vol. 1 of *The mystery of being*. Trans. G. S. Fraser. Chicago: Gateway Editions, 1960, p. 113.)

statistical data for the further objectification and intellectualization of man. Marcel argued that secondary reflection is a vital and living process for it serves the same organizing and integrating function at the psychological level that the nervous system accomplishes at the physiological level.

Marcel's empirical method of reflection led him to the discovery of certain basic dimensions of the human condition. The most fundamental distinction he makes is between life as a "problem" and life as a "mystery."[15] He argues that we cannot answer the central question of our human identity by reducing it to a problem and trying to analyse its parts as if they were objective components of a complex machine. To reduce the psychology of man to the status of a "problem" is to assume that an answer to the question of our human identity merely awaits some new statistical data or information that will eventually be discovered by more sophisticated methods of scientific research. Now it is true that a problem can be solved by the accumulation of additional data and information because a problem deals with objects or a particular relationship between objects. But the question of our human identity cannot be reduced to the status of a problem because the "I" of man is not an object or an "it." Marcel certainly recognized that man's consciousness and his subjectivity were grounded in his physical being, and so man could be considered a specific type of natural object. Still the consciousness and subjectivity of man that make him distinct can never be eliminated and it is precisely these unique human attributes that make man a mystery rather than a problem. Marcel further argued that a mystery cannot be examined by the same empirical method of investigation as a problem since consciousness and subjectivity, which are attributes of a mystery, cannot be objectified as if they were "out there," isolated from the investigator and separate from the reality of his being-in-the-world.

This basic contrast between problem and mystery parallels a second and related distinction: "Everything really comes down to the distinction between what we have and what we are."[16] This second contrast between "what we have" *(having)* and "what we are" *(being)* clearly expresses Marcel's common existential concern with the alienation of man and the "broken world" produced by modern socialization and institutionalization.[17] He agrees with the other existentialists that this increasing objectification of man and society is destroying the possibility for man to survive as a creative and loving being—and even the possibility of his surviving at all. Man has been reduced to a mechanical "thing" who is fitted to a certain industrial task, located in a particular social class, and even given a specific statistical number. Society is dominated by industry and technology, and men have become prisoners in a world that they themselves helped build. Now society has succeeded in reducing everything, including men, to the category of mere "problems" whose behavior can be controlled and whose questions can be answered by easy calculation and simple manipulation. The "having" of material property, of social status, and even of knowledge becomes more important than the goal of personal "being" itself. And it is this obsession with "having" that tends to "blot us out" and to produce the alienation that is so characteristic of our modern society: "Having as such seems to have a tendency to destroy and lose itself in the very thing it began by possessing, but which now absorbs the master who thought he controlled it". The things that we acquire—a man's automobile, a woman's jewelry, or even a scholar's books and ideas —turn back upon us and come to "own" the one who first thought that he owned them: "Our possessions eat us up."[18]

Those persons who permit themselves to be thus devoured by their own possessions and become obsessed with "having" are cut off from themselves and from relationships with other people. "The man who remains on the plane of having (or of desire) is *centered,* either on himself or on another treated as another" and can no longer respond to the "being" or "thou" of meaningful human relationships.[19]

This loss of the capacity to be "present" in a meaningful way to our own self and to the personal self of another is the loss of our basic human identity and the loss of our capacity to be "faithful."[20] Marcel agrees with the common philosophical insight that only man can make a *promise* and he sees in this unique human potential the foundation of our "Being." The capacity to promise enables us to establish a special type of relationship between our own private self and the private self of another that is distinct to man. Marcel follows out the full implications of this human potential to make a promise and concludes that the ultimate character of man is grounded in "fidelity."[21] The potential to make and keep a promise therefore gives us a way back into "Being" and gives us a means to overcome human alienation in a world reduced to a problem and motivated by the principle of "having." Fidelity is at the heart of any relationship that demands our personal responsibility and Marcel argues that human existence finds its deepest meaning in the subjective affirmation of life as "being" through commitment and fidelity: "In these, man is recalled into the presence of mystery, that mystery which is the foundation of his very being, and apart from which he is nothingness."[22]

JASPERS (1883–1969)

Jaspers begins his approach to philosophy from the same point of departure and with the same basic goal as the other existentialists. His primary concern is with those aspects of our human existence that have been neglected, if not totally obliterated, by the destructive impact of modern science and technology. He insists that the goal of existentialism must be to correct this philosophical and psychological error that has manifested itself in the objectification and institutionalization of man and his world. He rejects the naive suggestion that a universal science could integrate the many fragmented disciplines and produce an effective body of knowledge that would both correct this methodological error and heal the psychological damage that has been done to modern man. He rejects this simplistic notion because a universal science, even if one could be established, would still fail to provide the crucial cure and the necessary corrective. He argues that each separate science can function only within the limits of its own chosen methodology. Consequently, any integration of all the sciences would still be restricted to the reality of those same chosen limits. And these limits placed on science are not due to the number of sciences considered or to their relationships with each other, but rather to the restrictions that science imposes upon itself by the use of only one method of investigation—the rational-empirical method. Such a method forces science, whether as a loose confederation of separate specialties or as a universal discipline, to reduce human experiences to impersonal objects in order to measure and quantify them. But the total reality of Being does not restrict itself to the arbitrary and artificial boundaries that science has established; nor can this reality be contained in the superficial statistical data that is forced into these narrow and rigid categories. Jaspers also warns that the complex subject matter of psychology—the concrete individual himself—is a factual part of existence, and the reality of his Being cannot be rejected merely because it does not fit an arbitrarily chosen and artificially structured methodology. Jaspers recognizes the contribution of science within the limits of its own methodological boundaries but he insists that psychology must move beyond these constricted limits if it is to encompass the authentic reality of man. Otherwise, psychology must content itself with a superficial and distorted view of its own subject matter and accept the fact that those aspects of life that are most meaningful will always remain hidden from us and beyond our scope.

Jaspers therefore focuses his attention on the same basic problem as the other existential philosophers—the concrete individual in existing situations. And Jaspers argues that this subjective and personal ground of Being which embodies the creative source of all life and all experience can and must be illuminated and encompassed. But this creative source of existence cannot be reduced to an object and studied within the methodology of empirical science for it is the very "source of my freedom" and, as such, it leads me to the ground of "being itself."[23] It is this personal and subjective source or "core" of human existence that gives direction and meaning to the reality of the concrete events in our daily life. The basic philosophical error of empirical science is that it attempts to substitute an object that can be measured by an impersonal observer for this subjective source that can only be illuminated and encompassed by the intuitive involvement of a concerned participant. Jaspers argues that philosophy must pass "through this nihilism" of sterile scientific objectification and begin to develop new and more creative methods of research if authentic psychological knowledge is to be discovered and explicated.[24]

Such new approaches to science and psychology must be based on methods of thought and research that permit the investigator to discover and experience his own self in that very process by which he advances knowledge. They must promote "a *different thinking,* a thinking that, in knowing, reminds me, awakens me, brings me to myself, transforms me."[25] And these new methods must not merely analyze the scientist or psychologist as another "object" but rather they must present and describe the ground of his professional stance as well as the subjective dynamics of his personal "being-in-the-world." These new methods must also reject and challenge any attempt by science to manufacture abstract general laws of behavior that reduce the unique individual to a statistical average of those universal laws. They must reject and challenge any such attempt in the name of science itself for the fact is that reality never arises as a universal or statistical abstraction but is always embodied in the concrete consciousness of an existing individual.

Jaspers outlines three "stages" of knowledge in his own philosophical approach to science and psychology. The first stage includes the lowest forms of knowledge such as statistical data based on the measurement of objects. The second stage of knowledge develops when the investigator recognizes within himself the basic dimensions of his own concrete existence. The third and final stage of knowledge emerges when man actualizes himself in relation to Being as transcendence. The second and third stages of knowledge are possible only when the investigator becomes conscious of his own finitude and the "limiting situations" that confront him, such as his own ultimate death. This personal encounter with our own finitude reveals to us the underlying nature of Being as transcendence. But the subjective encounter itself is an inward experience that is not amenable to rational or empirical proof. It is simply an encounter with the reality of existence that forces us to an awareness that the world in all its manifestations is grounded in transcendent Being. And we discover our freedom in that same encounter, for we find that in the actualization of our self we are free to affirm or to deny our relationship to the possibility of transcendence. Jaspers argues, however, that authentic existence does require that we affirm our relationship to transcendent Being even though there is no rational or empirical foundation for such an affirmation. But, unlike any formal religious commitment, this philosophical affirmation "has no holy object, no sacred place, no fixed form. The order which we give to it does not become a rule, it remains potentiality in free motion."[26]

Thus Jaspers confronts man with the same basic dilemma that is the common denominator of all existentialism. He places man in an existential stance where he must choose his own destiny beyond the limits of rational knowledge and scientific proof guided only by his own consciousness and his own subjectivity. Jaspers concludes that man can fulfill his human destiny only in a philosophical "leap of faith"* beyond reason into the transcendence of Being that lies at the existential depths of life.

CAMUS (1913–1960)

Camus was, as much as and perhaps more than any other modern existentialist, the authentic rebel who attacked the abstract systems and sciences of philosophy. He contrasted the intellectual claim to truth made by philosophy with the poverty of its actual contribution to the constructive development of man and society. He argued that the only valid way to assess philosophy was in terms of the concrete meaning it gives to the life of the existing individual. That is, only in terms of those concrete goals and values for which the existing individual is willing to live, to struggle and, if necessary, even to die.† Camus further ar-

---

*"This faith, which appears in many forms, becomes neither authority nor dogma; it remains dependent on communication among men . . ." (Jaspers, K. *Philosophical faith and revelation.* Trans. E. B. Ashton. New York: Harper and Row, 1967, p. 60.)

†Kierkegaard put this same goal to philosophy and man: "The thing is to find a truth which is true *for me . . . for which I can live and die.*" (*The journals of Kierkegaard.* Trans. A. Dru. New York: Harper Torchbooks, 1959, [date of entry, 1835] p. 44.)

gued that these passionate *commitments* to truth have more emotional integrity and philosophical authenticity than all the abstract intellectual *ideas* that make up the sterile history of philosophy. Still there is no safe and easy way to existentialism. Camus places a heavy burden on those who would choose such a philosophy. He demands that all our existential values be grounded in a radical commitment to absolute and unconditional freedom. That is, our existential choices become valid philosophical truths only when a man is willing to declare and defend his personal freedom at the risk of his own life. But we cannot take that existential risk among the abstract thoughts and speculative ideas of philosophy where nothing is ever personal and nothing is ever at stake. It is only by concrete acts of open rebellion against the destructive power of tyranny and oppression that we can proclaim our freedom and bring down the wrath of "the gods" upon us. It is only by such concrete acts that our existential commitments become valid philosophical truths, for then we know in our deepest self that we can suffer the "dreadful punishment" demanded by a philosophy of passion and revolution.*

So is it consistent with such a philosophy, based on radical commitments and concrete acts, that Camus did not develop in his own work any formal system and did not restrict himself to any one philosophical model or style. His personal involvement in philosophy remained too spontaneous and immediate to tolerate theoretical digressions into the ontological or epistomological implications of his position.

It is also true that Camus was more concerned with the

---

*Camus uses Sisyphus as an example of the passionate rebel and his fate: Sisyphus rebelled against "the gods" and was condemned "to ceaselessly rolling a rock to the top of a mountain, whence the stone would fall back of its own weight. They had thought with some reason that there is no more dreadful punishment than futile and hopeless labor." (*The myth of Sisyphus.* Trans. J. O'Brien. New York: Vintage Books, 1960, p. 88.)

revolt of individual man against his fallen and estranged condition than with social revolution as an organized political activity. No one can deny that political revolution emerges out of this basic individual struggle against human estrangement and social alienation but Camus focused only on the dynamics of the basic existential struggle itself, i.e., the rebellion of the individual against the "system." He even argues that most political revolutions organized as social movements to overthrow an authoritarian system only substitute their own totalitarian system in the end. The oppression is still the same as before and only the style, slogans and rhetoric have changed. These slight variations on the same old theme of tyranny give no comfort to the authentic rebel and so he must continue in his private revolt against the world.*

Camus, therefore, focused his attention on the dynamic struggle of the private individual in his revolt against the futility of a world in which there are no rational rules to guide us and no authority to give us an excuse to live. The recognition of this futility forces us to make one of three choices—we can adjust to the routine of a socialized and objectified world and "desensitize" ourselves to the reality of estrangement and alienation; we can take up the challenge to exist and revolt against our "thrown" condition; or we can escape both these alternatives and commit suicide. The analogy Camus uses to describe our human dilemma is that of Sisyphus ceaselessly pushing a rock to the top of a mountain from which it rolls down again to the plain. Sisyphus, like each one of us, is confronted with three

---

*Revolution must be the personal responsibility of each individual but it is grounded in a compassion and responsibility for all: "Then we understand that rebellion cannot exist without a strange form of love. Those who find no rest in God or in history are condemned to live for those who, like themselves, cannot live: in fact, for the humiliated. The most pure form of the movement of rebellion is thus crowned with the heart-rending cry . . . if all are not saved, what good is the salvation of one only?" (Camus, A. *The rebel: An essay on man in revolt.* Trans. A. Bower. New York: Vintage Books, 1956, p. 304.)

choices in relation to his fate. He can adjust to the situation and become a slave hoping to gain some momentary relief at the whim of the gods whom he has appeased by his submission; he can ask no quarter from any god or man and take on the endless burden of tension and struggle that the life of revolution demands; or he can choose neither to adjust nor to revolt but to escape the brutal dilemma by his own suicide.

Now existentialism is considered a pessimistic philosophy because it confronts man with the reality of these three "dreadful" alternatives. Yet it is seen by existentialists themselves as a constructive and creative philosophy because it gives us the hope of a personal victory over our "thrown" condition and our "cruel" fate. Sisyphus does choose to rebel and in his fight against the gods he does become "stronger than his rock . . . his fate belongs to him . . . he knows himself to be the master of his days." Still Camus must leave Sisyphus "at the foot of the mountain for one always finds one's burden again." Camus uses the analogy of Sisyphus and his battle against the gods to point us toward the creative thrust of existentialism that teaches us a "higher fidelity that negates the gods and raises rocks . . . the struggle itself toward the heights is enough to fill a man's heart."[27]

Camus insists, again like the other existentialists, that man can find in his rebellion a value that is his own and one that will give meaning and purpose to his individual life. And it is this value that must be maintained against all odds, for surrender leads to death either in the act of adaptation or in the act of suicide. But such rebellion does not promise us any sudden or total victory over the course of human history. It offers us only the uncertain hope of making a limited contribution to its positive development. Even these slow and gradual changes demand a great price from each individual, for revolution can be maintained only by a constant tension and a constant discipline that never rests.* This process of ceaseless revolution is crucial to the future of man because all the intellectual and social systems that it attacks are but new and varied forms of the same oppressive tyranny. Camus concludes that only in the constant tension of a disciplined rebellion by each individual against objectification and socialization can we find hope for the survival of authentic values and for the survival of man himself. It is a "dreadful" struggle but that struggle itself "is enough to fill a man's heart."

BERDYAEV (1875–1948)

Nicholas Berdyaev must be considered one of the most colorful and dramatic of the modern existential philosophers. The intensity of his personality and his existential commitment to freedom led to his exile from Czarist Russia before the revolution, and then to his exile again by the Bolshevik government after the revolution. His clear insight into the nature of freedom and his equally clear demand that he and others be permitted to live it made him an enemy of both the old and the new political systems. Berdyaev was more a philosopher in the sense of a prophet than a scholar, and more "religious" in the sense of a faith in the human spirit than a belief in any omnipotent God. He was a true champion of the spiritual dignity of man in all his battles against positivism, materialism, and totalitarianism.

Now Berdyaev was colorful and dramatic not only because of his direct involvement in a particular revolutionary phase of history but also because of the nature of his philosophy itself. He attempted to combine and merge widely divergent traditions such as theism and atheism, personal-

---

*Sisyphus gets only a temporary respite from his labor each time "the stone falls back of its own weight," and he descends the mountain to begin again.

ism and socialism, and even eastern and western views of life and man. It was Berdyaev's personal embodiment of this complex mixture of forces that contributed, more than the life and work of any other existentialist, to the development of modern movements toward an ecumenical world order. His appeal was grounded in this convergence of forces which made his philosophy a meeting point for many diverse and varied human potentials. And he attempted to encompass this totality of the world in the concrete experience of the existing individual:

> Personality cannot be recognized as an object, as one of the objects in a line with other objects in the world, like a part of the world. That is the way in which the anthropological sciences, biology, psychology, or sociology would regard man. In that way man is looked at partially; but there is in that case no mystery of man, as personality, as an existential center of the world. Personality is recognized only as a subject, in infinite subjectivity, in which is hidden the secret of existence.[28]

He further argued that "only the subject is capable of knowing reality," and declared that "what concerns, and absorbs, and haunts me is the destiny of the subject, the microcosmos, in which there stirs and throbs the whole universe, and which bears witness to the meaning of its own and the world's existence."[29]

Berdyaev can be best understood as a spiritual "anarchist" for he was against all forms of objectification and even committed to the position that " 'objective' things are devoid of ultimate reality; they are an illusion of our consciousness."[30] Berdyaev's lust for something more substantial than rational or empirical knowledge led him, like the other existentialists we have discussed, to an encounter with Being itself. And Berdyaev found his salvation and his ground in that Being which is freedom: "Freedom is the ultimate: it cannot be derived from anything: it cannot be made the equivalent of anything. Freedom is the baseless foundation of being: it is deeper than all being. We cannot penetrate to a rationally-perceived base for freedom. Freedom is a well of immeasurable depth—its bottom is the final mystery."[31]

BUBER (1878–1965)

Buber agrees with the general consensus among most existentialists that the objective method can lead to certain types of knowledge about the nature of external reality, and even about the nature of man as far as he can be observed and understood from an *external* point of view. But such an objective method of investigation can give us only "relative" truth about nature and man because it depends only on the arbitrary perspective chosen and the arbitrary scientific vocabulary adopted. And more important still, such an objective method cannot even ask questions about the meaning of our human destiny—let alone try to answer them. Only the subjective method can discover and comprehend man's inner experiences and transform them into an "absolute" knowledge of which each of these individual experiences is an integral part. Absolute knowledge can be discovered and comprehended but only in the concrete reality of an existing individual and, therefore, this absolute knowledge about factual reality cannot be used as a basis for scientific abstractions and generalizations.

Buber develops a method of investigation from this basic theoretical position that can lead us to factual knowledge about the subjective reality of man and his world. He sees in the dynamic process of "interpersonal relationships" a basic point of departure for his investigation and makes it the central focus of his philosophy. Buber's work is based primarily on the distinction between two types of relationships, which he defines as "I-It" and "I-Thou." He uses this basic distinction because, he argues, man cannot declare the reality of his own "I" in isolation but only in relation to some other object or person. Therefore the basic existential "I" is always relational; and the way that "I" is experienced depends on the way that the particular individual chooses to relate himself to the other object or person. The two choices open in every case are to treat the other as an "It" or as a "Thou." In the first case we see the other as an object analysed from outside and treat him or her as an "It." In the second case we enter into the immediacy of a subjective awareness of the other as an existing individual and experience his being as an authentic "Thou." These two choices are generally equivalent to the parallel contrast between an objective and a subjective approach to psychology and to man. Yet Buber's sensitive articulation of the contrast between "It" and "Thou" has given us new insights into the significance of this basic philosophical distinction. Therefore we must examine his argument in some detail.

Buber asserts that the choice we make in our relationship to the other determines, in turn, the nature of the self that we declare as "I." The "I" who experiences an "I-It" relationship can never experience the whole of his own being because to observe the other as an object necessitates the use of only certain perceptual faculties, and thus excludes basic parts of his own self. Buber argues that we distort the reality of the other as well as the reality of our own self as soon as we fragment the other and observe isolated aspects of him, such as the color of his hair, the pitch of his voice, or even his attitudes and his ideas. Man can accurately perceive the reality of another person, and authentically experience his own subjective reality, only when he enters into the fullness of an "I-Thou" relationship. Only then is the whole of the "I" fully involved with and responding to the subjective presence of the other as that other emerges and makes himself intuitively known. Now the "I" that participates in the relationship is no longer a "broken" self observing a fragmented "It," but an existing "I" living in the intimacy and presence of an existing "Thou."

Buber insists that any authentic investigation of subjective reality must be based on this type of personal "meeting." And such a meeting can take place only if the "I" suspends all artificial, social and professional modes of relationship in order to immerse itself in the subjective and intuitive reality of an interpersonal experience. The self must be so deeply and so completely absorbed in an emotional reach for the inner subjectivity of the other that all objective considerations are eliminated from awareness. And we do discover when we succeed in entering into this type of subjective, intuitive and personally vulnerable relationship that the other does emerge as an authentic "Thou." It is this open and vulnerable response of one sensitive being to another that produces the "I-Thou" relationship, which Buber calls an existential meeting. And it is only in such a "primary" meeting that we can discover the reality of our own self and the reality of our relationship with the self of another.[32]

Now one necessary characteristic of the "I-Thou" relationship is that it must be experienced in the present. Those who have tried to enter into the reality of the present realize that this is a very difficult thing to do. Our practical obligations force our attention to the past where we find our practical solutions and our practical guides for the future. Then the present quickly escapes through the thin line of "now" and becomes part of our practical past. But it is obvious that if we are to exist in any authentic sense we must be able to enter into the reality of the present and experience that reality as fully and deeply as possible. And such a venture entails a personal effort and a personal risk, for we must become so involved in and attentive to the concrete moment that we find ourselves merging into a new subjective experience that dissolves the objective

world and replaces it with another mode of existence. It is
this merging into the concrete "now" of another mode of
existence that Buber calls an "I-Thou" relationship or a
"primary meeting."

One further aspect of the "I-Thou" relationship is that
it not only enables us to discover the deeper reality of the
other, but it also leads us to a deeper knowledge of our own
personal being. Each time we enter into a subjective relationship and gain intuitive knowledge of the self of another
we better understand the distinction between our own accidental objective characteristics and those deeper aspects of
our personality that are the "core" or "heart" of our being.
It is also in this deeper discovery of our own selves that we
discover at the same time the existential ground of Being
which is *common to all men.* And that existential ground of
Being encompasses both our uniqueness as existing individuals and our shared experience of a common human
destiny. One is the "spiritual form" of individuality and the
other is the "spiritual form" of communality. Buber argues
that it is possible to establish an authentic interpersonal
"bond" only on the existential ground of such an "I-Thou"
relationship.

Buber's stress on the subjective method, the personal
meeting, and the existential present do not mean that he
rejects the significance of the objective method. He recognizes that we cannot live constantly in an "I-Thou" relationship nor constantly in the present. He insists that it is
an illusion to feel that we could perpetually sustain the
intensity demanded of an "I-Thou" relationship or of an
existence entirely in the present, for "life would be quite
consumed if precautions were not taken."[33] An objective
intercourse with the world is therefore necessary in order
to sustain us in our everyday actions and give us a realistic
"situation" in which to express the deeper existential
meaning of our lives. Consequently, an objective view of
both science and the world are indispensable aspects of

existential reality and can serve a useful purpose—as long as their limits are clearly understood. Buber seems to conclude that objectivity is necessary for our practical survival, but that "Thou" is the primal source and the authentic ground of our human existence.

The "I-Thou" mode of being-in-the-world is difficult to grasp and difficult to hold because it cannot be generalized into a scientific abstraction nor categorized within a logical system. It is a volatile mode of being that must be constantly created and experienced anew; but at the same time it is the most concrete of all realities, and those who have experienced it will bear witness to its authenticity. Still, the "I-Thou" mode of being cannot be observed and measured as an object in the natural world for that would reduce the "Thou" to an "It" and the existential dynamic expressed by the relationship would be destroyed. Nor can this unique mode of existence be contained within any logical or rational intellectual system for the "I-Thou" experience begins beyond the limits of reason and science.

Buber also declares emphatically that the "I-Thou" relationship cannot be contained within any structured or institutionalized social order, for "a world that is ordered is not the world-order."[34]* Any type of totalitarian or dictatorial political system can produce the illusion that an ideal order has been established, but Buber insists that man must rebel against all such political systems just as he must rebel against all closed intellectual systems. He even goes further and argues that while the "Thou" cannot be contained within a social system it can point us toward the conditions that any human community must try to fulfill. He presents the "I-Thou" relationship as a model that can serve as a corrective to the contemporary social dilemma

---

*We shall see in Ch. 17 that Skinner's utopian community named *Walden Two* is an "ordered world," but the "Thou" has been eliminated and so it is the exact opposite of the ideal "world-order" toward which Buber points us.

that has left man with two equally inappropriate alternatives—modern individualism and modern collectivism. He takes the position that both of these views are the result of the same conditions and that they are only different stages of development. They are both reactions to the isolation, loneliness, despair, and alienation experienced by modern man. But individualism grasps only a part of man since it ignores his communality, while collectivism acknowledges man only as a part or a component of a social system, and thereby ignores his individuality. Both destroy the authenticity of man, for the first distorts his unique human character beyond recognition and the second tries to suppress it completely. The only solution is a community in which each citizen knows the depths of his own individual self as well as the common roots of that identity in the shared destiny of all men. Buber concludes that there can be no authentic answer to our human and social problems until each one of us learns to say "Thou."

chapter 5

BINSWANGER AND BOSS: THE FOUNDATIONS OF EXISTENTIAL PSYCHOLOGY

The work of Ludwig Binswanger and Medard Boss provides us with a meeting ground for existential philosophy and existential psychology. These two men were philosophers as well as psychologists and psychotherapists. They combined Heidegger's theoretical insights into the nature of Dasein with Buber's insights into the psychological and therapeutic significance of the "I-Thou" relationship. And it was the metaphysics of the "I-Thou" relationship that Binswanger described in his challenge to Freud and to which Freud responded by presenting his manuscript of *The Future of an Illusion.* So it is essential to the development of any new psychology that we understand the work of these two "pioneers," for that work embodies the challenge to traditional science and psychology, as well as the dynamics and the foundations of existential psychology itself.

BINSWANGER (1881–1966)

Binswanger combined the philosophical sophistication of Heidegger with the philosophical sensitivity of Buber.

He expressed this new combination in a distinguished career of medical practice as an associate of Bleuler, Jung, and Freud. This new mixture brought to the discipline of psychology the existential and phenomenological corrective so essential to its future development. Binswanger called his new approach to psychology "Daseinsanalyse," and applied the phenomenological method directly to his investigations of psychiatric patients in his clinical work.[1] But Binswanger's most important contribution to the history of psychology was his profound critique of his own discipline and his outline of its limits and possibilities. His goal was to make the new discipline of psychology conscious of its unique potential, and aware of its essential structure as a science.

He began his attempt to outline the basic structure of psychology as a science at that point in the history of the discipline when the traditional paradigm of science and psychology had, in his opinion, "collapsed" under the pressure of new advances in existential philosophy. He argued that the method of natural science first adopted by psychology was oriented toward a "reality" and "objectivity" that was defined in terms of separate areas of facts arranged into patterns and systems (e.g., Kraepelin's categories of psychopathology or Freud's Id, Ego, and Superego). Such a demarcation of experience into isolated regions made events placed into these separate areas amenable to objective inquiry and determination. But the basic contribution of existentialism to the development of modern science and psychology has been to demonstrate that this artificial demarcation of experience is too constricted an approach to encompass psychological facts, and that its scope must be broadened and its horizon extended. This methodological challenge to science and psychology stems from the existential insight into the transcendent nature of man as Dasein. That insight forces psychology to abandon the methodological "dissection" of human experience into isolated regions, because phenomenology has shown that such an approach produces a world-design that does not correspond to those human experiences which it claims to represent and to measure.

Binswanger recognized that it was not sufficient just to demonstrate this methodological error of science and psychology but that the "what" which had been eliminated must be described and understood so that it could be included in any future psychological paradigm. Binswanger described this "what" that had been eliminated by empirical science as the ability of the organism to "call itself I."[2] Any science of psychology which reduces man to a chemical or mechanical organism so that he cannot use the authentic existential "I" in the description of himself destroys its own empiricism because it no longer studies man as an existential reality. The phenomenological investigation of man as Dasein has revealed that Dasein is distinguished by the fact that "in its very Being, that Being is an *issue* for it."[3] Phenomenology has provided us with a new approach to the basic anthropological fact that Dasein is "in its very Being" concerned essentially with its own being and is directed toward itself. Any world-design of psychology that eliminates the potentiality of the organism to say "I" or "me" or "mine" destroys itself as a science, for it destroys the very "what" of man that it pretends to investigate. Such a psychology is not a science for it only constructs rational systems or accumulates empirical data on the behavior of an objectified organism that is but an artificial symbol of man. Consequently, it cannot be considered a serious enterprise because it does not even undertake a factual investigation of the reality of its own subject matter. Such a "science" of man as organism results from the "*reduction* of man to his bodily existence and the further reduction of his bodily existence to a mere neutrally present, 'ownerless,' object."[4] Binswanger gives a concrete example[5] of such a reduction when memory is studied as the isolated process of a brain that is neither "yours" nor "his" nor "mine." He warns that in reality the mnemonic process, like any other human process, can be understood only within the perspective of a particular Dasein's power to be in the world as retentive, forgetful, and recollective. Memory cannot be understood simply as a physiological mechanism. It is a basic phenomenological fact that the isolated brain of an isolated organism does not "remember." Only man as an existential being, man as Dasein, has the power of "recollection." And it is equally obvious that any scientific paradigm that eliminates the reality of "I" destroys human freedom at the same time, for only an "I" can choose and will its own existence.

The existential revolution in psychology today can be understood only as a rebellion against this attempt of "science" to destroy Dasein and its freedom. The elimination of the "I" and its freedom makes the relation between man and his environment a fixed and determined one in which facticity alone controls his destiny. He has been reduced to an object by the loss of his "I," and so it follows that in such a helpless, "thrown," condition the physical causality and psychic determinism of psychology are applicable. Psychoanalysis and behaviorism are therefore valid sciences for man *only after* he has been reduced from a reality to an illusion and when Dasein is determined only by the facticity of its thrownness because it has lost the power to choose and create itself. But this is exactly the existential definition of psychopathology: "In all these cases, the Dasein can no longer freely allow the world to be, but is, rather, increasingly surrendered over to one particular world-design, possessed by it, overpowered by it. The technical term for this state of being surrendered over is: 'thrownness'."[6] Thus, psychoanalysis describes in endless theoretical detail, and behaviorism accumulates endless statistical data on—nothing but psychopathology. And so these "sciences of psychopathology" that claim to explain everything can, in fact, tell us nothing about the existential reality of man and his "being-in-the-world."

The "I" of man and his freedom give Dasein the power to stand over against the facticity of its environment and to choose and create a responsible relationship to the reality of its own thrownness. But in the system of psychoanalysis, in the science of behaviorism, and in the state of psychopathology, the Dasein is surrendered over to a world-design for which it assumes no responsibility and to which it does not actively relate itself. Dasein in these instances becomes subservient to and is controlled by its facticity. It is reduced to a state that Binswanger describes as "self-chosen unfreedom." This state of "self-chosen unfreedom" results from the destruction of "I," and the "sole task of psychotherapy" is to assist man to encounter the finite limits of his human existence and then gain " 'power' over his existence within this very powerlessness."[7]

The "sole task of psychotherapy" described here by Binswanger is, basically, the same goal of psychotherapy proposed by Otto Rank, which we have already discussed. Rank argued that the instinctual and biological relationships between parent and child were but the accidental facts of his "thrownness," and only constituted the existential ground upon which the child must discover his own freedom and create his own destiny.

Binswanger explicitly states this same position in the conclusion to one of his many carefully documented case studies. A female patient with a pathological relationship to her father had plunged her hand into the hot coals of a stove and then cried: "Look, this is to show you how much I love you!"[8] Binswanger warns us not to interpret this history, in the manner of psychoanalysis, merely as "a history of the libido, of its fixation onto father, its forced withdrawal from father, and its eventual transference to the world-around." He argues that, rather, a person's history and his relationships are but the existential ground upon which he discovers and creates his being, and that parents are, in most cases, a usual part of that ground: "But that Ilse got just that father and that mother was her destiny, received as a heritage and as a task; how to bear up under this destiny was the problem of her existence. Hence, in her father complex were destiny *and* freedom at work."[9]*

Binswanger argues, again like Rank, that only from the proper philosophical perspective can we understand the authentic meaning of life and, thereby, the authentic meaning of psychotherapy. And it was from the existential view of life and relationships that they both came to recognize that psychotherapy occurs only when there is a genuine meeting and a common understanding between the patient and the therapist in a relationship based on personal care and love. The psychotherapist, therefore, must venture beyond objective knowledge and beyond those technical skills that are its manipulative tools into the transcendence of an "I-Thou" relationship. And Binswanger most clearly expresses Buber's profound influence upon him in his own conception of knowledge. He concludes that a purely "objective" psychology eliminates the existential meaning of man's relation to himself and to others, and that all authentic knowledge has its ground in the person "as a self but also as a being-together with one another—relatedness and love."[10]

BOSS (1903–   )

Boss, like Binswanger, brought to psychology a distinguished career in medical practice as well as a sophisticated

---

*It is obvious that in his theory Binswanger did not reject any of the clinical facts that have been observed by all psychotherapists, e.g., personality conflicts concerning incest and homosexuality. He rejected only the psychoanalytic reduction of these observed facts to the determined categories of a closed biological system.

background in philosophy. He was associated in his professional work with Freud, Bleuler, Horney, Goldstein, and others. Even more important to our specific task of building an existential science is the fact that he was a close personal friend of Martin Heidegger, and that his translation of Heidegger's philosophy into psychological theory and practice was developed in collaboration with Heidegger himself. Let us try then to understand the basic dimensions of Boss' version of Daseinsanalyse.

The most important dimension of existential psychology (or Daseinsanalyse) is its insistence on the freedom of man. Consequently, any theoretical model of existential psychology must reject the concept of causality that is at the base of traditional systematic and scientific psychology. Boss articulates this rejection from many perspectives. Yet his essential argument is that while the principle of causality has been a useful assumption for the physical sciences, the attempt to transfer that same principle to psychology is the reason for the crisis in our discipline today. Boss asserts that there are *no* causal determinants in human relationships and human existence. Such a complete rejection of the principle of causality follows from the insistence that man is totally free and totally responsible for his acts. Thus we are forced to an either/or choice between determinism on the one hand, and freedom on the other. Boss agrees, of course, that there are events which have related existential significance in the life of an individual. Still this does not mean that one of these events "caused" the other—like the force of one physical object causes a second physical object to move. He argues that a traumatic emotional experience in the life of an individual may be related to a subsequent withdrawal reaction (e.g., an automobile accident may be related to a subsequent phobia of cars). But the trauma (the accident) did not "cause" the withdrawal (the phobia). Only the interpretation or meaning that the individual himself chose to ascribe to the accident can adequately account for the subsequent phobia. It is obvious that another choice could have been made regarding the accident, and that a different choice than phobia usually is made in similar circumstances. The different choice would have, in turn, expressed itself in a different behavioral reaction. Boss, therefore, rejects causality and determinism in his search for a more viable science and insists that the concepts of choice and motivation give us, in fact, a much more accurate and a much more empirical description of human behavior. His argument is similar to that given by Merleau-Ponty: there is no one-to-one correspondence between stimulus and response (and consequently no causal determinism in human experience) because conceptual and symbolic forms of behavior that can be freely chosen and actively willed mediate between any given stimulus and any given response to it. Boss contends that the study of motivation—which assumes that one either understands, or has the potential to understand, the relation between events—gives us a much more accurate and much more valid empirical description of behavior. Even a simple behavioral act, such as picking up a book from my desk, can be accurately and meaningfully understood only in terms of my intentions and my awareness of the consequences of the act. Thus the phenomenological articulation and description of my behavior would not be content with a simplistic causal explanation, i.e., the movement of my arm "caused" the movement of the book like one billiard ball causes the movement of another. Instead, a phenomenological description would try to clarify or "illuminate" the dynamics of the behavior in terms of my choices and my intentions or, in other words, in terms of my total motivation. The analysis of behavior into mechanical cause and effect sequences that are isolated from conscious awareness only fragments the reality of human experience and makes it impossible to explicate behavior, for "articulation is possible only in the context of a whole that has been left intact; all articulation, as such, derives from wholeness."[11]

Another basic existential theme stressed by Boss is that man is distinct from all other natural phenomena. Consequently, the reduction of man to a natural object makes it impossible for us to establish a science that can explicate and articulate his reality as being-in-the-world. Furthermore, such reductionism has contributed to the fragmentation, estrangement, and alienation of modern man. Such reductionism has left modern man helpless and at the mercy of technology, mechanization, and institutionalization. Existentialists even assert that the objectification of man by psychology, in an attempt to predict and control his behavior, has been one of the major contributing factors to his present state of helplessness and exploitation. And they further wonder what man and society might be like today if psychology had been a challenge to the mechanization of man rather than one of technology's most destructive intellectual tools. Therefore, the basic thrust of existential psychology is to reject this reductive and destructive function that psychology has served up to this point in its history, and to turn psychology back against itself—and forward to new human horizons and new creative goals.

Just as the attack on conventional psychology stems from a rejection of that causal determinism which strips man of his dignity, responsibility, and authenticity, so must the development of any new psychology be based on the existential ground of freedom, care, and love. Boss argues that no event in the life history of an individual ever "causes" that person to become "neurotic" or "psychotic." Rather, a pattern of experiences in the life history of an individual may discourage that person from actively and creatively carrying out all his possible relationships to himself, to other persons, and to the world. The goal, then, of any therapeutic intervention consists in the establishment of an interpersonal relationship within which the patient becomes aware of and assumes responsibility for all his own possibilities and relates himself to these possibilities "whether they please him or his fellow men or not."[12] No genuine knowledge of the self and, consequently, no meaningful actualization of the self, are possible until an individual assumes this responsibility for *all* his possible and chosen actions in the world. Thus the goal of psychotherapy is to "illuminate" the past, present, and future life of the patient to the point where he becomes aware of his basic existential responsibility to himself and to the world. Such an awareness emerges only from the pain of human crisis and human encounter for it is only at such depths that man can recognize the possibility of freedom and take that possibility "upon himself." These authentic possibilities of Dasein can be "illuminated" only from within the being of the patient as he encounters himself and learns to listen "to the call of his conscience."[13]*Such a process of inward exploration and discovery enables the patient to take over responsibility for those possibilities which are illuminated, stand by himself in relation to them, and make those possibilities that are his own a real part of himself.

Boss argues that the existential "cause" of psychopathology is only this *refusal* of an individual to recognize his own possibilities and to assume his own responsibility for them. Once a person fails to take responsibility for those possibilities that are his own and fails to integrate his own possibilities into an authentic self, he "falls prey to the demands, wishes, and expectations of others."[14] The individual then abandons his own unique possibilities in order to meet the "foreign expectations" of others in the hope that those who hold these alien standards will not abandon him. He vainly attempts to find safety and protection in

---

*"Conscience" as used here is similar to "Daemon" in the original Socratic sense of that term.

passive submission to the will of others rather than suffer the anxiety of separation and find his own base of security within the reality of his own individual being. But the more he abandons his own possibilities, and the more he submits himself to the possibilities of those around him, the deeper he sinks into the existential guilt and despair of having failed to encounter and become his own unique and authentic self. Boss argues that pathological feelings of guilt are due *only* to this failure on the part of the individual to choose his own freedom and to fulfill his own possibilities.

Boss further argues that it is possible to relieve these pathological feelings of guilt, because they do not originate within the patient but are imposed upon him by his passive submission to arbitrary external authorities. He becomes a victim of modes of life alien to his own possibilities, and these artificial external "voices" deafen him to the authentic call of his own individual conscience. Thus, it is the goal of the existential encounter in psychotherapy to awaken the patient to his own *personal* conscience, and to free him to rebel against the authority of others and to express his own unique and authentic self. It is by such an open act of individual rebellion and self-expression that pathological feelings of guilt are eliminated. But the elimination of *pathological* guilt is by no means elimination of the primal reality of *existential* guilt itself. Here again we see the link between Rank and existentialism, for Boss asserts that both our freedom *and* our guilt start with the trauma and separation of birth. We recognize at some vague level of awareness as we experience the pain and "thrownness" of our birth that it is now our own burden and our own responsibility to maintain, develop, and integrate that life which has suddenly and unexpectedly become "mine." Boss argues that it is with this vague recognition of our own responsibility for our own existence that man begins his indebtedness to carry out "all the possibilities for living of which he is capable."[15] And death is our only relief from this primordial existential guilt, for no authentic individual can escape the mandate to create his own destiny and to fulfill his own possibilities.

It is now clear why existentialism must reject the principle of psychic determinism in order to establish the reality of that human freedom and that human responsibility which are the foundations of existential psychology. Boss argues that man's existential guilt, disclosed by the "call of his conscience,"[16] and his freedom to respond to that call, are the structural foundations of Dasein. This primordial indebtedness, or guilt, of Dasein is distinct from and precedes any symptomatic manifestation of pathological guilt. The danger of reductive theories such as psychoanalysis and behaviorism is not so much that they will irradicate this primordial indebtedness or guilt of Dasein (although this must be seriously considered as an evolutionary possibility), but that these systems and methods of treatment simply substitute new symptoms for the old ones—or, what is even worse, they "deafen a patient to his pangs of conscience."[17] Boss describes the destructive consequences of such systems of treatment in his description of an iatrogenic*disease called "psychoanalytis." He argues that this syndrome is "by no means rare," and seems to imply that it is more the rule than the exception. Those who suffer from this new iatrogenic syndrome engage in

> ritualistic thinking and talking in psychoanalytic terms and symbols. Circles and sects are formed of similarly afflicted persons. While many such adherence may lose old symptoms, the neurotic nature of their new conduct is easy to detect. Instead of staying close to the immediately observable appearances of the world, they disregard them and speculate about what is "behind" them, unaware that their observations do not support their deductions. Instead of dwelling in openness toward the things and people they encounter, they "interpret" these same phenomena, human

*doctor-induced

and material. Generally such people cling rigidly to their theoretical convictions and take great pains to avoid people with different ideas. Their symptoms indicate their inability to penetrate beyond the concepts and interpretations of psychoanalytic theory; they have failed to arrive at an open and immediate world-relation.[18]

Boss further argues that the destructive outcomes of these "authoritarian" systems and treatments are but an expression of the nature of the relationship between the practitioner and the patient. Daseinsanalysis calls for a dramatic reformulation of the relationship between therapist and patient, just as it demanded a dramatic reformulation of the theoretical foundations on which any treatment is based. Boss argues that the psychoanalyst assumes an authoritarian stance of silence and abstinence as a technical device in order to produce transference by frustrating the patient and forcing him to regress to earlier infantile stages. He further argues that no creative human growth can ever result from such an artificial relationship and from months of "working through the transference" during which time the "supposed meaning of the patient's relationship to the analyst and his acting-out are drilled into him."[19]*

Daseinsanalysis, on the other hand, insists that there must be a genuine human relationship between therapist and patient. The two participants, as the process of their "being-together" unfolds, must come to understand and experience that they are grounded in a common human

*Apologists for psychoanalysis would argue that this is only true of "bad" transference and that Boss has merely presented a biased caricature of psychoanalysis. Boss, on the other hand, would answer that all transference, no matter how skillfully executed, is "bad" transference, and that his description is not a caricature but a precise and accurate insight into the destructive nature of any relationship "whatsoever" that is based on a "transfer of affect." He would further insist that transference cannot be "worked through," as claimed by analysts, but only "drilled in" (no matter how subtly done), once the patient has been "maneuvered" into a passive-submissive relationship to the transference authority.

destiny. They must each recognize and communicate, either directly or indirectly, that they are the same kind of
being and that each of them is an equal partner in the
common venture toward change and growth. Boss insists
on the rejection of all such concepts as "the 'transfer of
libido' from a 'primarily narcissistic ego' to the 'love object,'" or "the transference of an affect from a former
object to a present-day partner," etc. It is the very nature
of Dasein to disclose its being to itself and to others, and
so any artificial "transference" or "regression" only destroys the potential for authentic interpersonal communication. Boss concludes that there is "no interpersonal
relationship whatsoever" that requires or necessitates "a
transfer of affect."[20] The fact that the patient may misjudge
the actual situation because of his emotional immaturity
does not alter the reality that his feelings are his own, are
genuine, and that they are to some extent a function of the
professional attitude taken by the therapist himself. The
feelings of the patient cannot be simply explained as objective facts within a closed biological system and then dismissed as due either to "transference" or "resistance." For
the patient will begin to enter into an authentic love relationship with the therapist only when he comes to recognize that he is in the presence of someone who will take his
innermost feelings seriously, can understand their unique
subjective meaning, and accepts him as a person in spite of
his emotional immaturity. He comes to love the therapist
even more because the therapist gives him the occasion to
discover and experience, in the security of a trusted relationship, those deeper aspects of his being that up until
now have been beyond his reach. And Boss argues that all
genuine love of one person for another is "based on the
possibility which the loved one offers to the lover for a
fuller unfolding of his own being by being-in-the-world
with him."[21] So is it equally clear that "transference" destroys this possibility for a genuine love relationship, be-

cause the patient will hate the analyst as long as he is restricted to the limited perception of a child-father or child-mother relationship. Boss further concludes that he will hate him even more—and with good reason—if the analyst, because of his own limited world view and his own restricted emotional attitude toward the patient, "actually behaves like one of the formerly hated parents."[22] Thus, Boss offers those of us interested in existential approaches to psychology and psychotherapy the hope that we will be able to gain insight into the authentic nature of man, and will be able to help not only patients in particular but mankind in general to move "beyond the relief of symptoms to participation in a human freedom and openness."[23]

It is clear that the work of Binswanger and Boss has provided us with the basic foundations for the development of modern existential psychology and psychotherapy. Other psychological theorists and therapists such as Bugental, May, Moustakas, Burton, Gendlin, Laing and Jourard have for the most part added interesting and valuable translations or variations to these basic existential themes and theories. And today the number of psychologists turning their attention toward existential and humanistic approaches is rapidly increasing as part of the general rebellion against the modern objectification and institutionalization of man. So let us start now with our primary task—to outline a model of human science that can guide and monitor the development of these new existential and humanistic approaches to psychology.

Part II

BIOLOGY

chapter 6

THE BIOLOGICAL ASSUMPTIONS
THAT UNDERLIE PSYCHOANALYSIS
AND BEHAVIORISM

Psychology is essentially a study of life, and so we must begin at the beginning with a study of the origins of life. The two basic postulates which underlie the history of philosophy—material determinism and spiritual vitalism—provide us with alternate and contradictory models for such a study. The "atoms and space" determinism of Democritus has been developed in modern philosophy by Herbert Spencer, and the "flux and fire" vitalism of Heraclitus has been given contemporary significance by Henri Bergson. Darwin accepted the former deterministic model and praised Spencer as "the greatest living philosopher" and as "our philosopher."[1] It also follows that he would have accepted the deterministic model of psychoanalysis and praised Freud as "our psychologist."* Bergson began

---

*Of course, there would be some specific differences concerning such concepts as the unconscious, etc. But Darwin would have accepted Freud as "our psychologist" because of his basic theory of personality as a determined biological system, regulated by adaptation to the environment—and that is the only point of our argument here. Freud himself even claimed that he and Darwin had each dealt successful biological "blows to human narcissism." He believed that Darwin had shown that "man is not a creature different from animals," and that his

as a disciple of Spencer but soon rejected the whole Spencerian system and devoted himself to the development of
a new and creative theory of evolution and of life itself. We
shall use these two models and these two men to contrast
the biological assumptions of general psychology and existential science

We stated earlier that it was not our purpose to review
in detail what psychology is or has been, but rather to
concentrate on the outline of a model for what psychology
can become. Therefore, we shall provide only a brief sketch
of the biological assumptions that underlie psychoanalysis
and behaviorism as a background against which to present
a biological model for existentialism and existential
science.

Now biology was the dominant theme of nineteenth
century philosophy, and Spencer presented the basic theory of evolution in an essay entitled "The Development
Hypothesis" (1852), and followed it up in his *Principles of
Psychology* (1855). Darwin did not present his detailed and
documented account of evolution until publication of *The
Origin of Species* in 1859. Spencer was more concerned with
generalization than with documentation and he attempted
to explain not only the origin of species but of everything
else—society, politics, morality, aesthetics, religion, etc.—
in terms of his mechanistic formula of evolution. It was this
mechanical system of determinism which Darwin accepted
and which led him to claim Spencer as "our philosopher."
The reductive system of Darwin and Spencer was followed
up in modern psychology by psychoanalytic theory, and its
material determinism is succinctly expressed in Freud's
statement that "the intellect and the mind are objects for

---

own system of psychological determinism had shown that man is controlled by
biological instincts and that "the ego is not master in its own house." (*Gesammelte
Schriften*, X, pp. 352, 355. In Binswanger, *Being-in-the-world*, p. 178 n.)

scientific research in exactly the same way as any non-human things."[2] This same reductive materialism was expressed in Freud's answer to Binswanger concerning *metaphysics* when he said that given time, "I could find room for these noble guests in my little subterranean house."[3]

Spencer's basic formula was that *"Evolution is an integration of matter and a concomitant dissipation of motion; during which the matter passes from an indefinite, incoherent homogeneity to a definite, coherent heterogeneity; and during which the retained motion undergoes a parallel transformation."*[4] He meant by "integration of matter," that separate items merge into masses and groups and wholes, e.g., separate bones fuse into structural units after birth, and families merge into clans, cities, states, etc. The "dissipation of motion" results from the restriction on the independent function of each part as it becomes one member of a larger functional system. The integration results in a transformation of matter from "an indefinite, incoherent homogeneity to a definite, coherent heterogeneity," as in the division of labor and specialization of function in a developed political system, or when homogeneous protoplasm evolves into coherent and heterogeneous organs of nutrition, reproduction, locomotion, and perception.

Spencer also argued, as did Darwin and Freud after him, that the deterministic theory of biological adaptation was based on the natural operation of mechanical forces. There was, first, a certain "Instability of the Homogeneous,"[5] i.e., similarity among parts breaks down because even similar parts are inevitably subjected to different external pressures. There is a "Multiplication of Effects,"[6] i.e., the intricate and varied differentiation of life forms can be explained by the fact that one single cause can produce a multitude of effects. There is a "Law of Segregation,"[7] by which differentiated parts once separated into new locations are shaped into dissimilar products by the unique pressures of diverse environments. Finally, there is the

"Law of Equilibration"[8] which causes every motion and every rhythmic oscillation which is not externally reinforced to come to an end and dissolve in nirvana and death. This mechanistic view of evolution leads Spencer to his definition of life as "the continuous adjustment of internal relations to external relations,"[9] with all higher forms of consciousness mere products of this mechanical adjustment between rival and conflicting impulses. Nothing could state more clearly the Freudian reduction of higher psychic processes to impulse conflict, and the psychoanalytic notion of life as a biological "adjustment of internal relations to external relations." Nor was Darwin's influence on the progressive development of behaviorism any less profound. The functionalists used his theory of biological adaptation to defend their study of *adaptive functions,* and to reject the structuralists' preoccupation with "mental chemistry." Then behaviorists proper evolved from functionalism, and used his theory of species continuity to defend their study of animal behavior and to reject the argument that man himself must be the unique subject matter of psychology. There is no need for more detail. Our point is clear. The two approaches that dominate general psychology—psychoanalysis and behaviorism—are but variations of one common philosophy of material determinism and biological adaptation. It is against this Darwinian background of modern psychology that we now want to present another view of science and of man.

chapter 7

ADAPTATION VERSUS CREATION: THE SCIENTIFIC FOUNDATIONS OF EXISTENTIALISM

Existentialism and science are generally regarded as irreconcilable antagonists. This is true only if existentialism is grounded in religion and science is grounded in physics. Neither of these latter assumptions is necessary, nor even defensible. Both of these arbitrary assumptions are impediments to the development of an existential science. The purpose of this chapter is to eliminate these obstacles which now block further progress in psychology. The method used is to ground existentialism in the concreteness of biological science, rather than in the abstractness of speculative religion.

I want to base the argument on a decisive example of existentialism in order to make the reconciliation with science more crucial and the ramifications for psychology more meaningful. Let us begin then with an unequivocal statement of the existential position:

> Creativity is inseparable from freedom. Only he who is free creates. Out of necessity can be born only evolution; creativity is born of liberty. When we speak in our imperfect human language about creativity out of nothing, we are re-

ally speaking of creativity out of freedom. Viewed from the standpoint of determinism, freedom is "nothing," it surpasses all fixed or determined orders, it is conditioned by nothing else; and what is born of freedom does not derive from previously existing causes, from "something." Human creativity out of "nothing" does not mean the absence of resistant material but only an absolute increment or gain which is not determined by anything else. Only evolution is determined: creativity derives from nothing which precedes it. Creativity is inexplicable: creativity is the mystery of freedom. The mystery of freedom is immeasurably deep and inexplicable. Just as deep and inexplicable is the mystery of creativity. Those who would deny the possibility of creation (creativity) out of nothing must inevitably place creativity in a certain determined order and by this very fact must deny the freedom of creativity. In creative freedom there is an inexplicable and mysterious power to create out of nothing, undetermined, adding energy to the existing circulation of energy in the world. As regards the data of the world and the closed circle of the world's energy, the act of creative freedom breaks out of the determined chain of the world's energy. From the viewpoint of an immanent world datum this act must always represent creation out of nothing. The timid denial of creation out of nothing is submission to determinism, obedience to necessity. Creativity is something which proceeds from within, out of immeasurable and inexplicable depths, not from without, not from the world's necessity. The very desire to make the creative act understandable, to find a basis for it, is failure to comprehend it. To comprehend the creative act means to recognize that it is inexplicable and without foundation. The desire to rationalize creativity is related to the desire to rationalize freedom. Those who recognize freedom and do not desire determinism have also tried to rationalize freedom. But a rationalization of freedom is itself determinism, since this denies the boundless mystery of freedom. Freedom is the ultimate: it cannot be derived from anything: it cannot be made the equivalent of anything. Freedom is the baseless foundation of being: it is deeper than all being. We cannot penetrate to a rationally-perceived base for freedom. Freedom is a well of immeasurable depth—its bottom is the final mystery.[1]

Nothing could present the challenge of our task more clearly. Such a stance points directly to the irreconcilable conflict between freedom (creation) in existentialism and determinism (adaptation) in science. Thus we begin with a categorical statement of the problem. Nor could there be any advance beyond this terminal impasse if we accepted as definitive the Darwinian-Spencerian model of biological science that produced psychoanalysis and behaviorism. But let us penetrate down through this mechanistic model of life and examine biological evolution within the framework of existential science:

> That adaptation to environment is the necessary condition of evolution we do not question for a moment. It is quite evident that a species would disappear, should it fail to bend to the conditions of existence which are imposed on it. But it is one thing to recognize that outer circumstances are forces evolution must reckon with, another to claim that they are the directing cause of evolution. This latter theory is that of mechanism. It excludes absolutely the hypothesis of an original impetus, I mean an internal push that has carried life, by more and more complex forms, to higher and higher destinies. Yet this impetus is evident, and a mere glance at fossil species shows us that life need not have evolved at all, or might have evolved only in very restrictive limits, if it had chosen the alternative, much more convenient to itself, of becoming anchylosed in its primitive forms. Certain Foraminifera have not varied since the Silurian epoch. Unmoved witnesses of the innumerable revolutions that have upheaved our planet, the Lingulae are to-day what they were at the remotest times of the paleozoic era.
>
> The truth is that adaptation explains the sinuosities of the movement of evolution, but not its general directions, still less the movement itself. The road that leads to the town is obliged to follow the ups and downs of the hills; it *adapts itself* to the accidents of the ground; but the accidents of the ground are not the cause of the road, nor have they given it its direction. At every moment they furnish it with what is indispensable, namely, the soil on which it lies; but if we

consider the whole of the road, instead of each of its parts,
the accidents of the ground appear only as impediments or
causes of delay, for the road aims simply at the town and
would fain be a straight line. Just so as regards the evolution
of life and the circumstances through which it passes—with
this difference, that evolution does not mark out a solitary
route, that it takes directions without aiming at ends, and
that it remains inventive even in its adaptations.[2]

Thus the "irreconcilable" conflict between existentialism and science begins to dissolve as these distinct approaches to life are mixed and blended within the crucible
of biological science itself. The existentialism of Berdyaev
and the biology of Bergson merge and fuse in the common
postulate that *creation* is at the heart of living matter—that
a vital impetus presses life forward to increasingly more
complex stages of evolution. The critical link, then, between existentialism and science is this creative thrust or
drive, which pulses at the source of living matter and makes
life an open inventive process rather than a closed adaptive
one. Therefore, it is this vital impetus pushing life up from
within that must be closely examined and carefully documented, for any viable model of existential science must be
grounded deep down in the biological roots of man.

MECHANISM AND VITALISM

Now the ingredients for the development of an existential science were present at the turn of the century.
Biologists as well as philosophers argued

that the biological studies of Darwin are static and cinematic;
that the science of biology studies only abstractions and
mechanisms; that the theory of evolution is no more than a
hypothetical assemblage of data which ignores the question
of how the energy of development provokes the formation
and differentiation of organs; that there is a need to recognize an "effort toward life" which manifests itself with re-

gard to all the organs of living beings; that the idea of vital
spontaneity is necessary to understand how the conflict of
organism with physical environment has made new functions always better localized in distinct organs; that the living world is no more than an always progressive
concentration of psychic energy diffused everywhere as the
organizing energy of the universe; that it is the power of
creation which characterizes life and not its physico-chemical properties.[3]

The forces of rebellion were present but the man who
mobilized them into a "Copernician Revolution" was a
philosopher/scientist named Henri Bergson. It does not
seem necessary to provide a biographical sketch of Bergson, but a few dates will put his work into historical perspective. He was born in 1859 and published his major
scientific works between 1889 and 1911. He published a
more speculative work in 1932 before his death in Paris at
the age of 82. Nor is it necessary, or even possible, to
describe Bergson as a philosopher and scientist, since his
work changed the meaning of both these terms.

SCIENCE AND PHILOSOPHY

Bergson insisted that philosophy must assume its own
responsibility for investigating directly those facts that tra-
ditionally were considered the subject matter of the positive sciences. Philosophy could no longer take the data and
conclusions handed to it by the positive sciences as a "final
verdict,"[4] and then merely add its own metaphysic or critique to that verdict. Such a division of labor assigned the
study of matter to physics and chemistry, and the study of
life to the biological and psychological sciences. The
philosopher was but a technician in the scientific process
whose only function was to reword more precisely the ideas
and conclusions that were handed down to him "pro-
nounced and irrevocable."[5] It was true that he could study

these given facts and laws in order to speculate on their deeper causes, or he could engage in a philosophical analysis of the scientific data presented to him. Yet in both cases his function was reduced to that of an outside observer who can report and comment on the conclusions reached by others but is denied direct access to the original phenomena under investigation. The problem with this secondary role in the development of knowledge is that in reality it is no role at all. Philosophy becomes only a technical system for the enumeration and registration of facts, because the very metaphysic and critique which it claims as its own are already implicit in the attitudes and methods of the positive sciences that designed and conducted the original investigation. Nor can the positive sciences ever get beyond their own closed circularity, because the explicit facts they discover were already implicit in their own assumptions and procedures on which the original investigation was based.

Bergson recognized this closed circularity of positive science, and challenged philosophy to break that circle by its own entry into the "domain of experience." Philosophy had been reduced to the mere technical role of stating in more precise terminology the implicit assumptions of positive science because it had not demanded any critical role in the initial investigation of the phenomena themselves. It was thereby reduced to the secondary function of making more explicit the careless and inconsistent metaphysic and critique by which positive science cut into nature and divided her into elements amenable to its own arbitrary systems and methods. But science cannot escape responsibility for these implicit philosophical assumptions under the guise that it deals only with facts that are independent of such judgments. Any "laws" of nature are internal to the specific "facts" that a particular method of science abstracts out of the complex ebb and flow of nature itself. Consequently, these specific facts are relative to the particular method chosen by a specific investigator, and to the types of data that the chosen method has artificially cut out of the real world. Nor can it be denied that the particular method chosen was merely a function of the philosophical assumptions, implicit or explicit, that form the basic metaphysic and critique of positive science. We cannot escape this necessary relationship between philosophy and science because we cannot employ a particular scientific method without at the same time making a particular philosophical assumption. Psychology cannot claim to be a science that deals with facts independent of philosophical judgments, for both its definition of itself as a "behavioral" science, and its use of "operational" methods, are based on *a priori* philosophical assumptions. We are forced to recognize this necessary relationship between philosophy and science because we cannot study the movement of objects or the behavior of organisms by the use of any specific scientific method without making implicit philosophical assumptions about the inner nature and organization of those objects and those organisms. Psychology can no longer escape responsibility for its own implicit philosophical assumptions, and philosophy itself can no longer escape responsibility for its own surrender to them.

This was Bergson's challenge to science and psychology on the one hand and to philosophy on the other. He insisted that philosophy must "invade" the realm of concrete experience and attack the superficial assumptions and methods of science and psychology. Philosophy and science must interact and merge, and neither the intuitive philosopher nor the analytic scientist can avoid the strain and burden of that reconciliation and reorganization. It was because Bergson embodied within himself this remarkable combination of intuitive and analytic talents that he was able to create a turning point in the history of modern philosophy. But let us trace the development of Bergson's work right from its beginning when he was a young disciple of Spencer.

SPENCER AND BERGSON

Bergson clearly realized that the intellectual current of his time demanded a scientific philosophy that was grounded in concrete biological facts rather than abstract theoretical speculation. There was also a new focus on embryology which dominated the biological sciences and pointed toward the need to study growth and process rather than static immobility. These new forces pointed toward an inwardness in nature which endures, and that can be studied and understood only as constituted by motion and becoming. It was in terms of these convergent philosophic and scientific forces that Bergson explained his initial attraction to Spencer,* for "a philosopher arose who announced a doctrine of evolution, in which the progress of matter towards perceptibility would be traced together with the advance of the mind toward rationality, in which the complication of correspondences between the external and the internal would be followed step by step, in which change would become the very substance of things."[6] All eyes were turned towards the man who made such a promise, for his theory of evolution embodied the contemporary hope for a bold new philosophy based on process and change. Bergson followed Spencer until this bold new vision dissolved into nothing but broken and mechanical fragments of the original promise. Then his defection came quickly and abruptly, for Spencer "had no sooner started to follow the path than he turned off short. He had promised to retrace a genesis, and, lo! he was doing something entirely different. His doctrine bore the name of evolution-

*It is a relevant parallel that Kierkegaard, in his early student days, was a disciple of Hegel: "Let a doubting youth, an existing doubter, imbued with a lovable and unlimited youthful confidence in a hero of thought, confidently seek in Hegel's positive philosophy the truth, the truth for existence . . . The admiration and enthusiasm of the youth, his boundless confidence in Hegel, is precisely the satire upon Hegel." (Kierkegaard, S. *Concluding unscientific postscript,* p. 275.)

ism; it claimed to remount and redescend the course of the universal becoming; but, in fact, it dealt neither with becoming nor with evolution."[7] Bergson argued that Spencer merely reconstructed evolution with mechanical fragments from the already evolved, like a child who pastes a picture on a card, cuts the card into pieces, regroups the pieces again, and has the illusion that he produced the original picture. But to reassemble the fragments of a picture has nothing to do with the creative process of drawing and painting the original work itself. To put together a puzzle has nothing to do with the creation of color and design that produced the original picture of which the puzzle is only a cardboard copy. And so it was with the mechanistic evolution of Spencer that only assembled the most simple *results* of evolution and thereby produced an accurate cardboard copy of its most complex effects. But since you began with the cardboard pieces of the puzzle you can never retrace the genesis of the color and design that are the artistic core of the original picture itself. You can never get to the creative process and movement of evolution merely by assembling the mechanical fragments of facts already evolved. Spencer took the end results as already given, and started at the conclusion, rather than make any attempt to determine the movement of the creative process that produced those results.

Bergson agreed with Spencer that the laws of thought reflect the integration of relations between facts. But that initial mechanical assumption was little more than a simplistic truism. The real problem was to determine the complex causal relationships between the present structure of mind and the present subdivision of matter. The complexity lies in the realization that evolved modes of thought could themselves have determined the nature of the facts cut out from the whole of reality and the relations among them, just as easily as the facts and the relations could have generated the laws of thought. Spencer never gets beyond the initial mechanical truism that thought and facts are related, because he only analyzes the cardboard fragments already cut out from the whole of the picture puzzle. He cannot discover by such a mechanical analysis the complex process of creation by which intellect evolved and matter was subdivided, any more than can the child who assembles a puzzle discover the complex process of creation that produced the original picture. These were the reasons for Bergson's defection and the grounds on which he rejected the simplistic reductionism of Spencer and the superficial mechanism of his philosophy.

INTELLECT AND TRUTH

Bergson rejected Spencerian scientism and then proceeded to break through this mechanistic impasse in philosophy to develop his own theory of creative evolution. He entered into the process and becoming of evolution and tried to describe the inward movement of life just as an older child might reject the mechanical puzzle in favor of direct entry into the dynamics of the original picture itself. Bergson began his attack on mechanism and his defense of vitalism with a description of the development and function of the intellect and the role of the intellect in philosophical knowledge.* He argued that the faculty of reason is but an extension of the faculty of action. It is but a more and more complex, more and more flexible, and more and more exact adaptation of the consciousness of man to the environment within which it has evolved. The function of the intellect is therefore made clear and specific by the very

---

*Bergson uses the terms "intellect" and "intelligence" interchangeably to designate the narrow and specialized rational function of consciousness. Consciousness itself is a broader and more generic concept that includes all the different forms of awareness, e.g., intuition, will, love, etc., that express the vital impetus of life.

nature and purpose of its origin and emergence. The rational intellect is but a more complex and more flexible stage
of action, and its function is to perfect the most efficient
"fit" of our body to its environment. The intellect was
evolved to calculate with maximum skill and expertise the
relations of objects among themselves, and so our reason
has developed and emerged as geometrician *par excellence.*
The rational intellect is a superb tool and it does beautifully
the task for which evolution designed it. It moves and works
with consummate precision among the impersonal and
inanimate objects in the environment. It moves and works
with maximum efficiency among the solids in our world
that form the basis for our action and our industry. Thus
it follows that our rational concepts have been forged and
shaped on the model of objects and solids, and that our
logic is essentially the "logic of solids." The rational intellect was evolved "to think matter," and so it is master of
physics and geometry, where the fit between logical categories and inert objects is an exact one. The intellect is at
home in this domain and needs only make limited contact
with actual experience because the objects and solids
within its jurisdiction follow the logical movements of reason with no significant variation.

But it is the very fact of this exact fit between rational
intellect and inert matter that points to the circumscribed
function of intellect in the pursuit of philosophical and
psychological knowledge. The same precision tool that was
specifically designed to analyze and measure solids cannot
be used to fathom and chart the fluid current of evolution
that deposited it along the way. The pebble deposited upon
the shore by the dynamic flow of ocean tides cannot explain
its own history, since the whole cannot be understood in
terms of one isolated part, and the effect of a process cannot absorb and explain its own cause. The intellect is no
more than this kind of precision tool, for it was produced
by concrete environmental circumstances to act on con-

crete environmental objects, and so its function and capacity were limited and circumscribed by those same conditions of evolution that created it. The intellect is but an appendage or fragment of evolution, and such a fragment deposited by a process to serve one restricted purpose cannot then be used in retrospect for a very different and even paradoxical purpose—to explain the process that deposited it along the way. We are forced to conclude that the categories of our rational intellect (unity, multiplicity, causality, finality, etc.), that were specifically designed to fit objects and solids, can tell us nothing of the dynamic forces of evolution and life that underlie all philosophical and psychological knowledge. General psychology tries to contain human experience within these rigid categories, but all the molds crack because they were made for objects and solids rather than for the dynamic "flux and fire" of life and evolution.

But the faith that general psychology places in its rational and empirical methods to "solve all human problems" cannot be easily shaken. Psychology bases its exclusive use of these methods on the assumption that "in the long run" man and society will prove as amenable to prediction and control as have objects and solids in the physical world. Such an assumption seems to involve a basic contradiction concerning the origin, function, and power of reason and logic in psychological knowledge. Mechanistic theories of evolution first describe the "perhaps even accidental" emergence of intellect as a local effect of adaptation with a specific dependence on the goal of practical action. Then they completely contradict the essence of their own mechanical description of the origin, function, and power of the intellect, and imbue it with the wisdom to solve every moral, social, and political problem that confronts psychology and man. These mechanistic theories ignore the basic contradiction in their own argument to the point that they even proceed to reconstruct the flow of life and evolu-

tion, that produced the intellect in the first place, in terms
of the intellect's own rational and mechanical categories.
They find, as they proceed with this task, that the initial
contradiction binds them into increasingly complex contradictions until they are forced to abandon their original goal
of providing us with absolute knowledge about nature and
life. Still, even at this point, they do not concede that the
power of reason is circumscribed and limited, but argue
rather that nature and life themselves cannot be fully understood. They assert that the true meaning and essence of
life must always escape us and that absolute knowledge lies
beyond the limits of human comprehension—"we are
brought to a stand before the Unknowable."[8]

It would seem at first glance that reason had been
humbled by recognition of its own limited function and its
own shallow wisdom. But this is not the case. Reason remains convinced that it possesses within its own methods
and assumptions all possible approaches to truth. It may be
confronted with an object or process that it cannot explain
but it will only admit that it does not know at that particular
moment into which of its rational categories the object or
event fits. It only needs to further analyze and subdivide the
phenomena until it can properly categorize it, label it, and
then know it. Reason always assumes that a rational category is available into which an event can be placed and by
which it can be identified if only enough information about
the event is given. There is no way for reason to admit that
a novel phenomenon outside its own limited boundaries
may have emerged, and that new concepts, new methods,
and even a new language may be necessary to understand
the unique event that has been discovered.

Now it is obvious that such a simplistic mechanical
solution to the complexity of philosophy and life must be
challenged. Such a challenge is inherent in the very history
of philosophy, which presents the inevitable conflict between competing logical systems and the failure of these

rational attempts to force the real world of experience into rigid systematic categories. And reason at first even appears to back down in humility, for it makes a final pronouncement that rational intellect and logical systems deal only with *relative* truth and not with absolute knowledge. But this apparent humility soon reveals itself as pride, arrogance, and even certainty about the essential nature of truth and knowledge. It soon becomes clear that any feigned humility about the relativity of truth is but a ruse behind which the intellect continues "to apply its habitual method of thought without any scruple, and thus, under pretense that it does not touch the absolute, to make absolute judgments upon everything."[9]

ADAPTATION AND CREATION

We thus see the main outline of Bergson's attack on the philosophy of mechanistic evolution. But Bergson's unique contribution to the advancement of science was the result of his unique combination of talents. So let us follow the more crucial dimension of his work and examine his attack on the *biology* of mechanistic evolution. The specific question now raised by Bergson forces us into a more detailed argument: "Can the insufficiency of mechanism be proved by facts?"[10] He begins with an explanation of the principle by which he wants to demonstrate in biological detail the need for a theory of life and evolution based on vitalism rather than mechanism. The basic assumption of vitalism is that from its origin life is the continuation and expression of one single force or impetus scattered along the different paths of evolution. Life has grown and developed along these divergent paths by a continuous series of transitions and creations. This process of creative development even produced its own divergent paths when specific growth tendencies became mutually incompatible and the vital growth energy had to be dispersed along different routes to continue its creative course. It is a legitimate rational hypothesis that evolution might have occurred by a continuous series of transformations in one single individual spread over eons of time, or by transformations in many individuals stretched out over time in one single unilinear series. Such an hypothesis would, in either case, assume that the evolution of life developed along one dimension only.

But the fact is that evolution has actually occurred through the transformation of millions of single individuals, and on numerous single individual paths with new directions of growth radiating out from numerous crossroads in a complex and endless pattern. The principle of proof, then, for the hypothesis of a primitive impetus at the origin of this complex network lies in showing that each of these endless paths has something in common, even though they have been forced into countless separations and into disparate and mutually exclusive channels of growth. Such proof would establish that dissociated elements had evolved by separate and independent means, but that the creative development of these dissociated parts is due to a primitive psychological impulse at the origin of the whole. The validity of this hypothesis would be demonstrated if something of the common psychological element at the base of the whole undeniably revealed itself in each of the disparate and mutually exclusive parts. There would be proof of a vital impetus at the origin of the whole if the same identical organ appeared in very different and widely separated species at ends of disparate and mutually exclusive paths. It would be difficult to account for this remarkable production of the same identical organ at the ends of mutually exclusive paths by any simplistic and mechanistic explanation. Such a mechanistic theory explains the evolution of life as a series of accumulated accidents, with each new accident preserved by selection if it has survival value for the already accumulated sum of former accidents. We are then forced to accept the chance probability that two widely separated series of accumulated accidents, on two widely separated paths of evolution, could produce the same end result and the same identical organ. And this probability, that accidental outer pressures or accidental inner variations, could construct identical organs, dramatically decreases in relation to the distance between the two paths of evolution and to the clear evidence that there was no trace of the two identical organs at the moment of divergence.

Mechanistic evolution founders when confronted with this fact of identical organs produced by divergent and mutually exclusive paths. Yet this same fact follows logically and directly from the assumption of a primitive impetus at the origin of the whole. It follows logically and directly from the vitalistic hypothesis that something of the original common impetus would express itself even in the most disparate and widely separated parts of the whole. This then is the model on which Bergson bases his refutation of mechanism and his proof of vitalism. He argues that a significant step toward such proof will have been taken if it can be demonstrated that life manufactures the same organ by different means on separate and divergent paths of evolution. He further argues that the degree of certainty of that proof will be proportional to the distance between the two paths of evolution chosen for the demonstration, and to the complexity of the identical organ that life has produced on both paths.

Now we can begin to appreciate the meticulous and scholarly research at the base of Bergson's work. First, he presents in detail all of the arguments and all of the evidence for the position of each recognized theorist of evolution—Darwin, Devries, Eimer, Lamarck, etc. Then he proceeds to show that none of these systems can adequately account for certain observed events, e.g., the manufacture of *"like apparatus, by unlike means, on divergent lines of evolution.* "[11] He concludes each presentation with a return to his original position that "whether we will or no, we must appeal to some inner directing principle"[12] in order to account for these events. Now it is not our purpose here to go through each of these presentations or even to go through any one of them in all its detail. Rather, we propose only to summarize one of these documented arguments in order to sketch a clear outline of the method used. Again, we want to select an example that is unequivocal and undisputed, so as to make the conclusions as meaningful as possible. Therefore, let us focus on the basic Darwinian assumption that environmental conditions bring about an adjustment of the organism to its circumstances by the elimination of the unadapted variations. Bergson agrees that the Darwinian idea of adaptation by automatic elimination of the unadapted is a "simple and clear idea."[13] But he then goes on to expose the major flaw in that "simple and clear idea."

The basic flaw in the Darwinian formula is that it attributes to evolution a merely negative influence which cannot adequately account for the creation and progressive development of complex organs. Bergson bases his rejection of mechanism, and his own defense of vitalism, on this failure of adaptation to account for the reality of creation. Now this failure of the Darwinian formula of mechanistic adaptation reveals itself most decisively when we examine the structural similarity of two extremely complex organs on two widely divergent paths of evolution. Mechanistic theories of adaptation are vulnerable at this point because the concept of even a minute accidental variation must assume the concurrence of numerous small physical and chemical causes. Consequently, the accumulation of accidental variations that could produce an extremely complex organ such as the eye must assume the concurrence of an infinite number of infinitesimal causes. Mechanistic theories are therefore confronted with a statistical "improbability" that leads to a philosophical contradiction, for they must assume that the concurrence of an "infinite number of infinitesimal causes" is entirely accidental—and yet appears in the same way and in the same order on divergent lines of evolution at different points in space and time. And no "simple and clear idea" of adaptation by automatic elimination of the unadapted can resolve this contradiction, because our concern here is not with what has been eliminated but, rather, with what *has survived.*

The crucial fact that must now be explained is the creation of identical organs on divergent lines of evolution by a gradual accumulation of accidental variations. Here mechanism destroys itself as a tenable theory of evolution because it cannot be argued that an infinite number of accidental causes that occur in an accidental order and have effects that are infinitely complicated can repeatedly come to the same result and repeatedly produce the same identical organ. Bergson rejects such a mechanistic explanation as no more tenable than the argument that two walkers who finally meet after starting from different points and wandering at random could have followed identical routes superimposable one upon the other if those routes were infinitely zigzagged and complicated. He rejects mechanistic evolution on the ground that even the hypothetical complexity of these infinite zigzags is simplicity itself, compared with the biological complexity of an organ that can be created only by the definite and systematic arrangement of thousands of different cells, each a kind of organism by itself, into a definite and systematic configuration. But let us now deal with a specific example and consider Bergson's defense of vitalism in terms of the concrete facts of biological science.

The complex organ that we want to consider, in our examination of biological facts, is the eye. The eye is the best example by which to prove "the insufficiency of mechanism,"[14] because it is the clearest instance of the manufacture of *"like apparatus, by unlike means, on divergent lines of evolution."*[15] We can examine the eye of a vertebrate and that of a mollusk because these two divergent evolutionary streams have both produced, "by unlike means," the same "like apparatus"—the same complex visual organ. The eye of the vertebrate and that of the mollusk both contain the same essential parts composed of analogous elements, i.e., they both contain a retina, a cornea, a lens of cellular structure like our own, etc. So does this example meet the other criterion of the proposed principle of demonstration, since it is agreed that vertebrates and mollusks separated from their common parent stem long before there was any trace of an organ so complex as the eye. Bergson attempts to prove "the insufficiency of mechanism" by his demonstration that mechanistic theories of evolution cannot account for this structural analogy along these two divergent lines of evolution.

The Darwinian theory of insensible variations* attempts to explain the manufacture of the eye by the occurrence and continual accumulation of small differences due to chance. Now it must be remembered that all the parts of an organism must be coordinated if the organ is to function and be useful so that natural selection has a chance to take hold. But the complicated development of the minute structures of the retina would *hinder* vision *rather* than favor it if the visual centers as well as other parts of the eye were not developed and coordinated at the same time. The mechanical model cannot explain how these accidental variations arise and are coordinated in every part of the organism at the same place and at the same time so that the organ can continue to function. Darwin clearly understood this aspect of the problem, and for that very reason considered variations to be *insensible.* Any very slight difference

---

*These refer to imperceptible changes that do not disrupt the function of an organ.

that arises accidentally in one area of the organ will not disrupt the visual function of the eye because that first accidental variation can wait for complementary variations to accumulate, and then raise the visual efficiency of the organ. Bergson agreed with the Darwinian analysis that this first insensible variation need not disrupt the function of the eye, but it was also obvious that it did not improve visual efficiency so long as complementary variations did not occur. Therefore, Bergson contended that because the insensible variation was of no use to the organism, its initial survival could not be explained adequately by the "simple and clear idea" of natural selection. He concluded that the same small variations that are infinite in number could not have occurred by accident in the same order along two divergent lines of evolution, and that these small insensible variations could not have been preserved by natural selection and accumulated when each of them taken by itself was of no use.

Bergson then proceeds in his presentation to demonstrate the *truth* of vitalism by explaining this complex manufacture of *"like apparatus, by unlike means, on divergent lines of evolution,"*[16] in terms of his basic assumption of a primitive impetus at the origin of living matter. He argues that the more closely we examine the data of biology itself the more we come to understand that this improbability of the manufacture of the same organ by two separate and independent accumulations of an infinite number of infinitesimal causes, forces us to reject mechanistic theories of evolution. The creative production of the same complex eye by species on separate and independent lines of evolution was used to demonstrate this theoretical failure of simplistic mechanism. But the same basic failure of mechanism can also be demonstrated by certain remarkable facts of regeneration within one single organism. The crystalline lens of a triton, for example, is built up out of the ectoderm of the organ, while the iris is of mesodermic origin. Yet the remarkable fact of biological regeneration is that a new lens can be manufactured out of the mesodermic iris when the original lens that was developed in the ectoderm is removed. An even more remarkable fact of regeneration can be noted in the eye of the salamander. Here, the typical regeneration of the lens takes place in the upper part of the iris when the lens is removed and the iris left intact. But the regeneration of the lens takes place in the inner, or retinal, layer of the remaining section when the upper part of the iris itself is removed. These remarkable facts of biological regeneration conclusively demonstrate that different parts of an organism that are located in separate regions, that are constituted by different structures, and that are normally meant for different functions, have the vitalistic potential to perform the same function and even to manufacture the same identical complex organ when some unexpected disruption of the normal process occurs.

We have cited these few examples from biological science in the preceding paragraphs only to demonstrate the biological fact that the same effect can be produced by separate and independent combinations of causes. Bergson argues that recognition of this basic fact which is inherent in the evolutionary process forces us "whether we will or no" to "appeal to some inner directing principle,"[17] in order to account for this convergence effect. He has demonstrated that such convergence cannot be explained adequately by the Darwinian theory of natural selection and by the accumulation of insensible accidental variations. We must therefore conclude that the variations of different organs are not simply accidental and mechanical but, rather, that these variations continue from generation to generation in definite directions. This does not imply that the evolution of the organic world is predetermined as a whole, but only that the spontaneity of life manifests itself by a continual creation of new forms that succeed one another in a progression toward more and more complex stages of development and integration. The development and integration of a complex organ like the eye (which was used as our example) can be explained *only* in terms of such a process of continual change and creation in a definite direction. There is no other way to account for the manufacture of the same complex organ in different species that have separate and distinct developmental histories. Accidental and mechanistic combinations and accumulations of physical and chemical causes are not adequate to explain these complex facts of biology and evolution. Bergson insists that only one hypothesis can fully account for these documented facts; and that is the assumption that a psychological cause or primitive impetus is at the origin of life and evolution.*

KNOWLEDGE AND LIFE

Thus Bergson comes to the historical impasse that is common to all those interested in the science and philosophy of existence. He comes to a recognition of the arbitrary and dictatorial closure that the mechanism of the rational-empirical method forces upon our search for knowledge. Bergson reached that impasse and then asked himself the basic question that is so crucial for the future of psychology and man: "Must we then give up fathoming the depths of life?"[18] Let us examine the answer and the challenge that Bergson has given us as a response to that crucial question.

Bergson first acknowledges that we would be forced to such a standstill in the advance of knowledge *if* life and evolution had exhausted all its potentials in the production

---

*Teilard de Chardin makes this same argument: "The impetus of the world, glimpsed in the great drive of consciousness, can only have its ultimate source in some *inner* principle, which alone could explain its irreversible advance towards higher psychisms." (*The phenomenon of man.* Trans. Bernard Wall. London: Collins, 1960, p. 149.)

of pure intellect and had been content to make man only a sophisticated geometrician. Then we would be left with only this mechanistic conception of knowledge which is, of necessity, artificial and symbolic, since it has reduced the total movement of life to one restricted function (namely, intellect) that is only a partial and local manifestation of the vital process of evolution. But life did *not* exhaust all its physical potentialities in the production of pure reason. There are many lines of evolution other than the one that has produced man. Other forms of consciousness have emerged from other divergent streams, and these modes of awareness also express something of the essential impetus and movement of life. The way to break through the artificial closure that pure intellect imposes on our search for knowledge lies in the integration and utilization of these various forms of consciousness. Such a convergence and amalgamation of consciousness would enable us to grasp something of the essential nature of life and to glimpse something of the absolute nature of knowledge—for such an integrated consciousness "turning around suddenly against the push of life which it feels behind, would have a vision of life complete—even though the vision were fleeting."[19]

But those psychologists who want to oppose such a methodological advance in science can argue that it contains a basic contradiction, i.e., the proposal assumes that we could transcend the limits of our own intellect. They can then reject such a proposal as logical "nonsense" on the grounds that it is only with and through our intellect itself that we could even recognize or understand these other forms of consciousness. Now existential science would be forced to concede the argument and admit the futility of its proposed method if it could be demonstrated that men were only pure intellect. But the methodological advance urged by existential science is necessitated by the undeniable fact that there remains around the crystallized nucleus

of logical and rational intellect, a vague and nebulous substance out of which that very nucleus emerged and by
which it was formed. And it is within this broader region of
awareness, which is the primordial ground for the condensed "figure" of intellect, that the forces of other intuitive and complementary forms of consciousness reside and
make themselves known to us as they push life forward in
the constant evolution of nature and man.

The existential argument that forms of consciousness
other than the intellect must be utilized in the pursuit of
knowledge can be stated more cogently as an insistence
that our metaphysical theory of *life* is as essential to science
and philosophy as is our rational theory of *knowledge*. To
challenge knowledge from the perspective of a theory of
life enables us to place the intellect in its proper role. We
can then begin to understand how the rational categories of
the intellect were themselves constructed, and even begin
to see how to break through these artificial structures and
go beyond their rigid limits. Accepting a theory of rational
knowledge without such a criticism and challenge forces us
to arbitrarily accept the artificial limits of logical categories
which can only enclose the facts within those restricted
boundaries that the theory itself sets as the final and ultimate reaches of scientific knowledge. It is true that the
passive acceptance of these rational categories enables us
to produce a superficial but useful symbolism that is necessary for the practical goals of positive science. Still, such a
constricted symbolism will never get us beyond these technical and utilitarian goals, for the rational intellect alone
can never penetrate to the true essence of its own subject
matter.

Thus we see that the basic problems of science and
philosophy can be approached only through a circular process that pushes our theory of knowledge upward by continuous challenge and interaction with the more
fundamental theory of life. Such an interaction between

knowledge and life would show us the very process by which the intellect itself was formed, and would penetrate to the very genesis of life which the rational categories of our intellect will never understand. Such a constant push and challenge from encounter with life itself will force science to abandon simplistic and mechanistic theories of evolution that can never discover anything new since they posit in advance everything that they later claim to explain. Such closed circularity follows of necessity from the analytic method of positive science which only cuts up a completed and evolved reality into little pieces, and then puts these arbitrary and artificial fragments back together again.

It is now obvious that our basic assumption that life and evolution are vitalistic rather than mechanistic demands a new scientific approach, one which can penetrate down into the process of creation and becoming that is the dynamic core of existential reality. Such a new scientific approach is necessary because we do not want merely to fit together the static and isolated fragments of the already evolved, but to discover and comprehend the dynamic inward process of creative evolution itself. We find that when we do eliminate these mechanical and artificial reconstructions of life, that the static and isolated fragments melt back into a simple flux of continuous process and becoming. Then we can begin to explore this deeper and more primal order of nature and begin to discover and understand the dynamic reality of concrete time and duration that is at the heart of life and of consciousness. It is true that positive science in its study of inorganic matter can afford to neglect the dynamism of creation and becoming without serious error, for objects and solids are dense and "weighted with geometry."[20] But animated inward movement is the essence of life and consciousness, and can be grasped and understood only by an active entry into the "flux and fire" of the creative process of evolution itself. We must thrust ourselves down into the very essence of the evolutionary movement in order to follow the results in the process of their creation, rather than simply recompose the already evolved results with artificial fragments of themselves. Bergson argues that this is the true function of philosophy, for it is the "turning of the mind homeward, the coincidence of human consciousness with the living principle whence it emanates, a contact with the creative effort." It is only by such a "turning of the mind" that philosophy can study the process and becoming of evolution itself, and thereby develop and emerge as "the true continuation of science."[21]

chapter 8

BIOLOGICAL VITALISM: ITS IMPLICATIONS FOR PSYCHOLOGY

The vitalistic concept of life and science developed in the preceding chapter has direct consequences for the future of psychology. Let us examine these consequences by a study of basic psychological issues from the viewpoint of existential science.

MEASUREMENT

The goal of psychology is the "control and prediction of behavior." Existential science shows how any "success" in the attainment of this goal is a meaningless illusion, since the operation which underlies "control and prediction," viz., measurement, is an artificial abstraction. This insight into the nature of scientific measurement explains why any systematic operation in psychology can yield "results", once man is reduced to a "thing" and personality to an object fixed in space. Such artificial results can *always* be obtained, simply because the "behavior" of an object fixed in space always expresses a consistent negative tendency, i.e., the tendency of matter toward rigidity and immobility. Each of these artificial results comes from the work of a particular psychologist who imposes upon man a materialistic bias, isolates certain specific variables, and then applies conventional units of measurement to these abstracted "facts." But it is exactly because of this artificial character of psychological measurement that our scientific knowledge of reality remains essentially superficial and symbolic. The conventional standards of measurement used by science and psychology correspond only to the inert and immobile aspects of matter and not to the spontaneous movement and fluid reality of nature. These conventional standards of measurement are nothing but an endless series of artificial impositions forced upon nature. The whole enterprise of measurement itself is nothing but an artificial human construction. Measurement is only the real or ideal superposition of two objects one upon another a certain number of times. But the vital flow of nature never intended to measure itself and to count itself; nor did it ever intend to superpose one object upon another in regular and mechanical sequences.

Still, science and psychology continue to count, measure and relate "quantitative" variations to one another in order to obtain laws—and they "succeed." Now these methods succeed only because the laws of the physical world have no positive reality but merely express matter's negative tendency toward rigidity and immobility. The intellectuality of rational analysis and the materiality of homogenous space coincide, and produce "results" exactly because the intellect evolved out of the materiality of the physical world and was made to "fit" it. Psychology need only reduce personality to the category of a determined material object, i.e., make it a rigid and immobile "thing," and the artificial intellectual operations of measurement fall automatically into place and fit the object investigated. And paradoxical as it may seem, we could never even begin to explain the "success" of science and psychology if this mechanical and mathematical order in nature was a positive fact rather than a negative tendency. We could never explain how our artificial standards of measurement could exactly fit that positive mechanical order and exactly isolate the specific variables from the total complexity of such a profound mathematical system. We could never be so presumptuous as to assume that we had discovered those specific positive laws and orders in nature that exactly correspond to our artificial symbols and codes. But it becomes easy to explain the "success" of psychological measurement if matter contains within itself the very means by which it can adapt itself to these artificial symbols and codes. Consequently, we are forced to the only conclusion possible: the order measured by science and psychology is a negative interruption of a positive process, rather than something positive within itself. The reduction of existential reality that is necessary to use scientific and psychological methods of analysis is exactly such an interruption of a positive process, and a return to the inertia and immobility of material objects.

Now we can understand why science and psychology "succeed" even though they are contingent, relative to the variables isolated, and relative to the systems that they have artificially imposed upon reality. These systems can even be varied endlessly and organized into an infinite number of complex orders, as is typical of the proliferation of theories in psychology today. Still, all of these endless and even contradictory systems can each yield its own "results," and each claim its own "success," exactly because there is no definite system of mechanical laws at the base of nature, and exactly because mechanics and geometry simply represent the inertia of matter when the spontaneous movement and becoming of life are interrupted. Bergson explains these artificial results obtained by science and psychology in the same way as the fact that we can always obtain "results" when we "put one of those little cork dolls with leaden feet in any posture, lay it on its back, turn it up on its head, throw it into the air: it will always stand itself up again, automatically." He argues that it is the same with matter and that "we can take it up by any end, and handle it in any way, it will always fall back into some one of our mathematical formulae, because it is weighted with geometry."[1] It is for this reason that each of the endless and often contradictory systems and theories of psychology can produce its own "results," for these results are a negation and have no more meaning for man and his existence than the automatic behavior of "those little cork dolls."

DETERMINISM

The definitive grounding of existential philosophy in existential science is made explicit by Bergson's *scientific* explanation of Berdyaev's *philosophical* statement that "a rationalization of freedom is itself determinism."[2] The scientific argument asserts that freedom is a factual reality but that it cannot be defined without reduction to deterministic categories since determinism, like measurement, is the expression of a negation. To analyze or rationalize freedom is to reduce a process to an object, and time to space, for only a thing or an extensity can ever be analyzed or rationalized. But freedom is a vital process that takes place in concrete time, because it is a relationship between the concrete self and the concrete act which that self performs. Now this relationship between the self and the act it performs cannot be reduced and analyzed because the *relationship itself* is a concrete existential fact. And we cannot study this type of existential fact by analysis unless we first substitute the completed act for the act that is in process and thereby break the reality of concrete time into pieces of abstract space. But this destruction of the reality of the concrete relationship destroys the vitality and reality of the self at the same time, because it substitutes inertia for spontaneity, and necessity for freedom. It thus becomes obvious that no rational or empirical definition of freedom can be given, because the very categories of analysis necessary to make such reductions are themselves the negation of freedom and would thus force the argument back into simplistic determinism. For example, the free act cannot be defined as "something that has been done but that might have been left undone," or as "something that was not done but that might have been completed," because each of these definitions implies a reductive equivalence between concrete duration and its artificial translation into spatial terms. This reduction of time to space then leads (by the very nature of the relationships that the reduction itself has constructed) to the most rigid determinism. Nor can the free act be defined as "that which could not be foreseen even when all the conditions were known in advance." Such a definition would be a contradiction, since concrete time forces us to place ourselves at the exact moment when the act is being performed, and "all the conditions" could never be given in advance of that moment.

The only alternative to such a contradiction would be to agree that psychic duration *can* be structured symbolically in advance, and thus to agree (in new words) that the reality of time is equivalent to its symbolic spatial representation. But such an agreement would then force the argument back once more into the dead end of simplistic determinism. Nor can the free act be defined as one "that is not necessarily determined by its cause," since such a definition means only that the *same* inner causes do not always produce the same effects; and thus we imply that the psychic antecedents of a free act can themselves be repeated. But to say that these psychic antecedents can be repeated is to say that *unique* moments of concrete time that have their own *original* history can, nevertheless, be reduced to symbolic moments in space, substituted for the reality of concrete time, and repeated. Such an implication leads us once again directly back to the artificial assumption of an equivalence between time and space, and our definition of freedom is forced back once more into the closed rational categories of determinism.

Thus, every rationalization of freedom leads to the factitious reduction of concrete time to symbolic space. Such a reduction may be useful when one deals with time that has already passed and become inert; but not when one considers time that is passing and is being experienced in the reality of the concrete moment. And the free act takes place only in this concrete reality of time that is passing, and not in time that has already passed, that has already become inert, and that can easily be categorized within determinism. Freedom is therefore recognized as a concrete reality which is embedded in the immediate experience of time; while determinism is an artificial illusion because it can be symbolically represented only *after* one has made a mechanical abstraction *from* the reality of concrete time. It therefore becomes obvious that the rejection of freedom in psychology is a rejection of concrete reality, and that the assumption of determinism is only the substitution of an abstract illusion.

ASSOCIATIONISM

Measurement, determinism and associationism produce explanations for symbols which have been abstracted from facts, but not explanations for the original facts themselves. Scientific explanations are thus irrelevant to experienced facts because the very operation of symbolic reconstruction inherently reduces and distorts the nature of the original data being investigated. The basic distinction between the multiplicity of juxtaposition, and that of fusion or interpenetration must be stressed again, in order to show the fallacy that is inherent in associationism and that is similar to the fallacies already pointed out in measurement and determinism. And to demonstrate this fallacy we must first understand that each of our feelings and each of our ideas contains an indefinite plurality of conscious states that cannot be observed as a composite of separate entities unless these conscious states are *first* fragmented and segmented by the method of psychological analysis. Only then can we perceive isolated elements external to one another, and the symbols used to represent them, rather than experience the fluid reality of the original fused states of consciousness. Thus the function of the method of psychological analysis is to translate the personal essence of an original conscious state into impersonal elements separated from one another and expressed by symbols. But just because our intellect can reduce the unique to the general and can represent that reduction by categories and symbols, it does not follow that these categories and symbols were contained in the reality of the original conscious state itself. It is obvious that the multiplicity of feelings and ideas contained within the original state merged and melted into one another and did not analyze, label, and categorize themselves. Thus associationism is another clear example of psychology's replacing the reality of a concrete phenomenon with a symbolic and artificial reconstruction, and then confusing the explanation of the substituted 'fact' for the reality of the fact itself.*

*This is similar to William James' concept of *"The Psychologist's Fallacy:* The *great snare of the psychologist is the confusion of his own standpoint with that of the mental fact* about which he is making his report." (*The principles of psychology.* New York: Dover Publications, 1950, vol. 1, p. 196.)

CONSCIOUSNESS

Existential science demonstrates that certain phenomena rejected by general psychology as "unscientific" are,
nonetheless, dynamic forces at the heart of living matter,
viz., *freedom* and *creation*. Consciousness is the embodiment
of these life forces; and evolution can be understood only
in terms of their progressive development. Bergson defines
consciousness as a *"need of creation"*[3] that can become manifest only when freedom is activated. It is dormant when life
is reduced to habit and mechanism, but becomes a crucial
reality as soon as, and to the extent that, choice and vitalism
are restored. Thus, the degree of consciousness in an organism without a nervous system varies according to the
degree of locomotion possible; and in animals with a nervous system, according to the sensory-motor complexity of
the brain. Now it is this relationship between the complexity of choice, and the complexity of the brain and
nervous system, that accounts for the illusion that
consciousness is "caused" by the brain. But consciousness
does not "spring" from the brain. The brain and consciousness correspond only because they both reflect the
complexity of choice available to a particular organism.
The correspondence is not due to a causal relationship
between the brain and consciousness, but only to a correlation between the nature of choice that is reflected by the
complexity of the brain structure on the one hand and by
the complexity of conscious awareness of the other. But
since this correlation is not based on a direct causal relationship between the brain and consciousness, the correspondence breaks down at its critical limit. And this is why
we cannot conclude that the consciousness of man and the
consciousness of the ape are comparable, even though
their brain structures are similar to one another. Both the
brain of man and that of the ape are made to set up motor
mechanisms, and to let us choose among them the one we

shall put into action at any particular moment. But the human brain differs radically from that of the ape and all other animals, in spite of obvious structural similarities, due to the complexity of the mechanisms it can set up at any one instant. The distinction is clearly manifest in the ability of man to learn any sort of exercise, construct any sort of object, or acquire any kind of motor habit, while the number of motor mechanisms and the number of movement combinations available even to the best endowed of the lower animals is strictly limited. Thus, the consciousness of man cannot be reduced to that of the ape merely because of certain similarities between the cerebral characteristics of the two species. The distinction between human and animal consciousness is categorical because the number of motor mechanisms (and consequently the number of choices) made available by the animal brain is limited, while the number of motor mechanisms (and consequently the number of choices) made available by the human brain at any instant in time is *un*limited. And the difference between the limited and the unlimited is not one of degree but one of kind, because it is the absolute difference between a closed system and an open process. It is this categorical distinction that makes the contrast between animal consciousness and human consciousness a radical one of kind rather than just a linear difference of complexity and degree. It forces us to recognize the radical *discontinuity* between animal and human consciousness which is the central philosophical assumption of existential science, and to reject the assumption of species continuity upon which general psychology is based.*

We can better understand this fundamental distinction between these two types of consciousness—a distinction

*Only one aspect of this crucial contrast between animal and human consciousness is considered in this section. But the implications of consciousness as "unlimited choice," or freedom, are examined in detail in other sections throughout the book.

that cannot be eliminated by simplistic reference to the similarities between cerebral structures in animal and man —by a closer examination of the significance of consciousness as defined by man's power of choice. Such an examination of consciousness makes the definition of a specific type of consciousness dependent upon the extent of *possible* action that surrounds any choice of *real* action in a particular moment. It is this process of open selection from among an unlimited number of potential actions in any moment of existence that makes human consciousness synonymous with invention and freedom. But in the animal, invention is never anything more than the variation of a routine response. The animal is condemned to the habits of its species, and the success of any individual initiative is extremely limited. Such initiative can enable the animal to escape automatism only long enough to create a new automatism, for "the gates of its prison close as soon as they are open; by pulling at its chain it succeeds only in stretching it."[4] But consciousness in man breaks that chain, and in man alone consciousness sets itself free. Bergson argues that the whole history of life has been the effort of consciousness to raise matter, and that "everywhere except in man, consciousness has let itself be caught in the net whose meshes it tried to pass through . . . man alone has cleared the obstacle."[5]*

PERSONALITY

Existentialism asserts that "personality is a breakthrough, a breaking in upon this world. It cannot be recognized as an object, as one of the objects in a line with other

---

*Teilard de Chardin states this same view of man's unique position: "In such a vision man is seen not as a static centre of the world—as he for long believed himself to be—but as the axis and leading shoot of evolution, which is something much finer." (*The phenomenon of man*. Trans. Bernard Wall. London: Collins, 1960, p. 36.)

objects of the world. This is the way in which the anthropological sciences, biology, psychology, sociology would regard man. In that way man is looked at partially: but there is in that case no mystery of man, as personality, as an existential center of the world."[6] Existential science makes this same distinction between the reduced and partial views of personality that psychology gives us, and the actual self which flows beneath these artificial reconstructions. Now this confusion between the reduced self and the actual self has arisen because the actual self comes into contact with the external mechanistic world at its own outer surface, and so the surface of the actual self retains the imprint of objects and the association of terms that it perceives in its contact with the socialized world. It is these connections of simple and impersonal sensations at the surface of the self that the associationist theory fits. But such a superficial theory becomes irrelevant as soon as we dig below the socialized surface of personality and enter into the reality of lived experience. Now the self becomes something more than an accidental juxtaposition of sensations, and we discover that states of consciousness do not function as separate entities but melt into one another so that each one is colored by the nuances of all the others. The interpenetration of these states of consciousness blends into a unique result in each personality so that each self has its own unique emotional existence. Each self has its own unique way of loving and hating and these unique styles of love and hate reflect the personality as a whole. But the language of psychology reduces these unique expressions of distinct personalities to the lowest common denominator leaving us with only objective and impersonal fragments of "love," "hate," and all those unique human emotions by which man seeks to identify and communicate himself. Psychology will always fail to grasp the essence of personality as long as it studies only socialized and categorized states of consciousness set side by side in systematic juxtaposition. Psychology will always fail because there is no common ground between its symbolic language on the one hand and the reality of human experience on the other. Such a symbolic language tries to explain personality as determined by emotional states that have been reduced to forces or vectors which press upon us like so many pistons and valves in a mechanical engine. But the fact is that each one of these states of emotion goes deep down into our being and makes up the whole of our personality. The whole of our personality is always expressed and reflected when we experience any one of them. We can even say that personality is "determined" by any one of these emotional states, since that is to say that personality is, in fact, created by itself.

Now the self that concerns the associationists is only an aggregate of conscious states that have been reduced to isolated sensations, feelings, and ideas. These psychological reductionists only examine the general categories and the impersonal aspects of emotional states. That is why their endless studies yield only data about a phantom self that is but the shadow of personality projected out into social space. But existential science studies each of these emotional states as a lived reality that is embodied in a concrete individual, and that is colored by the subjective nuances of his unique and original existence. Then there is no longer any need to add conscious states together in order to construct a symbolic personality, for we can study the real personality of the concrete individual which reflects all these emotional states in each single one. Now we can grasp the total self by a complete study of any one of these existential states, for each one of them is but a different expression of the same basic personality.

MOTIVATION

The motivational theory of existential science is based on the evidence of a vital impetus which pushes organized matter toward more and more complex stages of evolution. This motivational impulse is the *consciousness* of living matter, and it evolves through more and more complex stages until in man it becomes reflective consciousness.* The existential processes of willing and loving are but more complex emanations and integrations of this primal growth drive. This impetus for growth and development pulses through life and pushes up against inert matter, whose dead weight tends to pull life down toward fixed and immobile points in space. Consciousness in its evolved forms of willing and loving pushes up against inert matter whose rigid forms of habit and socialization tend to pull life back down from creation to adaptation.

Such a motivational model provides a scientific basis for existential theories of mental health that define pathology as *self-estrangement* caused by social adaptation, e.g., Otto Rank's view that *refusal* to adapt to society is the first step toward mental health and toward the development of a creative self. The image taken from existential philosophy which best expresses this motivational model is the description Camus gives of Sisyphus "ceaselessly rolling a rock to the top of a mountain whence the stone falls back of its own weight."[7] The gods wanted to destroy the spirit of Sisyphus because of his rebellion against them and so condemned him to this most "dreadful punishment." Now this motivational view of man, as ceaselessly pushing up against the dead weight of habit and socialization, is an optimistic one in spite of the pain and labor of such an endless task. Sisyphus discovers the deeper meaning of creative rebellion when he discovers that "he is stronger than his rock"

---

*Kierkegaard stresses the reciprocal relationships between reflective consciousness and the self and will of man: "Consciousness, i.e. consciousness of self, is the decisive criterion of the self. The more consciousness, the more self; the more consciousness, the more will, and the more will the more self. A man who has no will at all is no self; the more will he has, the more consciousness of self he has also." (*The sickness unto death.* In *Fear and trembling;* and *The sickness unto death.* p. 162.)

and that "his fate belongs to him." He teaches us "the higher fidelity that negates the gods and raises rocks . . . the struggle itself toward the heights is enough to fill a man's heart."[8] But let us describe this motivational theory and struggle in the language of existential science.

Bergson sees the living world best characterized as one great creative effort forward. Most often this primal creative effort is frustrated, and sometimes even temporarily paralyzed, by pressures and forces that block its movement. But the more critical danger to progress and human development lies in the fact that forward movement can be diverted from "what it should do by what it does." It can be absorbed by the form it must take to express itself, and it can be "hypnotized" by that form "as by a mirror."[9] Life is always burdened by the materiality which it must assume in order to express itself, and it can always be objectified and destroyed by that materiality even in those most perfect moments when it seems to have triumphed over all external and internal resistances. Each of us experiences that burden of materiality because each of us creates the potential habits that can destroy our freedom in those same moments in which our freedom itself is affirmed. Even our most perfect expressions of freedom are "dogged by automatism,"[10] because the potential habits embodied in the concrete forms necessary to express freedom turn back upon us and destroy the vitality of our freedom if we fail to renew it by a constant effort of the will. We see this failure of our will and the victory of materiality when a vital thought is destroyed by the rigid formula that expresses it, when an idea is betrayed by the words that communicate it, or when the letter of the law turns back and destroys its own spirit. Bergson argues that man can easily be led to nihilism and cynicism exactly because our highest aspirations are so naturally congealed and destroyed as soon as they are externalized into concrete action. And man might be led to fatally embrace materialism and even to deny the reality of his own inner aspirations—if he did not understand that the profound cause of this discordance between mechanism and vitalism lies in an irremediable difference of rhythm that only the constant effort of our will can surmount and master.

Now the constant effort of our will is necessary just because of this irremediable difference between the rhythm of vitalism and the rhythm of those particular material manifestations that are necessary for its expression. Most of these material manifestations of vitalism accept the mobility and becoming of life that activates them with reluctance and so they constantly lag behind. These reluctant material manifestations are therefore relatively stable, and in their lethargy they counterfeit mechanism and immobility so well that they are considered, by science and psychology, as objects rather than as processes. Science and psychology ignore the fact that the *apparent* permanence of their manifest material form is an illusion, and that the reality of these "objective" phenomena is the subjective vitalism of life that flows within them. Sometimes we get a direct glimpse of this inward subjective reality because it seems to emerge at certain moments, and to present itself "before our eyes" in its pure and pristine form. Bergson argues that we can experience such an existential encounter with the subjective reality of life if we but open ourselves to the meaning of these sheer subtle moments and these pure pristine forms. Such an insight into the existential meaning of evolution and life is available to us in the sudden illumination that we experience "before certain forms of maternal love, so striking and in most animals so touching, observable even in the solicitude of the plant for its seed." Bergson argues that the deeper mystery of life may be embodied in such a process of love, and that our devoted entry into a study of these existential experiences may yet "deliver us life's secret." And existential science does offer the hope that man may yet be able to fathom the meaning of his "thrown" condition by study of these processes of loving and willing that seem to be life's purest modes of expression and manifestation. The study of these motivational processes may yet give us some insight into the ultimate significance of "each generation leaning over the generation that shall follow," and may yet help us understand the profound motivational fact that "the living being is above all a thoroughfare, and that the essence of life is in the movement by which life is transmitted."[11]

FREEDOM

Existentialism does not try to "explain" freedom, because any attempt to rationalize freedom necessarily reduces it to those determined categories which are its negation. But existential science does *describe* the process of freedom which underlies our consciousness and manifests itself in concrete and critical moments of our lives. We can understand this process of freedom by further exploration of the basic distinction between personality as fragmented sensations juxtaposed and fixed in space, and personality as an active and creative consciousness. Now personality as an active and creative consciousness can be experienced only by a concrete self whose inward states have been left intact and not separated, categorized, and labeled. Personality can no longer be experienced as an existential consciousness once the subjective reality of that self has been reduced to a symbol and transformed into a static piece of sterile public property. And this transformation of the self, from personal subjectivity to public objectivity, is more than just a simple symbolic substitution. The mechanical system which science and psychology claim they use only to explain our behavior aims, in fact, to end up predicting and controlling it. The objective symbol is first substituted for the subjective reality, and then these reduced psychic states become solidified as permanent associations are developed between these crystallized ideas and our external movements. Then, gradually, a crusted automatism begins to cover over our freedom as our consciousness begins to passively imitate that same process by which nervous matter procures reflex actions. Those persons who permit this materiality to cover over and then destroy their own inward vitality have actually stood by and permitted their own reduction and objectification in the name of science and psychology. The reductive method that began as only a technique of investigation and exploration now fulfills its own prophecy, convincing the associationists and the determinists that they were right about the nature of man in the first place. They study only those public and impersonal aspects of consciousness that they can separate into distinct states which recur in time like physical phenomena and to which the law of causal determination applies as it does to nature. Once consciousness has been thus fragmented, and the self has been thus reduced and objectified, "the only thing left is to turn freedom out of doors."[12]

Existential science, however, insists that another course of action, and another method of investigation, are open to us. But to discover this deeper reality of our own existence we must take ourselves back in time to those exact moments in our life when we made some crucial decision. These concrete critical moments were unique and can never be repeated, any more than we can repeat critical past phases in the history of evolution or in the advance of civilization. Now we begin to understand why these past states of consciousness cannot be reduced to symbols and artificially reconstructed by a simple juxtaposition of quantified states. They were experienced and lived as a qualitative and dynamic unity that must be recognized and investigated in its own right. We can even begin to understand, by such a direct investigation of the dynamic unity within us, that our actions are truly free, because the relation of our actions to the dynamic state from which they issue can never be reduced to a law. The relation between our actions and the motivational state that accompanies them can never be reduced to a law because the psychic state itself is unique in the history of the individual and can never occur again. Thus, direct investigation of the concrete reality of human experience forces us to reject determinism as meaningless, because in any consideration of the existential moment there can be no question about predicting the act before it has been performed or about the possibility of some contrary action once the designated act has been completed. There can be no question of such prediction since, in the reality of concrete time, to have all the necessary conditions given is to place one's self *within* the very moment of the concrete act and thus preclude the possibility of external observation and prediction.

Now let us try to understand the origin and nature of the illusion of determinism upon which psychology is based. The illusion of determinism develops because the transition from existential reality to symbolic representation, and thus from freedom to determinism, is made by gradual and imperceptible steps. Little by little, the weight of habit and materiality tends to cover over and destroy the inward vitality of freedom and creation. Persons gradually and imperceptibly turn toward a passive surrender to the constant burden of existence, and gradually and imperceptibly they objectify themselves as they imitate the mechanical model of man that the analytic method of psychology has constructed for them. This transition from freedom to determinism is often so subtle and obscure that even those persons whose actions seem most obviously determined insist that their behavior is the result of free and independent choice. But such passive surrender and such passive imitation are accident and illusion, rather than real and essential, because they represent only the negative interruption of the positive vitalism of life and evolution. Thus we discover from a closer and more careful examination of freedom that it is real, but extremely difficult to experience and maintain, and that its actualization demands the constant effort of our own creative will.

CREATIVITY

Existential philosophy argues that creative freedom is its own energy source because it "breaks out of the determined chain of the world's energy" with "power to create out of nothing, undetermined, adding energy to the existing circulation of energy in the world."[13] So too does existential science describe this positive force of creation, as it breaks through the artificial symbols of its negation. But we must first remember that the concrete and living self is generally seen only as refracted through space with its conscious states fragmented into categories and crystallized into words. We have even explained that man tends to imitate these superficial reconstructions of personality, and tends to substitute the artificial symbols of psychology for the reality beneath them, just because such imitation and substitution promote social efficiency and adaptation. And our most simple daily actions confirm this efficiency of imitation and substitution because these simple actions are not elicited by our deeper personal feelings but by the images and symbols with which our feelings have been associated. The alarm that wakes us in the morning would no longer be efficient if it disturbed our whole consciousness and blended with the confused mass of impressions that fill our awareness. But rather the alarm merely signals the idea of rising that has been associated with it on the surface of our consciousness and thus produces the superficial but efficient action intended. The alarm and the idea have become so closely associated that the idea is automatically aroused without the self interpreting or interfering with it. Man is by conscious choice an automaton in this instance because there is everything to gain in this particular case by such efficiency. We can even agree that most of our daily actions are performed in this mechanical way and that the associationist theory is applicable to these numerous but insignificant acts. These mechanical actions are the substratum of our free actions, just as our organic functions are the substratum of our conscious functions. We have already explained that man often surrenders his freedom even in more important matters due to a tendency toward passive indulgence and passive imitation. But now let us go deeper into the self and try to understand the positive force of creation that erupts and breaks through the passive imitation and artificial solidification of reality.

Let us assume that we have been confronted with some crucial decision and our friends and acquaintances advise us on the issue. The attitudes which they express become lodged on the surface of our self and solidify there just as in the example of the alarm waking us in the morning. These suggestions accumulate, and gradually they form a thick crust which covers over our own deeper and more personal feelings about the issue. We may not be aware of this gradual erosion of our own personal involvement and may even believe that we are acting freely rather than being determined by the advice of others. We may even reach a decision and be convinced that it was a free one even though we recognize that it occurred after consultation with others and that it did express a composite of their attitudes. Then, at the last minute when the act itself must be performed, something inside us revolts against it. It is the existential self from deep below rushing up to the surface and breaking through the superficial outer crust of passivity and socialization. We must therefore conclude that a creative force deep within our personality, with an energy source of its own, was in action below this superficial 'rational' self which only pondered superficial rational pieces of advice. Then this creative force from down inside us that was gradually "heating up" its own attitudes and options at a deeper level of intuitive awareness suddenly "boiled over" into a free and spontaneous choice expressed in a personal and individual action. Let us try to understand this process of creative choice and action in more detail.

We realize, as we examine the decision making process, and reflect on our final choice and action in this specific case, that the inward ideas and feelings were our own but that we had kept them below the surface through some strange reluctance to exercise our will. This is why there is no rational or empirical explanation for the final choice and action: because there is no causal relationship between the final outcome and any observable circumstances which preceded it. Still, psychology wants to know the *reasons* for our final choice and action. But they are beyond reason, and even against reason—which may make them the best of reasons. These may be the best of reasons for in such cases the choice and action do not merely reflect some superficial passive socialization that is external to our deepest self and easy for psychology to predict and control. Rather the choice and the action are a creative eruption of the totality of our most intimate feelings, thoughts, and aspirations that express the unique personal meaning that we have given to our selves and to our lives. Thus we see that it is a mistake for psychology to model its study of man on the examination of superficial and meaningless events in order to "prove" that our behavior is determined, for these insignificant events do not mobilize the creative energy and the creative will within us. Rather let psychology study those solemn and critical moments in our lives when our very being was at stake and it soon becomes obvious that human behavior cannot be predicted and controlled. It soon becomes obvious that when our destiny is the issue, "we choose in defiance of what is conventionally called a motive, and this absence of any tangible reason is the more striking the deeper our freedom goes."[14]

DIAGNOSIS

General psychology is forced by its own scientific assumptions to classify unique qualitative experiences into generalized quantitative categories. The necessary consequences of such diagnostic operations are pointed out by existential science as it demonstrates that these labels and categories arbitrarily distort and destroy the reality of immediate conscious experience. This distortion and destruction of experience is nowhere so striking as in the case of our emotional life. A person may be overwhelmed by a violent love or a deep melancholy; one, even, that seems to take possession of his total being. There are a thousand different elements that dissolve, merge, and permeate one another as they are stirred about and boiled up by the intensity of the emotional experience. There is no possibility at all, during this intense emotional reaction, for these elements to separate and externalize themselves, and so the experience is a unique and original event created by the complex interpenetration of a thousand active elements. We distort and destroy the reality of that experience as soon as we reduce this unique and original complex of active elements to a generalized collection of passive fragments isolated from one another, and then force that artificial reconstruction into one of our standard diagnostic categories. The person who directly experienced the intense emotional reaction itself lived through a unique subjective crisis that was flooded and permeated by the "flux and fire" of those thousand active and original elements that created it. That unique and original personal reality is now labeled and crammed into a rigid, lifeless, and colorless category. The subjective crisis has passed and now psychology is left with only a sterile diagnostic symbol that tells us nothing of the original emotional experience that it pretends to have named. The emotional crisis itself progressed and developed as a constantly changing reality and only by gradual movement through these concrete changes can a person survive the crisis, and resolve the emotional trauma into some temporary or permanent new personality integration. Such a resolution and integration could and would be made immediately and mechanically if the emotional reality was of the same order as the sterile symbol that pretends to represent it. But the emotional experience itself is beyond such mechanism for it lives and progresses in terms of its own dynamic principles. The emotional reality is of an entirely different order than the artificial symbol, because the emotional elements that created the original experience permeated one another; whereas, the diagnostic symbol was produced by the separation and isolation of elements in order to analyze and label them.

It is this artificial separation and isolation of variables from their unique and original emotional context that transforms the existential reality of a violent love or a deep melancholy into meaningless words, names, and diagnostic labels. And now the psychologist reasons about these words and names, applies his simple logic to the diagnostic categories, and interprets behavior in terms of these artificial constructs and symbols. The real *crime* is that he then proceeds to manipulate each unique individual according to the routine method prescribed for that general "class" of diagnosed "objects," in the name of psychological treatment. Psychological diagnosis substitutes for the concrete reality of unique individual experience, "lifeless states which can be translated into words, and each of which constitutes the common element, the impersonal residue, of the impressions felt in a given case by the whole of society."[15]

Psychobiology

Existential science posits a psychological life force pushing up through the roots of biology which cannot be explained by or reduced to physico-chemical properties. It argues that the relationship between this psychical force and its physical correlate is one of dependence, but *not* one of equivalence. For example, a machine may be dependent on a screw for its operation but that does not make the machine a screw. Existential science may even concede that life *is* a kind of mechanism. But it is a mechanism of the real whole, and not a mechanism of separated and analyzed parts. The real whole is an indivisible continuity, and the arbitrary systems cut out from it are only partial and symbolic views of the deeper continuity from which they have been abstracted. And all these partial and symbolic views put end to end can never even begin to reconstruct the whole, any more than you can reproduce the reality of an object by adding together an infinite number of photographs of that object arranged in an infinite number of ways. Now it is just as true that you can never reproduce the reality of existential life by the addition of physico-chemical elements, even though artificial and symbolic substitutes for life can easily be produced by such mechanical manipulation. Yet it is obvious that scientific analysis will continue to dissect the process of organic creation into an endless number of physico-chemical elements, and that chemistry and physics will become more and more proficient at such analytic reductions. Still, it does not follow that these analytic reductions and operations will ever give us the key to existence and life. It is true that a very small element of a curve can be considered a straight line, for a curve coincides with its tangent at each of its points. So is it true that the physical and chemical forces of organic matter are tangent to the *vitality* of life at each of its points. But these points are in fact only snapshots, taken at regular intervals, of the real movement that generates the curve. In reality the movement of life is no more made up of physico-chemical elements than a curve is composed of points and straight lines. Bergson argues that such symbolic substitutes for the real movement of life are possible only in a science that restricts itself to the study of phenomena that are "repeated" continually in the living being, just as in a chemical retort. This explains in some measure the mechanistic orientation of physiologists on the one hand, and the vitalistic orientation of histologists, embryologists, and naturalists on the other. These latter specialists concern themselves with the *genesis* and *evolution* of the minute structure of living tissues, and consequently are interested in the retort itself rather than merely in its contents. Thus the focus of their work forces them to recognize that this retort creates its own form through a *unique* series of acts that constitute an *original* history, and so they believe "far less readily than physiologists in the physico-chemical character of vital actions."[16]

Part III

ONTOLOGY

chapter 9

LOGICAL POSITIVISM
AND THE
SPATIAL CONCEPT OF REALITY

The same basic struggle between "atoms" and "fire" that has characterized philosophy from its inception expresses itself in the conflict between materialism and vitalism, adaptation and creation, determinism and freedom, etc. But one of the formulations of this perennial controversy which is most crucial to the future of psychological science is the clash between an ontology of *space* and an ontology of *time.* The "atoms" postulate is based on the assumption that natural phenomena can be understood only as *objects* in space; while the "fire" postulate assumes that these same events can be understood only as *processes* in time. General psychology accepts the former assumption and therefore uses spatial models for its approach to man. Existential science is based on the latter assumption and therefore has developed temporal models for its investigation of man. We first described the existential revolution in science and psychology as a breakthrough from biological materialism to biological vitalism. Now we want to examine that same revolution as a function of the transition from a spatial ontology to a temporal ontology. Therefore, we must contrast general psychology and existential science in terms of the critical distinction between a philosophy of space and a philosophy of time.

Nothing could state the spatial ontology of the "atoms" postulate more succinctly than the modern analytic philosophy of logical positivism that underlies all of general psychology. It attempts to construct a logical language which directly corresponds to objects in the world. It assumes that all knowable events have various properties and that these properties stand in various relations to each other. The only facts are those properties and those relations which can be empirically observed and measured; i.e., reality is reduced to and defined as objects in space and the relations between those objects.

Analytic philosophy began with Comte's assumption that metaphysics was an obsolete form of knowledge which had been outdated by modern science. It also embodied Hume's assumption that everything but empirical observations based on quantity or number were "sophistry and illusion," and should be "committed to the flames." The logical positivists combined this radical empiricism with new techniques of logic, and attempted to construct a language in which all knowledge could be reduced to a small number of axioms and their consequences. The critical significance of logical positivism for our discussion is that it was adopted as the philosophical foundation for the science of general psychology. What appealed to psychology, in its effort to identify itself as a physical science, was the verification principle which logical positivism proposed. The argument against metaphysics was that its statements were meaningless because they did not express a proposition about a matter of *fact*. It then became encumbent upon the positivists to define a criterion which could differentiate a scientific proposition about a matter of fact from a meaningless statement. Consequently, the verification principle was proposed as the means by which the scientific relevance of propositions could be tested. This principle thus became the crux of logical positivism, because it provided an explicit formula by which science could be *defined*. Psychology adopted the philosophy and formula of logical positivism because it guaranteed recognition as a physical science and provided an operational definition to serve as a standard for the development of general psychology itself.

The verification principle declares that the scientific significance of a proposition can be assessed only in terms of its method of verification; i.e., the meaning of a statement *is* the method of its verification. Logical positivism further defines the intent of its verification principle in a corollary assumption that all verification must result from sense experience and empirical observation. It follows that any proposition whose events cannot be reduced to the category of observable objects in space must be rejected as scientifically "senseless." A special exemption is given to those statements whose meanings are derived from the logical implications of words or ideas such as in mathematics. But all statements about matters of fact must meet the criterion set by the verification principle. Those statements based on logical implications are termed *analytic* propositions while those based on facts are termed *synthetic* propositions. Any statement that cannot be classified as either analytic or synthetic is considered non-cognitive, or emotive, and rejected as unsuitable for scientific investigation. And so the most critical consequence for psychology which has resulted from its acceptance of logical positivism is the restriction imposed upon its own further development. It recognized the ontological reality of space and rejected the alternate, and equally defensible, possibility that time is the basic dimension of matter and of man. The price psychology paid for the political "security" and "respectability" of that choice was the abortive and fatal constriction of its own future as a meaningful human science.

chapter 10

TIME AND DURATION
IN THE DEVELOPMENT
OF A HUMAN SCIENCE

The alternative to a psychological ontology of space is the existential ontology of time. So let us present the argument for this alternate philosophical possibility and study its projected impact on the future development of psychology.

SPACE AND TIME

Twenty-five centuries of philosophy seem to have proved Heraclitus right. Time, rather than space, presents itself to us as the basic ontological reality. Existence reveals itself clearly to us only through a direct encounter with concrete time. Kierkegaard knew it and dwelt on the problem of repetition. Bergson knew it and dwelt on the problem of duration. Both of these seminal thinkers agreed that concrete time must be the starting point for any valid approach to psychological science. Kierkegaard asserts that "say what one will, it is sure to play a very important rôle in modern" psychology.[1] He states his own position on the nature of time in the guise of a humorous anecdote about "the voyage of discovery I undertook in order to investigate the possibility and significance of repetition."[2] He sets off on a journey from Copenhagen to Berlin to see if he can repeat any of the events which he experienced on an earlier visit. His first disappointment occurs when he reaches Berlin and hastens "at once to my old lodging in order to convince myself how far a repetition might be possible . . . but, alas, here no repetition was possible."[3] His bachelor landlord had married, and the style and atmosphere of the rooms occupied on his previous visit had been changed almost beyond recognition. Still there were the parks, the restaurants, and the theaters where he was sure to experience a repetition—but all his many and varied efforts failed. The only thing that seemed to repeat itself was "the impossibility of repetition."[4] He could get nothing repeated even though he tried in every possible way. Frustrated and exhausted he decided to cut short his experiment and return to the familiar setting of his own home where repetition seemed a natural certainty. He was like the "man who became so tired of his home, that he had his horse saddled in order to ride forth into the wide world. When he had gone a little distance his horse threw him. This turn of events was decisive for him, for when he turned to mount his horse his eye lit again upon the home he wished to leave, and he looked, and behold! it was so beautiful that he at once turned back."[5] So was Kierkegaard convinced that

> in my home I could reckon with tolerable certainty upon finding everything ready for repetition. I have always had a great distrust of upheavals, indeed I go so far that for this reason I even hate any sort of cleaning, and above all household scrubbing. So I had left the severest instructions to have my conservative principles maintained even in my absence. But what happens! My faithful servant held a different opinion. He reckoned that if he commenced the commo-

tion soon after my departure, it surely would have ceased before my return, and he was surely man enough to put back everything punctiliously in its place. I arrive, I ring the door-bell, my servant opens. That was a momentous moment. My servant became as white as a corpse, and through the half-opened door I saw the most dreadful sight: everything was turned upside down. I was petrified. My servant in his con-sternation did not know what to do, his evil conscience smote him, and he slammed the door in my face. That was too much, my distress had reached its climax . . . there is no such thing as repetition.[6]

But Kierkegaard and Bergson were committed above all else to the maxim of Heraclitus that "character for man is destiny." All three of these philosophers demanded a continuity of character or self that endures through the "flux and fire" of concrete time. Each of them demanded a commitment to existence that must be created and main-tained by a constant effort of the will. But such subjective commitment is possible only at the depths of existential freedom and creation—only at such existential depths did Abraham receive Isaac again.* And it is precisely the recog-nition of these deeper existential processes that makes the assumption of mechanical repetition that underlies science and psychology so superficial as to be only comical. Thus Bergson pointedly rejects repetition in his ontological con-cept of duration:

But . . . science is concerned only with the aspect of *repetition*. Though the whole be original, science will always manage to analyse it into elements or aspects which are approximately a reproduction of the past. Science can work only on what is supposed to repeat itself—that is to say, on what is with-drawn, by hypothesis, from the action of real time. . . .

---

*The term "again" as used here does not mean, of course, a mechanical repeti-tion because the relationship between Abraham and Isaac was radically altered by Abraham's act of faith. Abraham did receive Isaac again but Abraham, Isaac, and the relationship between them had already been dramatically transformed by the passion of that existential act. (See Kierkegaard's account of the story of Abraham and Isaac. *Fear and trembling.* In *Fear and trembling;* and *The sickness unto death.* pp. 26–37.)

For that reason . . . mechanism regards only the aspect of similarity or repetition. It is therefore dominated by this law, that in nature there is only *like* reproducing *like*. The more the geometry in mechanism is emphasized, the less can mechanism admit that anything is ever created . . . all fabrication, however rudimentary, lives on likeness and repetition, like the natural geometry which serves as its fulcrum. Fabrication works on models which it sets out to reproduce; and even when it invents, it proceeds, or imagines itself to proceed, by a new arrangement of elements already known. Its principle is that "we must have like to produce like."

That is why again they agree in doing away with time. Real duration is that duration which gnaws on things, and leaves on them the mark of its tooth. If everything is in time, everything changes inwardly, and the same concrete reality never recurs. Repetition is therefore possible only in the abstract: what is repeated is some aspect that our senses, and especially our intellect, have singled out from reality, just because our action, upon which all the effort of our intellect is directed, can move only among repetitions. Thus, concentrated on that which repeats, solely preoccupied in welding the same to the same, intellect turns away from the vision of time. It dislikes what is fluid, and solidifies everything it touches. We do not *think* real time. But we *live* it, because life transcends intellect. The feeling we have of our evolution and of the evolution of all things in pure duration is there, forming around the intellectual concept properly so-called an indistinct fringe that fades off into darkness . . . the bright nucleus shining in the centre. They forget that this nucleus has been formed out of the rest by condensation, and that the whole must be used, the fluid as well as and more than the condensed, in order to grasp the inner movement of life.[7]

Time as well as vitalism was a basic ingredient in the revolutionary mood at the turn of the century. Bergson had forged the general issue of biological vitalism into a concrete challenge, and so did he make time a critical reality for twentieth century science and psychology. He argued that the starting point for any authentic encounter with the reality of time was buried within our own subjective self. Knowledge of all things outside the self must be considered external and superficial, whereas the grasp and awareness of our own subjective self is internal and profound. Awareness of our own intimate self is the starting point of existence, because this personal self within us is the reality which we know best and the reality of which we are most definitely assured. We can discover the critical significance of concrete time as the ontological essence of nature and being only by an encounter with the inwardness of our own private and subjective self. Bergson described the precise meaning of the word "exist" in terms of this privileged case of our own personal inwardness. *Time* was the central discovery of that inward exploration.

STATE AND CHANGE

The fact is that inwardly each of us passes from state, to state, to state in a continual process. We move in a constant flow of feelings, ideas, sensations, choices, etc. These may include being warm or cold, feeling good or bad, looking or thinking, waiting or acting, etc. This process of continual change and movement from one state to another is what divides and colors the reality of our personal existence. We need only turn in upon the self for a moment to feel this continual movement from state to state, and to realize that the self is a continuous process that changes without ceasing. That initial discovery of the self as a process is but an introduction to the existential significance of time, for change is much more basic and radical than we can grasp by such a brief inward glance. We can describe that initial perception of inward change and movement in terms of a process that advances from one state to another in a constant and ceaseless progression. But such an introductory description assumes that each of these states in the progression is an independent block and a separate whole in itself. Such an initial assumption suggests that the process of change which is so basic to our existence resides only in the passage from one separate and independent state to another. It suggests that each of these separate states is itself a constant, and remains the same throughout the entire interval during which it prevails and occupies our attention. Thus our brief initial description suggests that movement occurs between states but not within states. Now let us look closer at the reality of inward time and duration.

We can penetrate deeper into the existential significance of process and time by an examination of even the most stable of internal states. We can begin this deeper penetration into time by a simple examination of the visual perception of a motionless external object. Let us assume that the object remains the same during the period of our examination, and that we look at it from the same side, at the same angle, in the same light, etc. Now the crucial fact that we discover by this experimentation is that the vision I now have of the object is different from the one that I just had of the same object in the previous moment. The fact of this difference is obvious, and even necessary, because the latter view is an instant older than the former, and contains within it an image of the older view, since our memory conveys that image from the past into the present. The mental state, in this case the visual perception of a motionless external object, continually swells with the accumulated duration which it gathers into itself as it moves through the reality of experienced time. Thus the mental state continually grows and develops as it rolls upon itself like "a snowball on the snow."[8] We find such an increasing accumulation of experiences even in this simple example of a stable visual perception of a constant external object. The significance of time and duration as the essence of our inward self becomes more crucial as we consider states that are much more personal and internal such as feelings, ideas, desires, choices, etc. These latter mental states, unlike our example, do not correspond to any constant external object, and so at these deeper subjective levels the reality of continual change within states as well as between states cannot be denied. Yet, it is more convenient to neglect this continual process within states and to take note of change only when its effects become sufficient to produce an apparent change between states, in the form of a new bodily attitude or a new focus of attention. Only then are we willing to recognize that movement has in fact occurred and that our mental state has changed. But the more basic reality is that our consciousness and our being are in constant flux and that we change without ceasing. The more basic reality is that there *are* no separate and independent states between which movement occurs. The constant flux and change *within* each of these "states" proves to us that the boundaries are arbitrary and artificial, and that the state is itself nothing but process and change.

REASON AND EXISTENCE

The ontological assumption that the self and life are grounded in time and change is reflected in Bergson's conception of personality as a process of becoming. He asserts that our personality "shoots, grows and ripens without ceasing,"* for each of its movements adds something new to its constant growth and development. He goes even further and argues that the something added is not only new but is unforeseeable, and could not have been predicted in advance. He concedes that the present mental state of an individual can be explained only by what was in him and by what was acting on him a moment earlier in

---

*Kierkegaard says this same thing: "A self, every instant it exists, is in process of becoming." (*The sickness unto death. In Fear and trembling;* and *The sickness unto death,* p. 163.)

time, and that analysis would reveal no other elements were involved. But it is equally true that no analysis of the factors involved would enable us to foresee the simple indivisible form which alone gives concrete organization and personal significance to these purely abstract elements. We can predict only if we are able to project into the future some pattern of elements that has already been perceived in the past or some new arrangement of those same elements. But no prediction can be based on the personal significance and concrete organization of experience that continually unfolds in the development of our personality, because this simple indivisible form arises in a unique moment, and could not have been perceived before it occurred. The indivisible form could not have been perceived in advance because it is a simple totality which concentrates in its concrete reality all that has been perceived up through the moment as well as what the moment keeps adding to it. Each unique moment of our existence is an original moment with an original history, and our personality "shoots, grows and ripens without ceasing"[9] because it is continually being modified by these continually unfolding states, and it is continually becoming the new form that is just emerging.

It is also true that our actions are an expression of our personality, and that our personality, in turn, is continually being formed by the actions that we choose. Our personality is continually being created in the image of our own specific choices and our own concrete actions. This creation of the self by the self is the more complete and responsible the more one is able to "reason" upon his choices and his actions. We do not refer here to reason rigidly fixed as in matters of geometry where impersonal premises force us inevitably to one impersonal conclusion. Complexity in the prediction of personality is confounded by the fact that the same reasons in human affairs may dictate to different persons, or even to the same person at different moments, choices and actions that are equally reasonable but profoundly different. The fact is that in human affairs there can be no impersonal premises and no impersonal conclusions. The fact is that in human affairs there can never be *any* reasons that are "the same," because they can never be reasons *of* the same person, nor *of* the same moment in time.

It is recognition of this uniqueness of human experience that provides the clue to the failure of general psychology. The concrete moment in the personal history of a specific individual cannot be understood in the abstract from an external and detached perspective. Nor can any general and systematic formula be provided to solve the life problems of a specific individual since the problems themselves are always particular and unique to each one of us alone. Existential psychology is based on this recognition that general laws and abstract systems cannot solve for the concrete individual those specific problems that confront him. It is for this same reason that existential psychotherapy rejects all methods of manipulation, interpretation, diagnosis, etc., since these techniques are derived from impersonal data and theoretical abstractions. Existential science as a therapeutic process aims only to construct an authentic exploratory situation within which the concrete individual can encounter the personal meaning of his own specific problems. It provides no answers and makes no suggestions, but rather it asks each individual to discover and create his own unique solutions, and to "follow himself" to his own unique destiny. We can agree that the identity of a rock is given to that rock as to a passive thing. But man must actively create his own identity and ceaselessly affirm his chosen self by the conscious effort of his own will. And so Bergson insists that the destiny of man and the fate of these creative life forces that manifest themselves in personality and becoming are not amenable to prediction and control, because "for a conscious being, to exist is to change, to change is to mature, to mature is to go on creating oneself endlessly."[10]

Dream and Will

The pivotal distinction between personality as a process in time, and personality as an object in space, is so crucial for the future of psychology that we must try to understand it as completely as possible. So let us again turn inward and concentrate our attention on that aspect of our personal experience which is furthest removed from the abstract and rational categories of science and geometry. Let us search into the depths of our subjective existence and try to discover that region of experience where each of us feels most actively involved in the movement of his own life, and most actively in control of his own destiny. Such an inward venture forces us down into the flow and stress of concrete time where our past constantly advances into a present that is constantly being made anew. Here the tension of our inwardness strains the "spring of our will,"[11] for only by a strong recoil of our personality upon itself can we take hold of our past and thrust it compact and undivided into a present which it creates by entering. These willed moments of self-control and self-possession are difficult to maintain, but it is in such concrete moments of existence that our actions become truly free and our life truly belongs to us.

Now let us continue the subjective experiment another step. Let us shift our inward focus and relax the effort and the strain by which we forced as much as possible of the past into the present. Let us shift suddenly from intense activity to relaxed passivity. It is true that we cannot reach a state of absolute passivity because we cannot completely destroy our memory and our will. Yet, even in this simple exercise we can glimpse the possibility of a partial existence that is devoid of concrete time, where the present begins endlessly and the moment ceaselessly dies and is born again. It is in such a passive state that our actions turn into dreams, and our self is scattered into an infinite number of fragments, each external one to another. These scattered fragments merge back into an organized unity only when we actively force ourselves back down into the reality of concrete time, and actively forge our whole personality into a sharp edge "pressed against the future and cutting into it unceasingly."[12] It is only by such a bold and willful entry into existence that we can take possession of our personality and make our self and our actions truly free. We become geometricians to the extent that we passively withdraw from the flux and strain of existential becoming and let our personality dissolve into fragments, and then let those fragments disperse and descend into space. The final limit of such passive withdrawal is the transformation of personality as an expression of life into personality as only a complex form of inorganic matter. It then becomes obvious that *any* system or *any* science can be imposed upon man and "succeed," because personality has already been broken into fragments and those fragments fixed in space. The basic error of general psychology is that it continues to study man as a complex object in space when even the simplest subjective experiment demonstrates that man is a unique being who exists and endures in concrete time.

SYMBOL AND REALITY

We can better understand this crucial distinction between personality as an object in space and personality as a subject in time by examining the two types of self which emerge from the respective ontologies. The subjective self is the reality which existential science wants to study; the objective self is its symbolic substitute upon which various systems and sciences are imposed by general psychology. The ontological attitude taken toward the self by general psychology is based on a perception of personality as refracted through space. It is necessary for psychology to reduce the reality of time to the symbolism of space because deep-seated conscious states in themselves are pure quality and have no relation to quantity. They merge in such a way, and their duration is of such a nature, that they cannot be said to constitute a numerical or quantitative multiplicity. Even to say that these states of consciousness encroach upon each other is to distort them, for it implies that they could be distinguished in the first place.

It is this inwardness of process and becoming that constitutes the reality of the existential self. But the artificial socialization of these inward conscious states pushes them outward, and slowly transforms these vital subjective forces into inert objects and passive things. They finally break off from one another and even from that inward subjective organization which we call the self. No longer experienced and lived as immediate emotional realities, they can now be recognized and explained only by the labeled categories into which they have been placed. Thus a second and artificial self is grafted on to the reality of the first. It is a self taken out of concrete time and broken into spatial moments, spatial states, and abstract spatial categories. This second artificial self does admirably what it was intended to do, for an inner self composed of efficient mechanical parts can respond well to the superficial demands of social life. General psychology can even "succeed" in its goal to predict and control behavior, as long as it remains preoccupied only with events that have already mechanically taken place, and refuses to study that reality which is in the process of becoming. But the price we pay for such preoccupation and such "success" is nothing less than the destruction of our deeper personal self, and the elimination of our inward subjective life.

Still, psychology continues to reject the reality of these deeper subjective processes, and continues to study the self as a mechanical association of separate states which are distinct from one another and set side by side in homogeneous space. And the assertion that it can study the reality of human personality by such a method forces psychology into endless contradictions which only multiply with each added effort to overcome them. The continued attempt of psychology to force all human experience into its own operational categories only brings into clearer focus the basic error and fundamental contradiction by which psychology reduces the reality of time to the geometry of space, and so, by its own method, destroys the reality of its own subject matter. Bergson insists that all the contradictions that are implied in the problems of causality, freedom, personality, etc., arise from this one basic methodological error. The only way to break through the impasse in psychology that these endless contradictions have produced is to reject this superficial analysis of the self as an object in space, and to search for new methods and new styles by which to study the self as a process in time.

This destruction of existential reality, by the symbolic substitution of personality as a spatial object for personality as a temporal process, is so central to the basic contradiction in general psychology that it would be helpful to examine a specific case. Behaviorism used as a method of applied therapy provides us with just such a precise and conclusive example. The client's presenting problem was "fear of being alone." She could not be alone at any time unless she knew exactly where to reach a friend by phone and how to get to that friend, if necessary, by car. Now *aloneness* is a basic reality in existential psychology. Different existential approaches describe its exact nature in different ways, e.g., "alone before death," "alone before truth," "alone before

God," etc. Yet, all existentialists agree on the undisputed reality of aloneness as a basic ontological category. Man's encounter with the reality of his own ultimate aloneness, and his mastery of that existential fact, is a source of strength for the existing individual. His mastery of the fear and dread of aloneness, where "time will not pass,"[13] is a source of strength for individual man and the existential foundation of his freedom and responsibility. There is no way for an existing individual to avoid this primal confrontation with his own aloneness.* Yet behavior therapy destroys the reality of aloneness as an inward experience endured in concrete time, for it literally "spreads aloneness out" into geographical space. The therapist in our example "locates" the client and her nearest friend at the seaside in cottages separated by ten minutes in geographical space, twenty minutes in geographical space, etc. He then proceeds to desensitize her to "aloneness" as symbolized in these increasing spatial distances between herself and her nearest friend.† The problem with such behavior modification is that it fails most where it succeeds best. The reduction of aloneness as an experience endured in concrete time, to its symbolic substitute in abstract space, destroys the reality of aloneness as an existential process. Then the desensitization of this symbolic substitute destroys the very source of anxiety which could have generated an authentic encounter with aloneness, and mobilized creative life forces within the client. The price the client pays for this

---

*The constructive potential inherent in aloneness has been carefully documented and described by Clark Moustakas. (*Loneliness*, New York: Prentice-Hall, 1961.) He succinctly states in a follow-up article that aloneness "exists in its own right as a source of power and creativity, as a source of insight and direction, as a requirement of living no matter how much love and affirmation one receives in his work and in his relationships with others." (Heuristic research. In *Challenges of humanistic psychology*. J. Bugental (Ed.). New York: McGraw-Hill, 1967, p. 102.)
†This example of behavior modification is taken from the work of Joseph Wolpe. *Desensitization Therapy*. The Tape Library of the American Academy of Psychotherapists, tape #30.

desensitization of anxiety is that she learns superficially to avoid the reality of her ultimate aloneness rather than encounter it, master it, and develop the constructive potential inherent in it. She has been taught techniques to avoid reality, rather than given the opportunity to discover it. Existential science finds the same anti-realistic and anti-scientific bias in the technical application of general psychology that it finds in its basic philosophical assumptions.

But let us explore further the theoretical significance of this destruction of existential reality by the reduction of time to space, process to object, movement to immobility, becoming as a concrete experience to becoming as a symbolic abstraction. Let us examine more closely this fundamental contradiction in the reductive method of science and psychology. We can best proceed by an examination of a series of views of a particular event that is in process. The first methodological step would be to connect this series of views or pictures together by a label such as "becoming in general." But we cannot stop with only the label, for it is merely a verbal symbol that represents a certain transition between a series of pictures or snapshots, just as the abstract symbol x represents some certain unknown quantity "whatever it may be." The symbol is convenient but it tells us nothing of the nature of that unknown quantity any more than "becoming in general," as a symbol for the transition between snapshots, tells us anything about the nature of the transition itself. Let us try, then, to concentrate totally on just the transition itself and to understand what is going on *between* any two snapshots.

We can begin this attempt to analyze the transition itself by the insertion of a third snapshot between any two others in the series. Now we can study the smaller units of transition that our insertion of a third snapshot produced. But we find that these smaller units are no more amenable to our investigation than the larger ones, and that they reveal nothing new about the nature of the transition process itself. We continue our method in the hope of a breakthrough, and insert views between views until the size of the transition is infinitesimal. Then an actual breakthrough appears to have occurred because we are convinced that our perpetual use of the method has reduced the distance between views to insignificance. We are also convinced that the instability caused by the perpetual insertions has produced real movement rather than only its symbolic imitation. But in fact such an operation does not advance us one step in our investigation of the nature of the transition itself. The method of perpetual insertions may strain our vision to the point that we no longer perceive the infinitesimal distance between any two snapshots; and the perceptual instability caused by that visual "giddiness" will then produce an illusion of mobility. But we can never get beyond this symbolic illusion of mobility, for the fact remains that each of these snapshots taken by itself is an immobility, and that no increase in their numbers nor decrease in the distances between them can change that given fact and produce mobility out of immobility. The only method by which we can investigate the reality of movement and becoming is to thrust ourselves down into the actual flux and flow of concrete time. Only from within the process of change can we grasp at once both change and the successive states into which it could at any moment be broken and immobilized. But these successive states into which change could be broken at any moment are only *potential* immobilities, when they are perceived from *within* the process of movement itself. The reality of that movement could never be constituted by the endless and ceaseless addition of these successive states, when they are perceived from without and are taken as separate and actual immobilities. You may label these immobilities as you choose, multiply their numbers as you will, perpetually reduce the size of the intervals between them—still you will fail. The reality of the movement will always slip through the intervals and you will always experience "the disappointment of the child who tries by clapping his hands together to crush the smoke."[14] The reality of the movement will always elude you, because every attempt to constitute change out of static states founders on the basic contradiction that a mobility could be produced by the addition of immobilities.

ZENO AND ACHILLES

Thus general psychology founders on this basic contradiction between movement as space and movement as time. It is such a crucial issue that we must examine the early origins of this philosophical paradox and try to correct the problem at its source. There are numerous examples of these classical philosophical arguments but they all point to this basic contradiction between real and symbolic movement. They all consist in reducing the actual movement of an object to the line traversed by the object, and then acting upon the line traversed as if it were the movement itself. It follows from this method of logical reduction and substitution that the symbolic and the real are now interchangeable, and that we can now perform the same act on either the symbol or the reality and get the same result. It follows from this method of logical reduction and substitution that we can now divide real movement into separate parts and it will always be the same movement, just as we can divide the line traversed into separate parts and it remains the same line. But such methodological reduction and substitution sets off an endless series of contradictions that are but expressions of this initial reductive operation which substitutes a symbol for reality and then tries to treat the reality as if it were nothing but the symbol. The only way to substitute the line traversed for the movement itself is to analyze the movement from outside and then mechanically "add together" the potential stops and the potential immobilities that can be artificially abstracted from it at any point and at any instant. But such a reductive substitution builds the initial contradiction between the real and the symbolic into the very nature of scientific method, and produces a chain of subsequent contradictions and errors that confound and eventually doom all attempts to make psychology a physical science. Now this initial contradiction between the real and the symbolic, e.g., a mobility made by the addition of immobilities, which is built into the very nature of scientific method, dissolves and vanishes as soon as we enter into the actual continuity of the movement itself, and directly experience that continuity as we lift an arm or advance a step in our everyday world. The symbolic curve my hand sketches like a graph when I raise my arm from a horizontal to a vertical position can be arbitrarily divided into an infinite number of artificial stops or points, but not the actual movement itself because the real motion that raised my arm was one continuous and coordinated act. Thus we begin to understand that real movement is an organized and integrated process, and that the line any one motion draws between two stops can only be made by the action of a single indivisible stroke. Now we see that it is impossible to arbitrarily break up this simple indivisible movement that traces the original line in the same way that we can arbitrarily break up that line once it has been drawn. The line traversed by the movement of a body can be arbitrarily broken into parts and divided into sections because it has no internal organization; but the movement that produced the line is articulated inwardly and has its own internal structure and integrity. Real movement is produced either by a simple indivisible motion with a particular duration, or by a series of simple indivisible motions. But the internal organization of these motions must be taken into account or the confusion between real and symbolic movement will lead us directly back to the classical arguments of antiquity. Examination of one of these classical arguments will provide us with a concrete example of this confusion between movement as space and movement as time.

Zeno asserted that Achilles would never catch the tortoise because with his first step he could only arrive at the point where the tortoise was, and with his second step only at the point to which the tortoise had moved while Achilles was taking his first step, etc. The method Zeno used to win his argument was to substitute the line traversed in space for the actual movement of Achilles in time, and then divide that line in accordance with routine mechanical laws. Such a method leads to the conclusion that Achilles would *never* be able to catch the tortoise, because he would always have one more step to take. But it is obvious that in the world of real movement rather than symbolic movement Achilles *would* immediately overtake the tortoise. Consideration of real, rather than symbolic, movement would force us to treat each step of Achilles, as well as each step of the tortoise, as a simple and continuous indivisible act. So in the world of real movement Achilles would immediately overtake the tortoise and that is all there is to the argument. It would even be possible to subdivide the steps taken by Achilles and those of the tortoise, and no contradiction will arise as long as you respect the internal organization and the natural articulation of the two courses. No contradiction will arise because you will have followed the real movement rather than its symbolic substitute, and you will have investigated the real world rather than its artificial reconstruction. The artificial reconstruction proposed by Zeno would correspond to actual experience only if we could arbitrarily divide and design real movement the way we can arbitrarily divide and design the line traversed by that movement. The endless contradictions in psychology today can be traced back to this classical contradiction between the science of actual experience and the science of its symbolic substitute.

chapter 11

WHY PSYCHOLOGY FAILS:
THE IMPOSSIBILITY OF
PREDICTION AND CONTROL

In the preceding chapter we examined and described the significance of time as the ontological foundation of reality. Now let us focus on the specific problems and challenges that such an existential ontology poses for the future development of psychology.

PREDICTION

The stated goal of general psychology is "the prediction and control of behavior." It "succeeds" exactly to the extent that it reduces the basis of experience from time to space, i.e., reduces the self as process to the self as object. The man whose behavior psychology "predicts and controls" is an abstract and symbolic reconstruction, but not man as he endures and exists in concrete time. Such a basic methodological error is called the "Fallacy of Misplaced Concreteness,"* because a symbolic abstraction has been

---

*The "Fallacy of Misplaced Concreteness" is a straightforward phrase used by A. N. Whitehead to describe the "error of mistaking the abstract for the con-

substituted for concrete reality. It is not by study of such an artificial and objectified *representation* of man that psychology will advance our knowledge of the human condition—the self is more than a passive shadow. The endless data on these ritualized and socialized projections of the self are irrelevant since they ignore man in the process of becoming. They ignore man as an existential reality engaged in the vital dynamics of creation and time. Existential science insists that the lived temporal self, not its spatial symbol, must be the subject matter for any meaningful psychology. But the main object of science is prediction and control, and it attains that goal only to the extent that it reduces consciousness as an experience in time to consciousness as an object in space. Such a reduction is necessary, since time as an experiential reality cannot be quantified and measured. Psychology ignores the complexity of this problem, and simply substitutes an abstract spatial symbol for the concrete reality of time. Psychology must objectify and solidify its subject matter in this way because prediction and control are possible only if we assume that the experience being investigated does not *endure*. Thus it is only the reduced and objectified symbol of experience, rather than the concrete reality of experience, that psychology has designated as its proper subject matter. Psychology defends this substitution of abstract symbols for concrete reality on the grounds that statistical data gathered by this method of investigation "prove" that behavior can be predicted and controlled. Existential science

---

crete." He argues that "the field is now open for the introduction of some new doctrine of organism which may take the place of the materialism with which, since the seventeenth century, science has saddled philosophy." He concludes that the physical science concept of organism "is obviously an abstraction" and that, instead of such an abstraction, "the concrete fact, which is the organism, must be a complete expression of the character of a real occurrence." (*Science and the modern world.* New York: Macmillan, 1925, pp. 41, 52.)

agrees that man does tend to reduce himself to a social object and to manipulate his environment for practical ends. But it does not confuse this objectified public self with the creative personal self that flows beneath it. Psychology succeeds in its attempt to predict and control behavior only to the extent that man lives *outside* himself and substitutes these social and public symbols for his own personal identity. Psychology succeeds only to the extent that individual man imitates these artificial symbols and fails to free himself by the creative effort of his own will. And each individual man must free himself by his own effort, for it is obvious that freedom can never be imposed upon man nor made into a simple habitual automatism. The existential freedom asked of man is a concrete reality but it is difficult to discover and maintain against the weight of matter that constantly manifests itself as pressure toward adaptation and socialization. Still, the fact remains that psychology can predict and control behavior only to the extent that man imitates the illusion of determinism imposed upon him by psychology, and substitutes that illusion for the reality of his own individual freedom.

But it is also true that psychology *will* succeed and personal freedom *will* die, if man imitates and becomes this mechanical shadow of life that psychology has projected into public and social space. Then man will only adapt, rather than create, and live only for the external world rather than for himself. Man will speak rather than think, and be acted upon rather than act himself. Existential science realizes how difficult it is for man to free himself and grasp his inner states as living realities that are constantly becoming and that are not amenable to psychological prediction and control. Still, each individual man *can* discover this existential reality and take possession of his own life by an act of will that thrusts him down into the "flux and fire" of his own self and his own becoming.

CAUSALITY

The assumption of causality which is a necessary pre-requisite for psychological prediction and control is based on a false conception of time. Consequently the validity of that assumption breaks down once the crucial significance of consciousness and duration are understood. Laws of causality cannot be established in psychology since the same cause never repeats itself. Thus each cause produces its particular effect only once. To say that the same inner causes will reproduce the same effects is to assume that the same cause can appear in our consciousness for a second time. But such a "repetition" is not possible, since no two psychic states can be the same because each one expresses a unique moment in time that has its own accumulated history and its own memory of it. A physical object does not *remember* the passage of experienced time, and so the physicist does not contradict himself when he speaks of identical causes, in spite of the fact that time has lapsed. But the passage of time is something concrete and real for our human consciousness, because man does store and preserve the past in his awareness and memory of it. Consequently, the psychologist contradicts himself when he speaks of identical causes that repeat themselves, because the same psychic state never appears in our consciousness a second time. The original state is altered the "second" time, even if only by our memory of its first occurrence. Nor can it be argued that this difference is "negligible," and that therefore psychic states can still be reduced to common general elements or to causes that are comparable. Such a naive attempt to dismiss the significance of time ignores the fact that each of these psychic states is a unique addition to the process of becoming, and that the same feeling experienced again becomes an entirely new feeling by the mere fact of being "repeated."

These arguments lead to the conclusion that the assumption of causality which is based on the possibility of repetition, proves useful in physics exactly because objects are *not* conscious of their own history. But that same assumption of causality is an obstacle to the psychological study of mental states because the consciousness of man eliminates the possibility of repetition, and thereby makes causality a meaningless concept. The physicist can still proceed on the mechanical assumption that the same cause always produces the same effect. But the psychologist must reject as illusion any "laws" based on such a simplistic concept of physical causality. The assumption of causality must be rejected by psychology, because in man a psychic state can occur only once and express its unique effect only once and never again.

MEMORY

The human personality is the only relevant subject matter for existential science. Consciousness is the dynamic foundation of personality; and memory is, in turn, the dynamic foundation of consciousness. Therefore any valid theory of personality must be based on a valid assumption concerning the primary significance and dynamic function of memory. Any valid theory of personality must establish that memory is not a *tabula rasa* (blank slate) on which recollections are inscribed, but an active process which advances ceaselessly and generates continuous personality change and growth. This process of memory is inherent in our consciousness of time, and unfolds beneath the artificial symbols and categories that conceal it. Time and memory are essential for the development and evolution of man, for without them he would be trapped in a meaningless present that has no past to contemplate and no projected and anticipated future. Time and memory are 'the continuous progress of the past which gnaws into the future and which swells as it advances.''[1] The past grows without ceasing, and there is no limit to the capacity of our memory to store and preserve it. Memory is not a mechanical faculty that puts things in a drawer or inscribes them on a register, for there is no drawer and there is no register. It is even more accurate to say that there is no "faculty of memory" at all. A faculty works intermittently, only when it will or when it can, but the past "gnaws into the future," and preserves itself without relaxation. It is this ceaseless and relentless survival of the past that eliminates repetition, thus making it impossible for our consciousness ever to experience the same state twice. The circumstances may be the same, but they no longer act on the same person because he has advanced to a new moment in his own history and to a new memory of his own past. Thus our personality changes without ceasing, and this constant process of becoming prevents the mechanical repetition of any single psychic state. It is this accumulated memory of our own history that makes the advance of time irreversible, and makes it impossible for us to live over again any single moment from our past. We could repeat such a single moment from our history only if we could first forget all that had followed it. But even if we could erase from the consciousness of our intellect the memory of all that had followed such a single moment in time, we could never erase that memory from the consciousness of our *will*.

HABIT

General psychology could well be described as the science of habits, for it studies only that aspect of memory which can be abstracted out of time. It is that very abstraction out of duration that defines the nature of habits and, at the same time, makes them irrelevant to the development of any meaningful science of man. The irrelevance of habits lies in the fact that their abstraction out of time destroys the functional significance of memory as the dynamic foundation of consciousness and personality. Thus, the irrelevance of habits to the development of existential science is obvious, since habits reduce memory from a dynamic process to "a fold in a material, as of an impress graven deeper by repetition."[2] But such a reduction of memory ignores the fact that most of our recollections bear upon unique events and details of our life that have specific dates and histories, and consequently can never be repeated. Those memories that we acquire by planned mechanical repetition are, in fact, the rare and exceptional ones. The spontaneous memory of facts and images that are unique in time takes place at every moment; but planned mechanical recollections are more noted because they are more useful and practical. Consequently, these mechanical memories or habits that are learned by a repetition of the same effort are set forth as the model for memory. Spontaneous memories or recollections are then considered only habits in a nascent state, and the beginning of lessons to be learned by heart. Psychology has once more contradicted itself because it has reduced spontaneous memory, which is unique in time and cannot be repeated, to mechanical memory that can only be acquired by artificial repetition. Spontaneous recollection is perfect from the outset because it occupies a specific place and date in the concrete time of our personal history, and its image can only be disfigured by mechanical repetition. The opposite is true of artificial recollection, because a habit becomes perfect only to the extent that it passes out of concrete time and is made more and more foreign to our personal history by systematic repetitions. This psychological reduction of memory represents a basic contradiction because spontaneous memory and mechanical memory are of different orders, and "repetition" can in no way convert the former into the latter. Repetition merely imitates and uses the *movements* by which spontaneity is continued in order to organize them into a mechanism and construct a bodily habit. This habit could not even be called a memory except that the person can remember that he did acquire it. And he can remember that he acquired it only by appeal to spontaneous memory that dates specific events and records them but once. Bergson argues that only this first type of spontaneous recollection can be considered memory, and that the second mechanical type of recollection studied by psychologists is not memory but "habit interpreted by memory."[3]

Probability

One of the critical distinctions between general psychology and existential science rests on the contrast between probability as determined by antecedent conditions, and probability as an expression of personality organization. The former is based on the hypothetical assumption of an infallible causal relationship between the past and the future.* The latter is based simply on a judgment of character and its most likely expression, without any assumption that the past determines the future. Rather, the basic assumption of existential science is that we are free when our acts emerge from the depths of our subjective self and express the whole of our character and personality.† No argument that we are determined by the influence of our

---

*The concept of "probability" usually connotes the possibility of error, or *fallibility*. But this is only because, in practice, all the facts cannot be ideally known. In theory, the logical assumption that underlies the concept of probability is that the prediction would be infallible if *all* the facts that determine the causal relationship between the past and the future could be ideally measured.
†The self, character, and personality are all used here as synonymous with the existential "I" of Dasein.

character is meaningful, for our character is still our self and our personality. And it is equally meaningless to argue that the self that feels and thinks determines the self that acts, because the latter would be only an expression of the former even if such an abstraction were possible. Nor does it alter the basic existential position to say that we are free to change our character. We change our character in many imperceptible ways every day, and our freedom would be reduced to a mechanism if these changes were grafted on to our self and not blended with it so that they were appropriated by us and belonged to us. We can then agree to consider every act that emerges from the self and is a direct expression of our personality as a free act. Such an agreement leads to the conclusion that free will is a fact, since it is a necessary condition for the decision which produces the free act itself. But the determinist recognizes that such an agreement would destroy his own position, and so he turns from examination of the act itself to examination of either the past that preceded the act or the future that follows it. He either goes back to some point in time before the act and explains the determination of the act from that perspective; or he takes a future perspective and assumes in advance of the act that it has already been performed and could not take place in any other way.

Now, the critical distinction that must be made here is between a knowledge of antecedents which would enable us to state a probable outcome; and the *hypothetical* assumption of an *infallible* causal relationship between these antecedents and the act itself. Both determinist and existentialist alike can agree that under certain circumstances it is possible to say of a friend that he will probably act in a certain way. But this is a judgment of his present character in terms of our past knowledge of him, rather than a prediction of his future conduct. It is also true that our self and our character are constantly changing and growing. Still a sudden reversal in that process is rare, so we can *usually* say of an individual that some acts would be consistent with his personality, while some others would represent a rare reversal or contradiction. We can therefore say that certain acts express the character of a person and others contradict it, without any assumption of a determined causal relationship between the past and the future. But the determinist argues that such causal relationships are a *fact,* and that predictions are only "probable" because we can never know all the antecedents of any particular act. It follows from this determinist argument that the probability of a prediction increases in direct proportion to the number of *known* antecedents, and that there is an infallible causal relationship between the past and the future (which we could discover) if only all these antecedents could be designated. General psychology sets as its goal just such a hypothetical closed system of prediction. But existential science rejects any assumption of a determined causal relationship between the past and future. Existential science agrees that predictions of behavior are possible, but says that such predictions can be based only upon concrete judgments of the present *character* of a particular individual, and upon consideration of those personality expressions that would be consistent with it.

DYNAMISM

The crisis of choice is a central issue and a basic reality in existential philosophy. Thus, existential science must distinguish between decision as the free outcome of a dynamic process, and decision as the determined result of a mechanical operation. Now the determinist proceeds in his analysis of this central issue by first reducing deep emotional states to fixed symbols and categories, in order to construct a mechanical model of the self. He then places this mechanical self between two contradictory alternatives, and analyzes its movements back and forth between these two alternatives until a decision results. Now the self and the emotions aroused by the two alternatives are analyzed as objects that remain identical during the decision process. This means that the methodological design itself negates the very principle of causality that it intends to prove. No decision can ever be reached as long as the self that deliberates remains the same, and the opposite emotional states that aroused it do not change. But the fact is that the self has *already* changed as soon as the first emotion was experienced and even before the second supervened, because the self is constantly modifying the emotional states that aroused it and is constantly being modified by them during the entire deliberation process. It is this dynamic interaction between an active self and its changing emotional states that leads by natural evolution to a free and creative act. But determinism substitutes objective symbols for both the personal self and the emotional states that impinge upon it so that any potential dynamism in the interaction and in the decision is eliminated in advance. It places an objectified self between two objectified emotional states, and the decision is simply determined by a mechanical formula in favor of the stronger of the two solidified states. Existential science rejects this mechanism, to which psychology condemns itself in advance, because such symbols and formulas break down under the testimony of an attentive consciousness that shows us inner dynamism and creative decision as a fact.

VITALISM

The driving force of vitalism is the power of our will, which is inherent in consciousness and is the taproot of all human growth and creation. Our consciousness as a whole moves in the same direction as the basic principle of vitalism that sustains and thrusts it forward. But the weight of matter tends to pull our consciousness back down toward fixed and immobile points in space, and this passive, backward, look is the natural inclination of our intellect.* Consequently, it is only by an active and intentional effort of our will that we can detach our intellect from the mechanism of matter, and make our consciousness coincide with the forward thrust of vitalism that sustains it. Only after such a radical separation can we then attach our consciousness to the forward movement of becoming and the vital processes of human growth and creation. But such a radical action demands that our intellect turn in upon itself and twist upon itself until the direction of our looking has been made one with the forward direction of our willing. Such a reversal of the natural function of the intellect demands of us an intense and painful effort that must be made suddenly and cannot be sustained for more than a few moments. But in those moments of pure free action we can contract our whole being and thrust it forward into the reality of our own becoming. It is in these pure moments of existence that we can grasp something of the vital forces. that motivate us, and even something of the becoming itself by which they are organized into an act. But now let us push still further into these moments of pure existence and try to install ourselves within the vitalism of life and the tension of willing that carries it forward. Now we can feel our whole being merge into our will and our will itself merge into that same vitalism of life which prolongs it. Now we can

---

*Kierkegaard succinctly states this contradiction between the "backward looking" function of our intellect and the "forward striving" motion of will and time: "It is perfectly true, as philosophers say, that life must be understood backwards. But they forgot the other proposition, that it must be lived forwards. And if one thinks over that proposition it becomes more and more evident that life can never really be understood in time simply because at no particular moment can I find the necessary resting-place from which to understand it—backwards." (*The journals of Kierkegaard.* Trans. A. Dru. New York: Harper Torchbooks, 1959, [date of entry, 1843] p. 89.)

feel and even know in these moments of pure existence that reality is a perpetual growth and a creation pursued without end. Bergson insists that this miracle of growth and creation performed by our will is manifest in every act of invention, every act of freedom, and every act of love that brings something new into the world.

SELF

The self is the primary datum of existential science, and so it must be studied and defined as an existential fact until it is recognized as an emergent reality distinct from the artificial and objectified "self" studied by general psychology. Psychology considers only this latter objectified self because such a symbolic reconstruction is amenable to the method of analysis and is adapted to the requirements of social and public life. But psychology has become so obsessed and preoccupied with its analysis of this symbolic self that it has lost sight of the real self beneath it, and finally has even denied that any such real self exists. Consequently we must separate the authentic personal self from its projected shadow so that the primal existential self at the heart of man can be studied and understood in its own right. Now it is difficult to make this separation because it is easy to overlook the difference between time as quality, in which the real self exists, and time as quantity, into which its shadow is projected. It is easy to overlook this difference because the intellect prefers symbols and language to emotions and experience, and most often people are preoccupied with practical adaptations to social life rather than with the meaning of their own subjective existence. But the real self is there to be discovered and experienced and people do seek to understand its meaning once they look into themselves and encounter the deeper reality of their own being. Then they no longer confuse the reality of personal experience with its solidified and symbolic representation, nor the reality of their own subjective selves with dead shadows cast out upon social space. Existential science provides us with specific models of psychotherapy (see sections on Rank, Binswanger, and Boss), and promotes specific modes of involvement that make such inward exploration a concrete possibility. And those of us who do turn inward discover that psychology has failed, and that the real self is this active process of creation and becoming that is the essence of our own individual lives and the essence of life in general.

GROWTH

Existential science argues that growth and development do not result from the accumulation of data and information. Such objective knowledge provides no means by which to go beyond itself. The only way that a personality or a science makes meaningful advances is by an emotional *leap* that breaks through the circular confines of constricted intellectual knowledge. But psychology and science tell us that you cannot go beyond intelligence because you could only do that by the use of intelligence itself as a method. They say that intelligence is the only tool that clarifies our consciousness, and that we are inside our thoughts and so cannot get beyond them. They say that the intellect can make progress, but that you cannot otherwise engender progress for it is with the intellect itself that you would have to do the work. It follows that psychology and science would raise such an objection because they are both based on the method of intellectual analysis. But it also follows that the logical consequence of this same reasoning is to prove that it is impossible to learn anything "new."[4]

The essence of logical reasoning is that it confines itself to the manipulation of given premises, and thereby shuts itself up in a circle of the known. The only way to break through that closed logical circle is to risk the venture of a concrete action. Only the concrete action of swimming convinces us that swimming is possible, because "learning to swim" is a logical contradiction—the first step is to hold one's self up in the water which means that you can already swim before you start to learn. Reasoning alone always traps us in these empty circles filled with nothing but rational and logical contradictions. Only the reality of a direct encounter with existence frees us, for we can throw ourselves into the water and struggle during the period of risk and fear until we creatively adapt ourselves to the new environment and thus learn to swim. So existential science agrees that learning other than by intelligence is a rational absurdity. But the fact remains that in reality only action can "cut the knot that reasoning has tied and will not unloose."[5] Reasoning on its own power will never discover new knowledge, even though that extension of knowledge would appear reasonable once it had been discovered. Such a discovery of new knowledge demands a risk and a *leap* that forces us beyond the mechanical limits of our own environment. Endless new systems and formulas that are but variations on the theme of walking will never produce a rational rule for swimming. Try as the logicians may, they can never get beyond the rational limits of their own intellectual methodology. Sooner or later each individual alone must risk himself in a direct encounter with the reality of the water and only in that personal venture can he master his fear and learn to swim. It is true that after such a venture he will understand how the mechanism of swimming is related to that of walking, and that swimming is only an extension of walking. But so will he understand something much more important: endless speculation on walking would never have pushed him into the reality of swimming. And this same principle holds fast for the discovery of philosophical knowledge: endless speculation by intelligence on the mechanism of intelligence will never get psychology and science beyond that mechanism. It is true that the method of intellectual analysis does yield an endless number of varied patterns and diverse arrangements of already observed data; but it can never produce anything new or anything of a higher order of complexity. Such new discoveries and advances in psychology and science are possible only if you "take things by storm" and "thrust intelligence outside itself by an act of will."[6]

VALIDATION

The nature of a science is determined by the operational standard which it sets for validation. General psychology sets the validation of *laws* as its operational standard, and so it must reduce all individual events to systematic generalizations. The significance of existential science lies in its ability to study unique events, since it sets the validation of *facts* as its basic operational goal. These two different and mutually exclusive aims of validation arise because of the fundamental contradiction between nature as mechanism and nature as dynamism. Dynamism starts with an assumption of voluntary activity inherent in our consciousness and our will. It then represents inertia as a disruption of this natural free activity. Consequently it can conceive of a creative mobility in nature that is not governed by mechanical laws, and yet still recognize the reality of inert matter that is determined by those laws. Now, psychology and science are based on a system of mechanism and they follow the opposite course. They assume that phenomena under their observation are governed by necessary laws, and that these observed data always operate inside the determined system of mechanism, even though combinations become more complex and even though that complexity makes prediction and control more difficult.

Now these two mutually exclusive conceptions of nature involve two very different hypotheses concerning the relation between facts and laws. Dynamism assumes that there are unique and specific facts that cannot be encompassed within a general law, and so it sets the fact as the absolute reality and the law as only a symbolic approximation of that reality. But mechanism discovers within specific facts a certain law, and then makes this general law the absolute reality and the specific facts but a manifestation of it. This contrast between the priority given to facts or to laws is based on the different interpretations given by mechanism and dynamism to concepts of simplicity and primacy. Mechanism defines any principle as simpler and more primary if events based on that principle are easier to predict and control. This very definition makes the assumption of inertia simpler and more primary than the assumption of spontaneity; the assumption of space simpler and more primary than the assumption of time; the abstract and the symbolic simpler and more primary than the concrete and the immediate, etc. But dynamism reverses these priorities laid down by mechanism because it breaks through the objectified symbol and discovers that it is only an artificial composite of many simpler and more primary facts. Those concepts which mechanism defines as simple and primary are actually a blend of several forces that have been neutralized, just as darkness may be produced by the interference and neutralization of two lights. It is for this reason that dynamism considers the assumption of spontaneity simpler and more primary than the mechanical assumption of inertia. The concept of inertia is a complex abstraction: "the tendency of a body to persevere in a state of rest or motion as long as it is not acted upon by any other force." And this abstract definition necessarily contains within it the implicit notion of its exact converse, i.e., spontaneous movement. But spontaneous movement itself is a simpler and more primary fact because each of us need but stand up from his chair in order to directly experience the reality of his own voluntary action. Now some of us may choose to reject this direct experience of voluntary movement as a distortion or an illusion. Nevertheless, we must all agree that each of us can have an immediate experience of his own spontaneity without the abstract definition of inertia having anything to do with it at all. And so spontaneity or freedom becomes a simpler and more primary datum than inertia or determinism. Thus, mechanism and dynamism lead us to opposite conceptions of science and validation, according to the way we understand the relation between the concrete and the abstract, the simple and the complex, facts and laws.

Part IV

METHODOLOGY

chapter 12

LIMITATIONS OF THE RATIONAL-EMPIRICAL METHOD IN PSYCHOLOGICAL RESEARCH

The methods of a science follow directly from the philosophical assumptions which underlie that science. The analytic method of general psychology follows from its spatial ontology and biological materialism. That is, analysis of events that have been reduced to objects and can be repeated is possible, so intuition as a method is not necessary. The intuitive method of existential science follows from its temporal ontology and biological vitalism. That is, intuition as a method is now necessary because only such a technique can encompass time and becoming, while the fixed categories of analysis distort and destroy the reality of these existential processes. Thus the philosophical assumptions of general psychology lead to reliance on the traditional scientific goals and methods of quantification, prediction, measurement, etc. General psychology assumes that these traditional approaches will contribute to our knowledge of man and the human condition as they have contributed to our mastery of the physical universe. But the philosophical assumptions of existential science lead, conversely, to a complete rejection of these traditional spatial and mechanistic models of man. Existential science insists on an overall reappraisal of the goals and methods of psychology, since the specific nature of living matter and of human experience demands something more. Existential science argues that only by such a *total* revision can we as psychologists hope to meet and solve the unique challenges and problems that confront us.

So far we have contrasted general psychology and existential science in terms of the distinctions between their basic biological and ontological assumptions. Now, beginning again with general psychology, let us contrast these two approaches in terms of the *scientific methods* which directly follow from their basic philosophical premises.

We can agree that the appropriate starting point for the development of any meaningful science must be the nature of the subject matter itself. Experimental methods then evolve which are directly relevant to the basic scientific and philosophical parameters of the phenomena which are to be investigated. Any deviation in the progression of this sequential development leads inevitably to the distortion of data and events to make them fit a model of science developed for another subject matter and for another purpose. But psychology did not merely deviate from this developmental progression—it completely reversed the process. Psychology started with an established experimental model that had been developed for the physical sciences, and worked backwards to make the philosophy of its subject matter and the data itself fit that model. The unfortunate result of such a developmental reversal is that now psychology cannot advance our knowledge of its own subject matter, because the method which defined psychology restricted *a priori* the very nature of that subject matter. Consequently, any dimensions of psychological phenomena that do not fit the method must be rejected, since a challenge to the method is a challenge to the basis upon which psychology defends itself as a physical science.

Thus the abortive historical and philosophical origins of psychology have trapped it in the dead end of a method that blocks meaningful investigation of its own subject matter.

No psychologist can deny the confused nature of these historical and philosophical origins, for they are well documented. Psychology developed as a reaction against certain modes of philosophical abstraction and speculation. The intent was laudable enough; but the remedy produced even more serious philosophical problems than those it was supposed to solve. It is true that psychology did achieve independence from philosophy, and recognition as a separate discipline, by its forced identification with the physical sciences. Yet, more important to the future shape of psychology than these initial political tactics were the scientific biases of its founders. Wundt (1832–1920) was the most significant of these early founders. He tried to develop an experimental model for psychology based on his own background in medicine and physiology. He argued that physiology had successfully adapted the methods of physics to its needs, and that now psychology could do the same. Most relevant to our presentation was his assertion that *all* psychological processes could be made amenable to the methods of physical science. He insisted that any philosophical criticism which attempted to restrict application of experimental methods was a "prejudice," and that "as soon as the psyche is viewed as a natural phenomenon, and psychology as a natural science, experimental methods must also be capable of full application to this science."[1] It is this basic assumption concerning the unlimited application of the methods of physical science that has consistently defined and characterized general psychology. This has been true of general psychology from its inception right down to the present: Wundt wanted to reduce the psyche to a "natural phenomenon"; Freud wanted to investigate the spirit and mind of man "in exactly the same way as any non-human things";[2] and Skinner wants to completely abolish "autonomous man—the inner man, the homunculus."[3] Thus, the one common assumption which unites all these widely varied approaches under one label called "psychology," is the assumption that human experience can be reduced or eliminated until all available data fit the rational-empirical method of physical science. In the next two chapters, we shall examine the psychological and scientific limitations of this method and of this basic philosophical assumption. It will be our contention that at this point in its history psychology must break through this artificial methodological barrier if it is to become a relevant and useful science. Otherwise, psychology will remain trapped within a vicious circle where every psychological inquiry that promises to advance our knowledge of man is rejected as "senseless," and every research project must begin with a distortion of the data to make it fit the system. Such is now the fate of general psychology, for its rigid methodological bias violates the one essential requirement of any science—an open and sensitive response to its subject matter. It is this distortion and destruction of authentic psychological data that forces us to recognize the fatal limitations of the rational-empirical method in psychological research, and to seek a new alternative for psychology.

chapter 13

INTUITIVE KNOWLEDGE: ITS SIGNIFICANCE FOR PSYCHOLOGY

Today many psychologists are beginning to reject the "security" and "respectibility" provided by identification with the physical sciences in order to explore another alternative. They want to study and examine the authentic data of psychology, and are no longer content to merely observe and measure artificial and symbolic substitutes. So let us try to understand the nature of scientific data within the framework of existential science.

PROBLEM AND MYSTERY

The "flux and fire" of Heraclitus reappears in existential science as "time and vitalism." These are the energy processes which underlie the directly observable behavior studied by general psychology. The fatal error of psychological science is its failure to recognize that there are *two* distinct types of data, and to develop specific methods appropriate for the investigation of each. Existential philosophy describes this fatal methodological error in its own language:

> A problem is something which I meet, which I find complete before me, but which I can therefore lay siege to and reduce. But a mystery is something in which I myself am involved, and it can therefore only be thought of as *a sphere where the distinction between what is in me and what is before me loses its meaning and its initial validity.* A genuine problem is subject to an appropriate technique by the exercise of which it is defined: whereas a mystery, by definition, transcends every conceivable technique. It is, no doubt, always possible (logically and psychologically) to degrade a mystery so as to turn it into a problem. But this is a fundamentally vicious proceeding, whose springs might perhaps be discovered in a kind of corruption of the intelligence. The problem of evil, as the philosophers have called it, supplies us with a particularly instructive example of this degradation.
>
> Just because it is the essence of mystery to be recognized or capable of recognition, it may also be ignored and actively denied. It then becomes reduced to something I have "heard talked about," but which I refuse as only being *for other people;* and that in virtue of an illusion which these "others" are deceived by, but which I myself claim to have detected.
>
> We must carefully avoid all confusion between the mysterious and the unknowable. The unknowable is in fact only the limiting case of the problematic, which cannot be actualized without contradiction. The recognition of mystery, on the contrary, is an essentially positive act of the mind, the supremely positive act in virtue of which all positivity may perhaps be strictly defined. In this sphere everything seems to go on as if I found myself acting on an intuition which I possess without immediately knowing myself to possess it— an intuition which cannot be, strictly speaking, self-conscious and which can grasp itself only through the modes of experience in which its image is reflected, and which it lights up by being thus reflected in them.[1]

Let us now describe the same two kinds of knowledge in the language of existential science:

The fact is that there are two kinds of clarity.

A new idea may be clear because it presents to us, simply arranged in a new order, elementary ideas which we already possessed. Our intelligence, finding only the old in the new, feels itself on familiar ground; it is at ease; it "understands." Such is the clarity we desire, are looking for, and for which we are always most grateful to whoever presents it to us. There is another kind that we submit to, and which, moreover, imposes itself only with time. It is the clarity of the radically new and absolutely simple idea, which catches as it were an intuition. As we cannot reconstruct it with pre-existing elements, since it has no elements, and as on the other hand, to understand without effort consists in recomposing the new from what is old, our first impulse is to say it is incomprehensible. But let us accept it provisionally, let us go with it through the various departments of our knowledge: we shall see that, itself obscure, it dissipates obscurities. By it the problems we considered insoluble will resolve themselves, or rather, be dissolved, either to disappear definitely, or to present themselves in some other way. From what it has done for these problems, it will in its turn benefit. Each one of them, intellectual by nature, will communicate to it something of its intellectuality. Thus intellectualized, this idea can be aimed anew at problems which will have been of use to it after having made use of it; better still, it will clear up the obscurity which surrounded them, and will, as a result, become itself still clearer. One must therefore distinguish between the ideas which keep their light for themselves, making it penetrate immediately into their slightest recesses, and those whose radiation is exterior, illuminating a whole region of thought. These can begin by being inwardly obscure; but the light they project about them comes back in reflection, with deeper and deeper penetration; and they have the double power of illuminating what they play upon and of being illuminated themselves.[2]

We can now understand the difference between knowledge as problem and knowledge as mystery. We can also understand the appeal to our intellect inherent in the simplistic reduction of a mystery to a problem. It is so much easier to confine ourselves to concepts and categories that are well established within the commonplace structures of our language, than struggle to develop new and unique uses of that language. These concepts and categories were formed by the intellect to act efficiently on the environment in the service of practical needs for survival. That is why intellectual knowledge defines objects and facts according to the way they can be turned to practical account. Thus the intellectual standard for clarity is the degree to which reality can be reduced to these efficient and useful generalities. Those experiences in the real world that cannot be reduced to such commonplace categories are then dismissed as obscure and beyond the scope of science. Bergson explains the apparent inferiority of the intuitive point of view in philosophical controversy in terms of this pragmatic standard for clarity and obscurity. We have become so accustomed to think of clarity in terms of utilitarian goals that the philosopher who upholds determinism always seems to be "right," and the one who defends freedom always seems to be "naive." The determinist may be a beginner and his adversary a seasoned philosopher, but still the determinist can argue his case with ease and even arrogance, while the defender of freedom must "sweat blood" to present his own point of view. And still the latter will be criticized for being vague and ambiguous in his defense of freedom, while the former will be considered clear and easy to understand. It is true that the argument for determinism will be clear and easy to understand, but only because the ideas necessary to defend a *problem* are already embedded in the language of our science, our intellect, and even in the language of our practical common sense. Bergson says that it is so easy to attack the intuitive philosopher who must grope for new concepts and for unique uses of the language in order to defend a *mystery,* "that it will always tempt the beginner." But Bergson also warns that one may come to regret such a simplistic dismissal of the logos of mystery, "unless, of course, there is a native lack of comprehension and, out of spite, personal resentment toward everything that is not reducible to the letter, toward all that is properly spirit. That can happen, for philosophy too has its Scribes and its Pharisees."[3]

SCIENCE AND METAPHYSICS

Thus, both existential *philosophy* and existential *science* consider reductionism the "corruption" of knowledge. Yet psychology continues to reduce mystery to problem, thou to it, time to space, duration to extension, creation to adaptation, freedom to determinism, subject to object. If existential science is right that reductionism is the work of Scribes and Pharisees, then psychologists are just such modern day Scribes and Pharisees. But let us see if there are any definite grounds for such serious accusations by examining another concrete example taken from the dominant academic-professional approach in psychology today.*

The basic model of behaviorism is the white rat deprived of food and placed in a small cage. The physiological deprivation leads to motor activity which eventually leads to the *accidental* tripping of a lever which releases a pellet of food into the cage. The rat eats the pellet and the tripping of the lever is reinforced. Now let us follow a *behavioral* analysis of Jesus "turning the other cheek." First, let us eliminate one controversy by a rejection of the divinity of Jesus so that we can concentrate on his acknowledged humanity. The behavioral analysis goes like this: "That's why I insist that Jesus, who was apparently the first

---

*An example could as easily have been taken from psychoanalytic theory, with reduction in terms of psychosexual stages; but it is behaviorism which currently dominates psychology. (See: American Psychological Association. *Graduate study in psychology for 1973–1974.* Educational Affairs Office: Washington, D.C., 1972.)

to discover the power of refusing to punish, must have hit upon the principle by accident. He certainly had none of the experimental evidence which is available to us today, and I can't conceive that it was possible, no matter what the man's genius, to have discovered the principle from casual observation." The speaker is interrupted by a suggestion that the discovery might be explained in some other way than by accident—

> No, accident. Jesus discovered one principle because it had immediate consequences, and he got another thrown in for good measure. . . .
>
> To "do good to those who despitefully use you" has two unrelated consequences. You gain . . . peace of mind. . . . Let the stronger man push you around—at least you avoid the torture of your own rage. *That's* the immediate consequence. What an astonishing discovery it must have been to find that in the long run you could *control the stronger man in* the same way![4]

Behaviorism thus explains that Jesus "turned the other cheek" because, like the rat in the cage, his first accidental response was reinforced, i.e., the normal rage reaction did not occur. The behavior pattern was decisively "shaped" because the short-term reinforcement was accompanied by a bonus long-term reinforcement, i.e., he found that he could also manipulate the stronger man. We began with a rejection of the divinity of Jesus, so there is no objection to this reduction on religious grounds. Paradoxically, we object to such a methodological operation carried out in the name of science, in the name of science itself. We must ask if such a reductive operation advances science, or if this method of artificial reconstruction is anti-scientific because of the unavoidable distortion of the original datum, in this case human compassion, under investigation. The same question is raised by the reduction of freedom to determinism in a related sequence of arguments:

> Now that we *know* how positive reinforcement works . . . we
> can be more deliberate, and hence more successful, in our
> cultural design. We can achieve a sort of control under
> which the controlled, though they are following a code much
> more scrupulously than was ever the case under the old
> system, nevertheless *feel free*. They are doing what they want
> to do, not what they are forced to do. That's the source of
> the tremendous power of positive reinforcement—there's
> no restraint and no revolt. . . .
>   The curious thing is that in that case *the question of freedom
> never arises*. [5]

Now it would obviously be more accurate to say only that
the question of freedom never arises for citizens of Walden
Two, because existentialism considers such a reduction
and destruction of freedom to be the final reduction and
destruction of man and even the end of creative evolution
itself.

The destruction of reality inherent in these reductive
methods forces us to reject the definition of psychology as
a behavioral science, and then try to develop psychology
into an existential science. But let us first understand more
clearly the need for such an existential approach by further
exploration of the possible consequences of this indiscrimi-
nate application of the methods of psychological science.

General psychology tells us that we can advance our
knowledge of man if we now apply to him the same methods that have been so successful in our study of inert matter. It tells us that there are no different values and no
different goals, whether we apply the rational categories of
the intellect to matter or to life. But the only way to make
our study of man fit the frame of physical science is to
reduce the experience of life from an existential mystery to
a practical problem. And even then, the reality of life continues to assert itself as a mystery in the concrete world
outside our frame, until the frame itself begins to crack.
General psychology refuses to recognize the unique nature

of its own subject matter, and so in due course we come to regard "everything the frame contains with equal suspicion."[6]

Let us see what might be done other than merely continue this futile effort to force the mystery of life into a frame that was made for a practical and mechanical problem. Let us see if there is some alternate approach by which psychology could be established as an authentic source of human knowledge. Bergson argued that the first step in the development of such a new approach must be the reconciliation of science and philosophy. Philosophy must intermingle with science and superimpose upon scientific and problematic data another kind of knowledge that can be called metaphysics.* It is only within the concreteness of the real world that man finds his authentic being and his absolute existence. And so is it true that only by a creative combination of science and metaphysics can man reach toward a meaningful knowledge of that absolute world. The knowledge man now possesses of this absolute reality is, of course, partial and incomplete. But it does not follow that our ultimate knowledge of the real world must be limited to the external and the relative. Bergson was convinced that man could penetrate into the depths of absolute reality, and discover profound and absolute truth, by this combined and progressive development of science and metaphysics. But such a venture and such an advance is possible only if we first renounce the artificial unity that science and psychology have forced upon nature and man from outside. Only by rejection of these symbolic results,

---

*We recognize that metaphysics usually refers to abstract speculation, and science to concrete reality. But the argument presented here is that just the opposite is, in fact, the case. Science deals only with abstract symbols and signs, while metaphysics describes the concrete reality of immediate human experience.

and the superficial methods that produced them, can we clear a path for existential science and begin to explore the absolute unity at the heart of life and man.

RELATIVISM AND TRUTH

We must begin the development of such an existential approach to a science of the absolute by a clarification of the terms "relative" and "absolute." We have already made a distinction between two types of knowledge: problem and mystery. Now we must make a parallel distinction between two types of knowing: relative and absolute. We mean by a relative type of knowing, that we move around the object studied and analyze it from a variety of different perspectives. Our knowledge of the object then depends on the point of view at which we are placed, and on the symbols that we use to describe the object being investigated. A simple example will show us that our perception of an object that is moving in space will depend upon the perspective, moving or stationary, from which we decide to view it. And our description of the movement of that object will in turn depend upon the reference points, axis systems, and other symbols into which we translate our observations of it. Such a type of knowing can be said to stop at the relative because we are placed outside the object itself, and because our knowledge of the object is relative both to the perspectives taken and to the symbols used. The second type of knowing can be said to aim at the absolute, because it depends on neither perspectives nor symbols. Now we can speak of absolute movement because we can attribute to the moving object an internal organization, and even internal "states of mind." Now we can also speak of an absolute knowledge of that movement, because we can

place ourselves "inside" the motion by an effort of imagination and by a sympathetic resonance with those internal
states. Such a sympathetic entry into the internal flow of the
moving object enables us to experience the motion that it
makes, from inside the object itself. Now our experience of
the object no longer depends on the perspectives we take
in regard to it, since we have placed ourselves inside the
dynamics of its movement. Nor does our experience depend on any symbols into which we might translate the
dynamism of that motion, because we have rejected all
translations in order to grasp the essence of the original
movement itself.

So it is in this sense that we can speak of an absolute
type of knowing, because our grasp of the original movement depends neither on perspectives taken nor symbols
used. We do not remain at a distance and view the movement from outside, but we directly experience the original
movement from inside the actual process itself. And it is in
this latter sense that we can speak of the absolute as synonymous with perfection, because the original phenomenon
is always perfectly that which it is as a concrete reality in
itself. Endless photographs of a town taken from all perspectives will never be equivalent to the experience of that
real town "under my feet." A composite of the most skillful
translations of a poem into all possible languages can never
capture the intended meaning of the original work. So a
symbolic reconstruction must always remain imperfect,
compared with the original phenomenon that is always perfect in itself when taken as a factual entity. Thus experienced from *inside,* an absolute is always a very simple thing,
but it becomes "the gold coin for which we never seem able
to finish giving small change,"[7] as soon as we begin to
analyze it from endless outside perspectives, and translate
it into countless artificial symbols.

ANALYSIS AND INTUITION

The two types of knowledge that we have described and the two types of knowing that we have outlined bring us to the critical question about the future of science and psychology. It is easy to understand what the nature of science and psychology *has been* because it was based on knowledge as problem and knowing as relative. Now the burden of the modern crisis falls back upon us, for we must try to develop a science and a psychology that is based on knowledge as mystery and knowing as absolute. Bergson asks us to begin one step at a time, and not aim "at resolving at once the greatest problems," but rather "to define the method and to permit a glimpse, on some essential points, of the possibility of its application."[8] So let us try to understand the method of a new science and psychology that could provide us a glimpse into the nature of mystery, and a hold on the reality of the absolute.

It follows from our contrast between relative and absolute truth that the absolute cannot be discovered and studied by the method of analysis, since that method depends, by its very definition, on arbitrary perspectives and artificial symbols. Now it is clear that any new advance in science and psychology demands a method that can give us direct access to the internal organization and existential reality of phenomena themselves. Bergson argues that intuition is the only method of investigation that can provide us such direct access to the mystery of existence and to the absolute nature of reality. He means by intuition, a "kind of *intellectual sympathy* by which one places oneself within an object in order to coincide with what is unique in it and consequently inexpressible."[9] Analysis as a method of investigation can never comprehend the *unique* quality of any object or event, because it is a methodological operation which reduces any phenomenon investigated to elements that are already known and to elements that are common to other phenomena as well. Consequently, the method of analysis can explain a phenomenon under investigation only in terms of phenomena other than itself that have already been investigated. It translates the object or event that is to be explained into a symbolic representation constructed from successive perspectives that accumulate as many similarities as possible between the new phenomenon being investigated and phenomena other than itself that have already been labeled and categorized. It moves around the object under investigation, multiplying its perspectives endlessly in order to complete the always incomplete representation, and ceaselessly varying its symbols in order to perfect the always imperfect translation. The method of analysis therefore goes on to endless complexity and even ceaseless infinity—still the object investigated remains "the gold coin for which we never seem able to finish giving small change."[10] Nevertheless, the results of analysis are always taken to be realistic and scientific, while the results of intuition are always considered vague and abstract. But we have seen on closer examination that such assumptions do not hold up and that the reverse is actually true. Analysis yields only artificial data drawn from ceaseless and endless observations of an abstract and symbolic reconstruction, while intuition is a simple act that gives us direct access to the concrete phenomenological meaning of an object or event.

But it is easy to see from the above distinction that the method of analysis is dictated by the ordinary function of our intelligence. It is for this very reason that analysis has become the basic method of the physical sciences. Even the most concrete of the positive sciences, and those that are most concerned with life, confine themselves to the organs and anatomical elements of living beings. They reduce dynamic forces to static factors, and then make comparisons between the visible forms of these elements. Thus they focus their study of life processes only on those aspects of evolution that are its visible and symbolic manifestations. Any deeper and more meaningful study of these life processes is restricted by the very method of analysis on which science and psychology are based. Consequently, any advance in our study of nature and psychology can be accomplished only by the use of an alternate method of investigation. Such a method must seek to grasp and discern the reality of a phenomenon in absolute terms, rather than be satisfied with artificial and symbolic data that can never get beyond the relative. Such a method must seek to understand the internal organization of a phenomenon by permitting us to place ourselves within it, rather than to merely observe the visual and symbolic manifestations of the phenomenon from endless external perspectives. Nor will such a method be satisfied with the logical and rational analysis of an abstract symbolic substitute. Rather, it will seek to experience and assimilate the most profound inwardness of the phenomenon itself by a direct encounter with it. And this new method will not further multiply our already countless stock of codes and formulas, but rather it will seek to encompass the inward dynamics of a phenomenon without any artificial translation or symbolic representation.

Now, only metaphysics provides us with the means by which such a new research model can be developed, and the method by which such a new encompassing can be accomplished. Bergson defines metaphysics as *"the science which claims to dispense with symbols,"*[11] and therefore the only way to reconcile science and metaphysics is to use intuition as the basic method of scientific investigation. It is only by progressive development and creative use of the intuitive method that we can forge the critical union of science and metaphysics that is so necessary to advance our knowledge of psychology and of life. The use of intuition will then transform metaphysics into a positive science in the sense that metaphysics can become a progressive and indefinitely perfectible type of knowledge. The use of intuition will at the same time force positive science beyond the rigid limits imposed upon it by the method of analysis, and lead science toward a consciousness of its own wider range of potential discovery and contribution. Bergson argues that such a reconciliation between science and metaphysics will restore "the continuity between the intuitions which the various sciences have obtained here and there in the course of their history."[12] But let us turn now to the particular problem which concerns us here, and try to see how this intuitive method applies to our "essential point" of psychology as an existential science.

Bergson insists that there is at least one reality which we all grasp and hold from within by intuition, and not by any symbolic analysis from outside. That internal reality is our own personality that flows through time and our own self that endures and grows. We may be scientific and objective about everything and everyone else, but each of us can sympathize with the meaning and reality of his own personal self. We have seen that the abstract and artificial symbols used in psychological analysis destroy this inward reality of the existential self. But we must also realize that even the sensitive and subjective images of intuition can never reproduce exactly the original experience of this inward flow of our conscious life. The critical difference between analysis and intuition is that such a reproduction or reconstruction is not even the goal of the intuitive method of existential science. Each man must get for himself, in his own subjective encounter with existence, the intuition of the reality which constitutes his own personal being. No man can be forced by even the most persuasive of intuitive images to an encounter with the reality of his own existence. Abstract symbols and data from science and psychology contribute nothing to man's knowledge of his inwardness. But neither do the more subtle and sensitive intuitive images of existential science. Yet this is not the goal of existential science; the image is not to be taken as an end in itself or as a symbolic substitute for authentic knowledge. The single aim of the existential image, and the single aim of existential science, is to promote a certain effort and involvement which is destroyed by the abstract and artificial symbols of general psychology. The single aim of existential science is to place man in a stance from which he can venture into concrete reality and discover for himself the dynamic meaning of his own existence.* Then the scientist and the psychologist will no longer be passive observers who must remain outside their own reality and only analyze and measure the practical and utilitarian uses of life. And the intuitive image is the most efficient concept by which to accomplish this existential goal of personal involvement in the scientific process, since it most effectively points us toward the concrete reality of experience.

Now it is obvious that no concept or image can replace the actual intuition of our own inwardness and our own becoming. But the convergence of many diverse images *can direct* our consciousness to that precise point where there is an actual intuition to be seized. So is it obvious that the existential image must consistently direct us toward this "departure point" for the potential intuition, but at the same time resist its own tendency to become a sterile and symbolic substitute for the intuition itself. Consequently, many diverse and dissimilar images from different orders of things must be used, so that no one of these images will be indulged as an end in itself and usurp the place of the actual intuition toward which the images only tend. This convergence of diverse images that point toward one com-

---

*Moustakas calls this type of science "*heuristic research,* that is, a research approach which encourages an individual to discover and methods which enable him to investigate further by himself." (*Heuristic research.* In *Challenges of Humanistic Psychology.* J. Bugental (Ed.). New York: McGraw-Hill, 1967, p. 101)

mon intuition then produces a state of creative tension that keeps any one of them from dominance and keeps all of them directed toward the intended intuition. The dynamic involvement and creative tension produced by these convergent images gradually develops into a phenomenological stance from which consciousness can grasp the reality of its own existence. But consciousness must assume the stance on its own initiative, and must make the effort on its behalf, for nothing in fact has been done for it. The intuitive method has only presented to consciousness the attitude which it must take in order to come, by itself, to the actual intuition. It is only by such a phenomenological approach based on the method of intuition that psychology can study the reality of concrete human experience rather than endlessly analyze the abstract and artificial symbols that have been substituted for it. Only by development of a phenomenological approach can psychology study those *intra*-personal processes such as existential choice, will, commitment, etc., and those *inter*-personal processes such as existential love, compassion, communion, etc., that are so crucial for the future of man and his world.

System and Order

Let us try to understand this method of intuition in more detail, and see just how it "fits" the subject matter of existential science. The use of the intuitive method means essentially that we must think in terms of time rather than space. Science and psychology begin with the immobile and reconstruct a symbolic representation of becoming by an endless juxtaposition of immobilities. But intuition begins with the assumption that the movement and the becoming of life are reality itself, and so it sees immobilities as only artificial abstractions drawn out from the reality of process and mobility. Thus, science and psychology begin with static objects and consider change an accident which has been imposed upon them. But intuition begins with the assumption that change itself is the basic reality. And that is why it sees the static objects that have been abstracted out of change by the method of analysis as only symbolic substitutes for reality but nothing more. Now we can better understand the limits placed on science and psychology by the fact that the intellect analyzes the new only as the old placed in new molds or arranged in new juxtapositions. The intellect can never grasp the existential process of change and creation as the primal reality in itself. But intuition *enters into* this dynamic reality of change and creation, and perceives in its vital motion a fluid continuity of unforeseeable novelty. And only the method of intuition can thus penetrate down into existence, and grasp the fact that life "draws from itself more than it has, that spirituality consists in just that, and that reality, impregnated with spirit, is creation."[13]* But let us see if there is any order in this continual process of creation and becoming, and if it has a reality that existential science would be able to study and comprehend.

We must start our attempt to describe this reality of creation and becoming by an initial distinction between two kinds of order which are usually confused. The confusion has occurred because both these types of order, in their own way, satisfy our consciousness. Each represents a certain fit and agreement between subject and object; i.e., both of these orders represent a means by which the mind can find itself again in things. And the degree to which we consider reality ordered is in exact relation to the degree to which this fit between subject and object seems complete. The confusion between these two orders, as well as the common ground between them, lies in the total satis-

*This is similar to Berdyaev's concept of the "power to create out of nothing." (*The meaning of the creative act*, p. 134.)

faction that both orders give to consciousness. But the similarity between the two orders ends at that point; for the two types of satisfaction and the two orders themselves are disparate and distinct. Now both these orders are possible because the mind can go in either of two directions. The order that concerns and satisfies existential science emerges when consciousness activates its creative potential and expresses itself in the form of dynamic tension, sustained freedom, and continuous innovation. It is an order that emerges from the vitality of nature. It pushes life in the direction of the spontaneous and the voluntary. We can describe this creative order as a process that embodies the authentic expression of our willed existence.

The second type of order falls most properly within the domain of physical science. It prevails when the vital movement of our consciousness is inverted and this inversion spreads existence into space and disperses elements of life into fixed geometric patterns. This inversion of the creative movement of the mind seeks to find order based on relations of necessary determination between causes and effects, therefore it forces consciousness back to inertia, passivity, and mechanism. It is an order controlled by external pressures rather than created by internal tensions; and it is the original prototype for the authoritarian "system" against which existentialism long ago rebelled. We said that the first type of order was of the vital or the willed. It could now be said that this second type of order is of the inert or the mechanical. We refer to this second type of system when we say that astronomical phenomena manifest "an admirable order," and we mean by such a statement that they can be "foreseen and predicted mathematically." Thus Bergson makes the final contrast between these two types of order by use of a Beethoven symphony to exemplify the creative order, as opposed to the mechanics of a physical system. A Beethoven symphony is every bit as remarkable as any astronomical order, and yet it is "genius, originality, and therefore unforesecability itself."[14] It is this willed type of creative order as it manifests itself in the concrete processes of life and personality that existential science wants to investigate and understand. General psychology does not even try to grasp this process of creation and becoming which underlies life and evolution, because its method of analysis destroys the moving undercurrent of personality by reducing the vital and dynamic surge of existence to a static and symbolic representation.

INTELLECT AND WILL

We have shown that psychology proceeds like all other sciences by the method of analysis. It first breaks the existential self, which can be grasped only by a simple intuition, into fragmented sensations, feelings, ideas, etc., and then studies these reduced elements as separate and distinct entities. Such a reduction is possible only after the psychologist has rejected all those aspects of personality that cannot be expressed in known and common terms. He then isolates from this already simplified personality those specific aspects which are relevant to his particular investigation. He then treats these specific isolated aspects that have been abstracted from the total personality as independent and scientific "facts." But these isolated psychic elements are only the initial fragments or factors in his attempt to construct an artificial and symbolic representation of the personality as a whole. The primary error of psychological science lies in this rigid application of the reductive and analytic method to a subject matter that is not amenable to it. Let us see if the intuitive method of existential science can lead us back to the study of what is real in personality, and in psychology itself.

We understand that to achieve this type of existential "revolution" in psychology, it will be necessary to reverse the usual work of our intelligence. We must begin to "think" time and process, rather than space and matter. But we also understand the difficulty that such a reversal entails, because we realize that the basic distinction between analysis and intuition is that the factors and symbols used in analysis are modeled on space and matter, and therefore must remain completely immobile while they are being investigated. Thus, psychological science first abstracts a specific aspect of personality from the totality of interior life and labels it a simple sensation. This sensation is assumed to remain a constant entity as long as it is being studied. It would be further isolated into several successive sensations if any change was noted in the original abstracted sensation. The same assumption of immutability would then in turn be imposed upon each of these successive sensations. The analysis must always be pushed to the point at which agreement can be reached that each of the elements considered is a constant and is immutable. Such conditions of constancy and immutability are necessary prerequisites for use of the method of intellectual analysis in science and psychology. Now we can reject these "necessary" conditions, and reverse the direction that science and psychology have taken, only by a dramatic reversal of the normal function of our intelligence. And we can make this critical reversal in the habitual pattern of our intellect, and recast all its concepts and categories, only by an intentional effort of our will. It is only by a violent and sustained act of will that we can force our intelligence out of space and into time, so that we can thrust ourselves down into the "flux and fire" of creative becoming, and merge with its ceaselessly changing states. And it is only by such an intentional effort of our will that we can hope to develop that *intellectual sympathy* called intuition, and thereby help psychology to discover and understand the inward reality of its own subject matter. Bergson argues that only by use of the intuitive method can psychology develop images and concepts that are sensitive enough to encompass the inward processes of personality and life. He insists that only by such a reversal of the habitual function of our intelligence "will a progressive psychology be built up, freed from the disputes which arise between the various schools, and able to solve its problems naturally, because it will be released from the artificial expression in terms of which such problems are posited."[15]

chapter 14

A NEW OPERATIONAL
METHOD FOR PSYCHOLOGY

We stressed in the preceding chapter the scientific significance of intuitive knowledge. Now let us contrast the methods of general psychology and existential science in order to evolve a new operational approach that can encompass such authentic psychological data.

PSYCHOPHYSICS

Modern psychology began as an attempt to measure qualitative experiences by quantitative methods—and this is still its goal. Early recognition of psychology as a science was based on the promise that higher mental processes could be measured by the same methods which had proved effective for the physical sciences. This was the one common assumption which unified the diverse interests and orientations of the founders of psychology such as Wundt, Fechner, Helmholtz, and Ebbinghaus. It provided a philosophical base for the new discipline, and this is still the one theoretical assumption which unifies the many diverse interests and orientations that are included under the label of general psychology today. Thus the need for an existential revolution in modern psychology depends exactly upon the extent to which this original methodological assumption is proved arbitrary and inadequate. Therefore, existential science must make its criticism directly relevant to the basic psychophysical model, since that model is a formal statement of the common theoretical assumption which underlies all of general psychology.

Now it was obvious that scientific standards of measurement could not be introduced into psychology until a model was presented that could define what is meant by the equality and addition of two simple states, such as two sensations. The controversy inherent in any proposed definition arises from the fact that every phenomenon presents itself under a qualitative as well as a quantitative aspect. It is easy to eliminate the qualitative aspect, and then measure the quantitative residue of the phenomenon by some arbitrary but conventional method; e.g., degrees of temperature measure the quantitative dimension of heat. But the ambitious claim of psychology and psychophysics was that this qualitative element of experience need not be eliminated in order to measure a phenomenon, and that the new psychological science would even measure the qualitative element itself. Now all their attempts to measure this qualitative aspect of experience were based on two facts: that sensation varies by sudden steps while the stimulus increases gradually; and that these differences of sensation could all be labeled minimum differences, since each corresponded to the smallest noticeable difference in the external stimulus. Now each of these successive steps had the same common character of being *minimum;* and so a definition of equality was provided, and these "equal" minimum differences were then added together. It is true that there have been endless technical debates by mathematicians and psychologists about details concerning the exact nature of the psychophysical model. Still, our concern is not with these endless disputes over technical details, but rather with the validity of the fundamental postulate upon which the psychophysical model is based. Existential science must successfully challenge the validity of this basic postulate, or else accept the ambitious claim made by psychophysics and psychology that qualitative experiences can be measured by quantitative methods.

Now the basic assumption under attack is that each of these minimum differences can be considered as a quantity, and that each sensation can be considered a sum obtained by the addition of these minimum differences. It is true that I can experience a sensation and then perceive an increase in that sensation after a certain time if the stimulus has been increased continuously. But it does *not* follow that this perception of an increase can ever be considered an arithmetical difference or an objective quantity. The one noted fact is that the original sensation is now a different sensation. However, the transition from one sensation to the other could be considered an arithmetical difference, or an objective quantity, only if the original sensation was felt to increase by the addition of something. But it is obvious that, in the psychophysical model, the only real events are the two sensations themselves, and that the interval *between* them is rejected as an illusion and considered neither a quality nor a reality. The psychophysical method breaks down because it eliminates the very qualitative experience of the interval between sensations that it claims to measure. Thus it becomes only another arbitrary and conventional mode of representation. But an intuitive investigation of the transition from one sensation to the other reveals the reality of an experienced interval between sensations like that between blended shades of the rainbow, and not one that could ever be reduced to numbers or magnitudes. Thus the psychophysical method in particular, and psychological measurement in general, both fail because the reality of qualitative experiences can never be reduced to the illusion of quantitative symbols.

Empiricism

Existential science rejects the artificial reconstruction of experience which is necessary in order to apply the empirical method to psychological phenomena. But empiricism remains the methodological foundation of general psychology, in spite of the fact that it necessitates the forced translation and symbolic distortion of experience. The explanation for this methodological error and for the dilemma it has produced can be found in a confusion between intuition and analysis. Psychological empiricism denies the reality of original experience, because the real experience itself cannot be found in the symbolic representation. Consequently, the method of analysis only leads to a series of negations, and these negations simply mean that analysis cannot do the work of intuition. Psychology passes immediately, from the vague intuition of some concrete original experience that provides its data, on to endless observations of that data from an infinite number of external perspectives. It then assumes that analysis of these empirical representations of experience will provide enough information so that the artificial symbol can be substituted without any significant loss. But it is obvious that an endless number of snapshots taken from an infinite number of perspectives can never reproduce the original object being photographed; and so the existential loss is not merely significant but *complete*. The empirical analysis of an objectified event can tell us nothing of the internal organization of that event, and so psychology must always watch the reality of its subject matter "fly before it, like a child that would like to make a solid plaything out of the shadows outlined along the wall!"[1]

RATIONALISM

The methodological error at the base of rationalism results from the same philosophical confusion which underlies empiricism. Consequently no significant distinction can be made between these two methods since they are merely two forms of one common analytic operation. Rationalism starts with the same confusion as empiricism and remains equally powerless to understand the internal organization and inward self of man. It first considers psychical states as fragments attached to a mechanical "self," and then tries to construct a dynamic symbol to represent that self. But just as empiricism always sees its subject matter "fly before it," so does rationalism always see this dynamic unity of the self escape the logical confines of its reductive method. Now empiricism is more easily exhausted by the futile struggle and so ends up declaring that reality is nothing but a multiplicity of psychical states and that the self is only a phantom and an illusion. Rationalism, however, is not so easily discouraged, and it continues to persist in efforts to affirm and establish a dynamic unity for the self. But a basic contradiction arises from the fact that rationalism seeks this unity only on the level of psychical states themselves and by the same method of analysis used by empiricism. Consequently rationalism can find nothing more positive than empiricism to substitute for the dynamic unity of personality; and therefore it ends with the introduction of something purely *negative*. It substitutes a mechanical device called the "self" that merely strings together artificial fragments of personality and binds them into a symbolic whole. But it has, in fact, only introduced another mechanical negation, because it has merely linked together these isolated pieces of personality with another empty symbol that has no positive content. Thus rationalism adds something to these attached psychical states whose accumulated sum was the equivalent of the self for the empiricists. Rationalism aims to reconstitute personality from these shadows of the self and so adds something that is even more unreal: "the void in which these shadows move."[2]

INTELLECT

The intellect evolved for a specific limited purpose, and so it functions effectively when applied to mechanical events which can be repeated. It fails when applied to living matter and creative processes because its rigid structures and categories were not meant for such use. It is this inappropriate application of the intellect to human problems which are of a different order, that explains much of the failure of our contemporary psychological and educational methods. We must look beyond the intellect if we are to comprehend and solve the urgent human and social problems that confront us today. This failure of the intellect is due to the fact that its specific function is to reconstruct reality with elements that are already given. Thus, that which is *new* in each moment of our history always escapes it. The intellect deals only with consequences that can be calculated as a function of known antecedents, and so it rejects the possibility of anything unique or novel. The intellect deals only with the known that is combined again with the known, organized into different patterns, and then repeated. The intellect uses the method of analysis to eliminate the potential for spontaneous creation from every event under its investigation. This elimination of all creation and novelty is necessary so that the intellect can substitute for the actual event an approximate equivalent in which things will be sure to happen as predicted. The intellect cannot do otherwise because it evolved for this specific purpose and to serve this exact function.

Now the predictions made by the intellect are based on

an assumption of causality that expresses the mechanistic goals of practical action and control. Prediction is possible within such a model, since the whole is always composed of the same parts, and the same movements are merely repeated to obtain the same mechanical results. Within this mechanical model, even invention includes nothing of creation because the model is already given in advance and invention, in that case, can mean only a different arrangement of elements already known. The intellect cannot admit real novelty or creation, any more than it can encompass real becoming. The very nature of its function is to reduce that which is new and could not be predicted to the already known whose different arrangements can be predicted in advance. Once again the intellect lets an essential aspect of life escape and once more science and psychology must recognize the rigid limits of intellectual analysis as a method of investigation. No one denies the consummate skill of the intellect when it is applied to inorganic matter because this is the function for which it evolved and for which it was intended. But the intellect becomes awkward as soon as it tries to deal with biological and psychological aspects of life, because "it proceeds with the rigour, the stiffness and the brutality of an instrument not designed for such use."[3]

EMOTION

We cannot discover existence with our intellect because existence is an emotional reality that must be subjectively encountered and experienced. Nor can we understand the nature of this emotional reality unless we study it as lived duration; for emotional experience occurs during intervals of concrete time, and not at fragmented *points* of time that are selected out and then measured by mechanical instruments. Our consciousness does not perceive time as a sum of these abstract units, for by itself it has no means and no inclination to measure time. Still, it is a fact that an emotional experience that lasted only half its actual duration would not be the same emotional reaction; but this is true only because a multitude of impressions would not have occurred that gradually thickened the substance and altered the color of the original experience. Now we also know that it is possible to take this same original experience, reduce it to a thing, label it, and then believe that we can cut its duration in half and it will be the same emotion only on a reduced scale. But such an analysis neglects the fact that emotional states are ever-changing processes rather than labeled things, and that not a single moment can be eliminated from any one of these processes without making a *qualitative* alteration in the emotional experience that does not parallel *any* simple quantitative mechanical division. We can understand how it is possible for an astronomer to make such quantitative divisions of time and to perceive the orbit of a planet all at once or on a reduced scale. Such mechanical divisions are possible in astronomy because the measured positions of the planet are the results of its movement, and the facts at issue are not the experienced duration of the intervals that separate the successive measured points. But it is meaningless for a psychologist to deal only with measured positions in time,* and ignore the experienced intervals between successive points, because it is exactly in these intervals of lived duration that the emotional experience under investigation actually occurs. An emotional experience has no precise "results" that can be counted and measured since the reality of an emotional state lies only in the fact that it has been experienced. Therefore, psychology can study and understand an emo-

---

*A. N. Whitehead considered such "a series of detached positions" as analogous "to the automobile which is found at successive milestones and at nowhere between." (*Science and the modern world.* New York: Macmillan, 1925, p. 40.)

tional state only if it examines the actual duration within which the feeling occurred and follows that duration through all its phases. It is true that this feeling may at some point in time produce a definite action or series of actions which might be compared to the definite positions of a planet in space. Still, the analysis of these positions or actions will not help us discover the influence of the emotional experience on the history and personality of the individual. And it is exactly that influence which psychology must understand.

INTUITION

Numerous arguments have been presented so far to demonstrate that the analytic method which psychology adopted from physical science cannot penetrate down into the reality of human experience. Consequently, *intuition* must be developed as the operational method for psychological science since it is the only methodological approach sensitive enough to probe dynamic life processes and advance our knowledge of the human condition. Now this need for an intuitive method of investigation arises because experience presents itself to us under two different aspects. It takes the form of facts set side by side with other facts which more or less repeat themselves, which can to a certain extent be measured, and which tend in the direction of distinct multiplicity and spatiality. But experience also takes the form of facts which permeate one another in constant motion, which can never be repeated, which are refractory to law and measurement, and which always retain their essential quality of pure movement and duration. It is obvious that the focus of an attentive consciousness is necessary to register either of these types of knowledge. But in the former case the intellect unfolds outward and externalizes itself in relation to itself, while in the latter case consciousness turns back upon itself and takes possession of itself in depth. It is this latter inward direction of consciousness that characterizes the intuitive method of investigation. It is only by such a method that psychology can penetrate down into the nature of human existence and understand its internal organization. Now such an inward intuitive movement of consciousness could tell us nothing of the reality of man and matter, if consciousness had been added to matter *only* by accident. But consciousness in its rudimentary form is at the heart of matter, and reflective consciousness as it has evolved in man is the vital core of our human existence. And this fact makes our human consciousness a primordial and essential life force, and not just a rational appendage added to man that calculates and measures. Human consciousness is at the center of life, and it cannot be banished to a corner of nature merely because it is a problem for science and psychology. Thus, we can probe down into our consciousness *with* our consciousness, and we will be probing deeper into the essence of life, because those forces that are alive in all things of the world are alive within each of us. We can thrust down into our deepest selves confident that we are probing the reality of nature and man, and confident that only by such an intuitive method of investigation can we discover and understand the real world.

DEDUCTION

The distinction between space and time underlies the distinction between general psychology and existential science. Thus the distinction becomes critical when existential science challenges the spatial foundation upon which the analytic method of general psychology is based. The challenge must be made because it is obvious that deduction succeeds in the psychological and moral sciences only to the extent that events within these sciences can be reduced and translated into spatial symbols. And in these sciences, it quickly becomes obvious that deduction is something very strange and even paradoxical. Deduction is a pure operation of the intellect; and so it follows that deduction should be most effective among these psychological and moral sciences that are also "of the mind." But the very opposite is the case for it is precisely in the domain of these unique human sciences that deduction is helpless, while its power cannot be questioned in the physical sciences where the objects and solids analyzed are foreign to the psychological and moral concerns "of the mind." We must therefore conclude that deduction is a pure operation of the intellect that is governed by the properties of matter and the ontology of space that underlies matter. Deduction has only to reduce reality to this fundamental principle of space, and then "let itself go," for all its conclusions and predictions will follow automatically from that initial operation. Now the only thing wrong with the method of deduction is that the assumption which underlies it is false, since time rather than space is the essence of nature and reality.

INDUCTION

The fact that time rather than space must be the actual starting point for science and psychology challenges the significance of induction as well as deduction, since both methods are based on a spatial ontology. Thus it follows that induction as well as deduction can be understood only in terms of the spatial assumption that underlies psychology. But it is also obvious that such an assumption is a naive one, since it asserts that we should expect from the same conditions a repetition of the same facts. Bergson argues that it is not necessary to think geometrically (or for that matter to think at all) in order to accept this simplistic spatial assumption. Even the consciousness of the animal, and the organic body itself, are so constructed that they extract relevant similarities from successive situations and then respond to these similarities by appropriate reactions. But any comparison to these near-reflex modes of reaction is only metaphorical because the method of induction is above all else an *intellectual* construction and operation. It first demands that we make the arbitrary intellectual assumption that there are causes and effects and that the same effects always follow the same causes. But this first assumption necessitates the elimination of time as a reality, because the system of today cannot be superimposed upon the system of yesterday, unless yesterday can wait without change for the advent of today. Such an artificial elimination of the influence of concrete time is possible in the abstract and intellectual operations of geometry, but not in the scientific study of man and evolution. And a second related assumption of induction is equally naive, for it asserts that qualities can be superimposed on each other like magnitudes. The only justification for such an assumption is that all qualities are based on an implicit numerical mechanism, and therefore that all qualitative differences can be easily reduced to this common numerical factor. Only such naive and simplistic assumptions as these would ever lead us to expect that the same conditions must always produce a repetition of the same facts. Thus the model of geometry and space is the ideal limit of our inductions as well as of our deductions, and we must conclude that both these methods have been laid out along the natural course of matter as it descends toward immobility and spatiality.

Mathematics

Mathematical models are useful in physical science because numbers correspond to objects. But there is no basis for the use of mathematical models in psychological science because human experience bears no relation to numerical categories. The very essence of our conscious experience of time and of motion is that these processes are ceaselessly in flux and are ceaselessly becoming. Now it is true that mathematics can represent the *results* obtained at a certain moment of time, and the *positions* occupied by the motion of a certain body in space; but it can never represent the concrete passage of time nor the actual process of motion. The number of measurements taken may even be increased without limit by making the interval between measured positions smaller and smaller. Still, no matter how small the interval becomes, mathematics must always place itself at the extremities of that interval and must always leave out of its equation the reality of time and motion experienced during the interval itself. The reason that human experience can never be made to fit mathematical formulas is that time and motion are processes rather than objects, and they cannot be represented like objects by points on a line. So these personal lived experiences that are the proper subject matter of psychology cannot be broken into numerical fragments that are identical and external to one another. This is so because the process of becoming that is at the base of existence is essentially fluid, continuous, and with no analogy to numbers and mathematics.*

Metaphysics

The descriptive language of metaphysics is an attempt to break through the abstractions of psychological science in order to get closer to the reality of experience. Such a

---

*This is true of the simple statistical models used by psychology, but it is also true for higher forms of mathematics as well. Mathematics can never reduce time as duration to time as space because numbers, like objects, can never be conscious of the concrete passage of time nor of their own histories as lived duration.

transition parallels similar advances in physical science itself when obsolete concepts that are blocking progress
must be rejected and new approaches developed. These
new approaches to psychology and science will need to
communicate much more of concrete existence than can be
expressed by the abstract intellectual ideas embodied in
formal symbols and codes. Consequently these new approaches must develop experiential ideas that are concrete,
but that still retain an outer fringe of images. It is this
combination of concrete ideas and intuitive images that will
express by comparison and metaphor that which cannot be
communicated by formal symbols and codes. And the introduction of metaphors and images will not constitute a
scientific detour, but rather will provide a direct path to the
scientific goals of clarification and communication. These
new concepts will not be a digression, since the actual
blockage and the primary detour to the advancement of
knowledge lies in a continued use of the abstract and symbolic language of science and psychology. It is these abstract artificial symbols which represent the illusion of
psychological knowledge, for they are imitations of matter
rather than intuitions of mind. They are only spatial *representations* of reality that have been objectified and made
external to us. Abstract ideas and symbols force us to study
psychological experience on the model of matter, and to
understand concrete reality by transposition into a substituted symbol—and that is the exact meaning of the term
"metaphor." So in the investigation of psychological experience it is the analytic symbols of science that are the
figurative and metaphorical detours, while the more sensitive ideas and images of intuition express the concrete and
literal meaning of psychological phenomena.

Thus it becomes obvious that the intuitive image
whose aim is only suggestive, gives us direct insight into the
nature of reality, while the abstract symbol that claims to be
representative, leads us into metaphor and illusion. Exis-

tential science merely wants psychology to make the same methodological advance that physical science itself has already achieved. Progress in the physical sciences was blocked for a long time by the use of a simplistic language that did not adequately describe the subject matter under investigation. Natural phenomena were explained, weighed, and measured in terms of the low and the high, the heavy and the light, the dry and the moist, etc. Positive science transformed itself from intellectual chemistry into dynamic physics only when it rejected these abstract categories and turned to a direct examination of the phenomena themselves. Even physical science had to revolt against the intellect in order to thrust itself forward. The aim of existential science is to make this same advance in psychology by eliminating abstract concepts and symbols in order to encounter and investigate the actual phenomena themselves. It will be difficult to find the most useful and effective language for this new phenomenological description of our inner experience. It will even be necessary, in our efforts to develop this new phenomenological language, to return to the use of concepts; but these concepts will have been radically altered by the addition of intuitive ideas and images. These concepts will now be more sensitive and more flexible, and they will indicate by the colored fringe of nuances around them that they only *suggest* the reality of experience and cannot be substituted for it.* This advance proposed by existential science only parallels similar advances already made in the physical sciences. But the introduction of new models and methods into psychology is so much more imperative because of the unique nature of its human subject matter, and because of the contemporary crisis in the evolution of man and society.

---

*Heidegger's original and creative use of language is one possible example: *Being-in-the-world, potentiality-for-Being, Being-towards-death, etc.*

Part V

ANTHROPOLOGY

chapter 15

THE ANTHROPOLOGICAL ASSUMPTIONS OF SCIENCE AND PSYCHOLOGY

The term "anthropology" has come to be interpreted in the limited sense of cultural anthropology, or the comparative study of societies, races, customs, etc. And this concept of anthropology is, in turn, grounded in certain philosophical and scientific assumptions. The purpose of this chapter is to sketch in some detail the nature of these basic assumptions by an examination of the anthropology of modern science and psychology. This description will be based on Binswanger's account of the history of the natural-science concept of anthropology as it developed in medical psychology generally and in psychoanalysis specifically.

Binswanger starts his description of the modern origins of scientific anthropology with the establishment of the "Magna Charta" of medical psychology that dates from the year 1861. Binswanger argues that the conceptual categories and methodologies, with their implicit philosophical assumptions, were structured into the development of medical science with the appearance of "the second edition of Greisinger's *Pathologie und Therapie der Psychischen Krank-*

heiten [Pathology and Therapy of Mental Illnesses]. "[1] The basic
formula of that original charter linked medical psychology
to science in general, for Greisinger insisted that psychic
and psychopathological phenomena must be understood
"in the light of empirical psychology." He further insisted
that all psychic phenomena could be reduced to a physical
organic base and, because of their essential "organicity,"
that these phenomena could be "interpreted" only by natural scientists.[2] He also argued that these psychic phenomena could be understood only in terms of the function of
one organ—the brain—and he thereby reduced psychology
to the study of a quantifiable process recorded in objective
time and analogous to "reflex action in the nervous system." Psychic phenomena were conceived as "motor-sensi-
tive" cerebral reflexes governed in complex ways by the
"intermediary zone" of imaginary representations.[3] Binswanger notes that "the theoretical part of Freud's interpretation of dreams as well as his whole doctrine of the
genesis of the reality principle out of the pleasure principle
is based on such a view."[4]

Binswanger described this "Magna Charta" of medical
science as a combination of Herbart's theory of "the dynamics and conflicts of representations," and the Leibnit-
zian notion of "unconscious representations."[5] And at the
base of this mixture was a philosophical realism easily
translated into a scientific materialism that accounted for
the natural-science approach to mental illness which asserted that "madness is only a symptom-complex of various
abnormal cerebral conditions."[6] Binswanger argues that
Greisinger himself, however, qualified his own presentation with a sober question: "The fanatics and priests of
materialism might do well to consider . . . the elementary
processes in neural matter are probably identical in all men
. . . how, then, could these processes directly and exclusively give rise to the infinite multiplicity of representations, feelings, and goals not only of an individual man, but

of a whole century?"[7] He concluded that medical psychology could not rush to a premature and simplistic organic concept of mental life but that "it must patiently await the time when questions as to the connection between the content and form of human psychic life become problems of physiology, rather than metaphysics."[8]

Binswanger interprets this caution and qualification presented by Greisinger as implying that the original "Magna Charta" of medical psychology left room to expand our understanding of the horizons of man beyond a simplistic concept of "organicity." Still, Binswanger recognizes that if his interpretation of Greisinger's intention was, in fact, an accurate one then this intention was not long respected by others in the medical sciences. He cites the work of Wilhelm Dilthey (1833–1911) as only one example of a philosopher/psychologist who did attempt to widen this narrow organic view into a broader phenomenological perspective—and was not only abused and attacked for his effort but ostracized as well. Binswanger concludes that, regardless of the intention of the framer of the original "Magna Charta" of medical psychology, the charter itself soon became a rigid dogmatic law that led to the condemnation and excommunication of any scientist who challenged or opposed it. And Binswanger traces this transformation of an open guide into a closed law directly to Freud and the psychoanalytic system. He contrasts the concept of Ego in Greisinger's theory with that same concept in the Freudian psychoanalytic system. Greisinger had understood that what was "unassimilated by" and "oppositional to" the Ego was not an Id or an "it" as in the Freudian system, but rather was "a human *thou.*"[9] Greisinger's model of man thus left open the possibility of an authentic intrapsychic dialogue that was closed "once and for all" by the reductive biological system of Freud. It was for this reason that Binswanger considered Greisinger and his original charter "more modern" than Freud. Still,

Greisinger's concept of the Ego, in spite of the restricted possibility for an intrapsychic dialogue, was also an "abstraction" and fell within the limits of his own original prediction that all psychic phenomena would eventually be understood "in the light of empirical psychology" and in terms of their essential "organicity."

Binswanger presents this history of the anthropological foundations of medical psychology in order to demonstrate the most basic characteristic of its original charter—the depersonalization of man. This depersonalization and objectification of man has now become such a dogmatic law in psychological science that no one uses the term "I" but always speaks of "it." And Binswanger argues that this depersonalization of man is not only the most basic characteristic of modern psychological science but that it is the one characteristic most at odds with the development of an authentic psychology. The extent of this depersonalization can be seen not only in the attempt to relate a reified psychic apparatus to a material organ but even more clearly in the attempt to understand the brain itself in terms of isolated, mechanical, and impersonal functions. Thus Greisinger's early warning to "the fanatics and priests of materialism" was bypassed because of rapid progress in brain anatomy and in the localization of brain functions. The fusion between medical psychology and brain pathology was no longer considered "premature and completely unfeasible" as Greisinger had claimed.[10] Therefore medical psychology simply became brain anatomy translated into a new psychological language. "Higher" parts of the brain were now considered "workshops of the good" and individual cortical cells were endowed with the capacity to be "ensouled." But even the more reasonable and more moderate speculation about cortical cells and localization pointed to the same complex problems inherent in *any* attempt to reduce psychology to a system of quantification and to base it upon anatomy and organicity.

Binswanger next traces the history of medical psychology from the investigation of mental illness as a brain disease to the investigation of mental illness as a pathology of the whole organism; i.e., the transition from neurology to biology. Attention was no longer focused on the relationship between psychic phenomena and processes in the brain, but on events "in the organism" as a whole. Psychology now became a branch of biology rather than neurology, and the focus shifted from a study of processes localized in the brain to the study of "instincts" as "special concentrations of partial manifestations of events in the organism" as a total entity. Medical psychology was no longer directed by a "neurological" materialism but rather it was now directed by a "biological" materialism. The assumption of "organicity" which was the basis of the original charter of medical psychology remained intact and was in no way changed; only a shift in emphasis had occurred. There was still no acknowledgment by medical psychology of the fact that man is more than his "organicity." Its modern version had only reduced morality, culture, individuality—and even philosophy itself—to "biological facts" instead of to "neurological facts."[11]

And it is at this modern juncture that Freud's "great idea" intersects and merges with the "great idea" of the original charter of medical psychology. Now medical psychology in general and psychoanalysis in particular *both* propose to reduce the dynamics of the human condition to instinctual and biological "organicity." Psychology for Freud was a rigid biological science, since he insisted that the only important elements of psychological research were "the instincts of the organism."[12] Psychic experience, in the psychoanalytic system, is not an authentic phenomenon that is autonomous or "presentational" in itself; rather, psychic life is said to merely represent "organic forces" or "effects stemming from within the body that are carried over to the psychic apparatus."[13] Only physiological and chemical processes are considered presentational or "real" in the psychoanalytic system, and these processes must be described in the "pictorial" language of psychology only because we still lack a "simpler" language for them. Freud argued that "the shortcomings of our description" would likely be overcome "if for psychological terms we could substitute physiological or chemical ones."[14] Psychology was thus considered by Freud as only a "temporary" discipline that new advances in biology would someday render obsolete. Such an attitude is easy to understand; it is consistent with the assumption of "organicity" that is at the base of the original charter of medical psychology. Still, the "open end" that had been left by Greisinger was now closed by Freud and his dogmatic biological interpretations of human psychic life.

Binswanger insists that to understand Freud's psychoanalytic system correctly one "must not" approach it from the standpoint of psychology—a mistake that Binswanger himself claims to have made "for a long time." Such a psychological approach "stumbles at every point against the thoroughly unpsychological" components of the psychoanalytic system that can be understood only as Freud intended them—"biologically."[15] And Binswanger argues that the biological foundation of Freudian theory cannot itself be properly understood without reference to the relation between neurology and biology that developed from Freud's research on aphasia. It was by integrating various theories and data on aphasia that Freud was able to define a connection between neurological and biological functions, and his whole theory is based on this connection. Binswanger argues that "the greatness of his conceptions and his destiny rests, in the last analysis," upon the validity of this connection between neurology and biology, and upon the fact that "he extended this kind of thinking to the entire psychic life of the individual, society, and mankind in general."[16]

Freud's systematic reduction of all human experience to neurological and biological "organicity" can be clearly seen in his developmental laws of the organism, and in his concepts of sexuality and the unconscious. We must, therefore, examine the origin of these developmental laws in some detail so that we can better understand the laws themselves as well as Freud's concepts of sexuality and the unconscious.

Freud supported the notion of development contained in the original charter of medical psychology with respect to the historical evolution of the brain from lower animal forms to higher human forms, and also with respect to developmental changes that occur within the life of a single organism. These latter changes followed a progression from gradual growth to maturity and then deterioration. Brain activity was seen to parallel all other organic functions and so it also was subject to these same developmental laws. Freud went even further and included not only the development and retrodevelopment of pathological disturbances of psychophysical brain functions, but also the pathological disturbances of "total human psychic development."[17] He had already learned from his study of aphasia that the brain reacts as an entity to a lesion that incompletely destroys the language apparatus. That is, the partial loss is an "expression of the general functional weakening" of the language apparatus, and *"it answers the incompletely destructive lesion with a functional disturbance which could also arise through non-material damage."*[18]* Binswanger interprets this last statement as central to the development of Freudian theory, for Freud concluded that these neurological reactions to injury represented a functional disinvolution or "regression" of the language apparatus to a lower level or earlier condition of its functional develop-

---

*Binswanger considers this sentence, that Freud himself underlined, as basic to the development of psychoanalytic theory.

ment. And it was this principle, based on the physiological and physiopathological function of the nervous system, that Freud took from his study of aphasia and applied to the study of neurosis itself. It was this bridge from aphasia to neurosis, or from "neurology" to "biology," that formed the basic model for his conception of the functional reaction of the biological system of the organism to psychological or "non-material damage."

Freud built upon this basic neurological model a theory of biological development that stressed the historical significance of early psychosexual stages of instinctual conflict. His main goal, therefore, was to trace everything he discovered in the history of an individual back to these early psychosexual stages of biological conflict and development. Now it is here that his neurological model of aphasia and his biological model of neurosis merge, for he interprets the neurotic symptom as "an expression of the general functional weakening" of the total organism, as its defensive reaction to partial instinctual or biological damage. The organism as a whole relates itself to this partial damage, just as the speech apparatus or the brain apparatus relates itself to a comparable injury. That is, it seeks to accommodate itself to the partial damage by a "regression" or a "functional *dis-involution* . . . to earlier conditions of its functional development."[19]* Neurosis and psychosis are therefore those disturbances in the brain apparatus that are "not wholly destructive" and that in purely functional cases leave the nervous system intact but force the psychic apparatus to "reach *back* (regress) to earlier modes of functional reaction,"[20] i.e., "to earlier conditions of its functional development."

The most important aspect of this model is, of course, the notion of regression, which is based on the functional

---

*Freud used this statement by Hughlings Jackson, an authority on aphasia, as the foundation for his own theory of neurosis and psychosis.

"dis-involution" of the language apparatus that Freud observed in his study of aphasia. Freud merely substituted the concept of "regression" for "dis-involution," and applied it to the psychic life of the organism as a whole. But regression is a much more dynamic concept than dis-involution, and serves as an "active" and "oppressing" force which can account for "fixation" as well as for "repression." Pathology was therefore defined as the regression to an earlier mode or stage of functional development, and the specific type of neurosis or psychosis could be determined by the degree and extent of the regression in any particular case.

Freud then applied this same principle of biological development to the area of sexuality and designed a conceptual system that proposed to explain the psychic determinants of human experience and behavior. Binswanger begins this description of Freud's concept of the sexual instincts and sexuality with the definitive statement that it has nothing whatsoever to do with "what the physiologist understands by the sexual drive, and especially not what the psychologist, philosopher, or theologian understands by love."[21] Binswanger stresses the radical nature of this distinction by attempting to contrast Freud's notion of self-love as narcissism with the Aristotelian or Christian meaning of self-love. But the distinction is so fundamental and so complete that no contrast can be made, since Freudian theory does not even contain comparable terms or meanings for "love" or for "self." These two concepts, which are the cornerstones of an existential anthropology, are "assiduously" avoided by the anthropology of psychoanalysis. Freud means by sexual instincts and sexuality simply a basic biological tendency that can be understood only in relation to the two primal instincts in psychoanalytic theory—the life instinct and the death instinct. And Freud expressly owed the conceptual formulation of these two instincts, that are at the base of psychoanalytic theory, to his "reliance upon biology."[22] The sexual instinct or "life" instinct is comprised of those biological processes which are assimilative or constructive in nature, while the aggressive or "death" instinct is comprised of those biological processes that inwardly lead the organism to death and that outwardly manifest themselves as "*tendencies* of *destruction* or aggression." Freud argued that the life instinct and the death instinct were ordinarily compounded or alloyed, but that their disengagement was also possible, so that life consists of "the expression of conflict or interference between the two kinds of instincts" with death the final "victory of the destructive instincts."[23] It is clear that the phenomenological and existential term "love" has no more to do with this biological and basically chemical struggle that ends in death than the psychoanalytic term "ego" has to do with the phenomenological and existential concept of "self."

The psychoanalytic concept of the "unconscious" is derived from the same basic laws of biological development. Binswanger argues that the unconscious in Freudian theory "represents primarily a developmental system in the psychic apparatus and serves only secondarily as an expression in the pictorial language of psychology." He further argues that this same primary biological and developmental significance is accorded to the oral, anal and genital stages of psychosexual development as well as to the terms id, ego and super-ego. Freud even defines the "individual" as "an unknown and unconscious Id,"[24] upon whose surface rests the ego that is essentially a representation of the outside world or reality, and over against which stands the super-ego that is the introjected representation of certain aspects of that outside world. Thus, the entire mechanism of the Freudian psychic apparatus is set in motion by these essentially biological and chemical forces that make up the "unknown and unconscious Id" or the "it" that Freud called man. And this "it" that is at the base of the natural-science concept of anthropology "knows no values, no good and evil, no morality," for the economic or quantitative factor of the pleasure principle dominates all its processes and experiences. Thus man in the Freudian psychoanalytic system is nothing but instinctual energy "seeking discharge."[25]

It is precisely this natural-science concept of anthropology, and its attempt to reduce the reality of psychic existence to a chemical or mathematical equation, that has contributed to man's present state of objectified and mechanized helplessness. This anthropological view of man as a natural object, so clearly exemplified in psychoanalysis and behaviorism, was founded on two basic philosophical assumptions. Freud confidently asserted and rigidly defended both of these postulates: "there is no appeal beyond reason";[26] and "there is no other source of knowledge of the universe but the intellectual manipulation of carefully verified observations."[27] Thus Binswanger concludes that Freud's rational-empirical approach to man, and his reduction of man as Dasein to man as a natural object, imposed a biological closure on the phenomenological investigation of the human condition that has been destructive to the development of both science and man. Consequently, we must assume that those neo-Freudians who try to "salvage" Freud with the argument that he was "misunderstood," are motivated by some anticipated practical gain rather than by theoretical integrity, and make the bizarre claim that he was "misunderstood" out of either hypocrisy or ignorance.

chapter 16

THE GENERAL OUTLINE
FOR AN
EXISTENTIAL ANTHROPOLOGY

We stated earlier that the term "anthropology" is generally understood in the limited sense of cultural anthropology, or the comparative study of societies, races, customs, etc. But such a concept of anthropology is based on a natural-science world view whose horizon is too limited even to encompass the reality of its own subject matter. Binswanger has criticized this natural-science concept of anthropology and the dogmas of modern medicine and psychology that follow from it. He insists that we must develop a more meaningful theoretical model if the science and knowledge of man are to be significantly advanced. Binswanger is guided in his attempt to build such a new anthropology by the imperative that Heidegger has given us: "Inasmuch as man appears not only as a natural being but also as a being that acts and creates, anthropology must also seek to know what man as an active being can and should 'make of himself'."[1]

Binswanger begins his attempt to build a new existential anthropology with a summary of four contributions that the natural-science model of man can make to the development of such a "project." The first of these contributions is simply a methodological one. The natural-science approach demonstrates that a considerable body of systematic knowledge can be accumulated by the application of one methodological principle of organization. Such an approach logically "maps" entire areas and delimits particular regions by direct application of the analytic method of selection and classification. Thus the rational-empirical method of investigation yields knowledge of the physiological, biological, and psychological factors that make up the "nuts and bolts" of the rudimentary machinery of life. Yet Binswanger warns that such information is useful only to the extent that we clearly recognize its limits, and clearly understand that such information can tell us nothing about the vital nature of life and the meaning man gives to his existence by the relationship he chooses to it.

The second contribution that this knowledge of the mechanism of life can make to the development of an existential anthropology is that such information can, paradoxically, convince man that he is *more* than a machine. Knowledge of the mechanism of life demonstrates to man that he is more than a machine because he discovers the fact that he can relate himself as he chooses to his own mechanism. Binswanger argues that "the reverse side of absolute mechanism, of iron necessity, is unquestionably the notion of absolute freedom" for "the more mechanically we interpret man, the more freely he is seen to rise *above* mechanism."[2] Binswanger regards this discovery as the most significant contribution of "scientific" knowledge, since it enables us to understand the anthropological tension that exists between "nature" and "spirit," i.e., between being passively driven by mechanical forces on the one hand and freely choosing our own relationship to our own destiny on the other.

The third constructive use of data gathered by the method of natural science is that it gives us psychobiological measures "against which man can test and examine his existential posture in the world."[3] Data gathered by the reductive method of natural science always 'proves' that man is determined, and so man must prove against these 'facts,' and in spite of these 'facts,' that he is free. Any evidence of mechanism always brings immediately into play the reality of our existential being as its adversary. Binswanger argues that nothing challenges science as convincingly as our own existence, for it is only the reality of our being-in-the-world that can ultimately refute and overcome the mechanism of science.

The fourth contribution of "scientific" knowledge to the development of an existential anthropology is that it demonstrates the failure of any method of investigation that rejects the reality of creative change and growth. Psychoanalysis, for example, assumes that instincts are the basic determining factors in psychic life, and asserts that these instincts are indestructible operational constants. It tries to reduce the complexity of life to "the expression of conflict or interference" between two constant operational factors—the life instinct and the death instinct.[4] The failure of such a mechanical simplification of existence contributes to the development of an existential anthropology because it forces us to recognize that man is not merely "mechanical necessity," or merely an object "in-the-world." It forces us to recognize rather that there is an existential tension between mechanical necessity and creative freedom, and that man and his existence can be understood only if we study him as an active and creative "being-in-the-world." This failure of mechanism to adequately account for creative change and growth forces us to recognize that freedom is a reality distinct from and oppositional to necessity, and that new structures emerge out of the dynamic tension between mechanical necessity and creative freedom.

Binswanger moves from this account of the contributions of mechanistic knowledge to a closer examination of the "rift or gap" between the method of science and the reality of that being-in-the-world which it pretends to comprehend. Binswanger argues that every time psychology reduces man to an object and measures him by the empirical method of science, there is a "rift or gap" through which "something" escapes and overflows. Now this "something" that escapes, and which natural science rejects as an illusion, is what existential anthropology takes as the one reality for its point of departure as a science. Behaviorism is at least consistent on this issue and uses a terminology that explicitly rejects the concept and reality of the self. Psychoanalysis, on the other hand, also rejects the reality of the self but is not consistent in its use of terminology, because Freud does refer to "our" psychic apparatus and "our" psychic life. The contradiction is that these possessive pronouns imply the subjective reality of an autonomous self that is simultaneously being objectified and "bracketed out" by the same psychoanalytic system within which it is being discussed. The existential reality of the self is implied when such personal pronouns as "I" think, "he" replies, or "we" remember are used. Common usage of such personal pronouns implies not only that the self has an existential reality that is "mine" or "his" or "ours," but that there is also a reality to the interpersonal relationship between one individual self and another individual self that is like him. A psychological system cannot use personal and possessive pronouns whose functions are well established in the language and yet simultaneously "bracket out" the reality they imply. It must either reject the reductive method of natural-science or the existential reality of the personal and possessive pronouns that it uses. Psychoanalysis has chosen the latter option for it uses personal and possessive pronouns but does not attribute any existential reality to the self or to interpersonal relationships. Binswanger states that Freud "investigates human beings with the same 'objectivity,' the same existential surrender 'to the object' that characterized his researches on the medulla of Ammocoetes-Petromyzon in Brücke's laboratory."[5] The only difference is that he worked in the laboratory with "an eye sharpened" by the microscope, while he worked in the clinic with "an ear sharpened" by his systematic attention to the reports of patients. But in place of a reciprocal interpersonal communication between two human beings with a common human destiny, there is an irreversible "one-sided" authoritarian relationship between "doctor and patient"—and an even more exaggerated impersonal and professional "relationship between researcher and object of research." Freud maintained this impersonal attitude toward the patient in his own work and insisted upon this impersonal attitude as the basis of the science and the profession of psychoanalysis. He was convinced that he had succeeded in demonstrating mechanism as a scientific reality, as well as mechanism as a professional technique to "repair" the damaged object—the "mind" was repaired by the psychoanalytic "mechanism of transference."[6] Binswanger concluded that in the psychoanalytic system "experience, participation, and confrontation between human beings in the present moment gives way to the 'perfect tense' of theoretical investigation."[7] And psychology loses its authentic character as a scientific discipline exactly to the extent that its research and treatment methods become more and more impersonal and more and more "objective" until the reality of its human subject matter has been completely "bracketed out." Then psychology is no longer a meaningful human science but only another branch of physics or biology.

Now, existential psychology has demonstrated that the reductive method of "bracketing out" the reality of the person, his relationships, and the meaning he gives to his life, only widens this "rift or gap" between science and the reality of its own human subject matter. The science of psychoanalysis, just like the science of behaviorism, systematically rejects and ignores the one fundamental tenet of an existential anthropology—"that Dasein is always *mine, yours,* or *ours,* and that *we ourselves* always stand in relation" to the active and personal reality of our own being-in-the-world.[8] And Binswanger further argues that "when this self is objectified, isolated, and theorized into an Ego, or into an Id, Ego, and Super-ego, it is thereby driven out of its authentic sphere of being, namely existence, and ontologically and anthropologically suffocated."[9] Binswanger therefore concludes that this natural-science attitude toward man forces us to make an either/or decision, since

> there are two ways to practice psychology. The one leads away from ourselves toward theoretical determinations, i.e., through the perception, observation and destruction of man in his actuality, with the aim in mind of scientifically "constructing" an adequate picture of him (an apparatus, reflex-mechanism, functional whole, etc.). The other leads us back into our self, but not in the mode of analytic-psychology (which would again make us into objects), nor "characterologically" (which would objectify us with regard to our individual psychological "class"). The second way is that of anthropology, which concerns itself with the conditions and potentialities of Dasein as ours, or—what comes to the same thing—that concerns itself with the possible kinds and modes of our existence.[10]

This latter path leads us directly "back into our self" and to the existential ground upon which the scientist himself as a person stands. There is no escape from the reality that science has been made by man and is not something "out there" separate from and independent of those particular individuals who design it and practice it.* Conse-

*Kierkegaard stresses this point in his attack on speculative philosophy: " 'Who is to write or complete such a system?' Surely a human being; unless we propose again to begin using the strange mode of speech which assumes that a human being becomes speculative philosophy in the abstract, or becomes the identity of subject and object. So then, a human being—and surely a living human being, i.e. an existing individual." He next argues that the philosopher or scientist who does "his utmost to forget that he is an existing individual . . . becomes a comic

quently, the only valid perspective from which any particular data or any particular ystem can be understood is the Dasein of the scientist himself and the nature of his own being-in-the-world.

Such a closer examination of the philosophical ground of science and the scientist forces us to recognize that psychology has only arbitrarily accepted the traditional model of natural science which contains its own implicit (and sometimes explicit) philosophical "attitude" toward . science and the scientist. But then for psychology to ignore the problems associated with this "attitude" and still continue to arbitrarily accept the natural-science model eliminates in advance any chance for psychologists themselves to examine the foundations of their own discipline and to develop psychology into a more viable and creative science. And yet it is obvious that the science of psychology would take on a very different meaning, and become a very different venture, if each of us did recognize the primacy of his own selfhood and simultaneously recognize the reality of other selves and other attitudes. We would then encounter and discover the unequivocal fact that these various attitudes toward knowledge and being-in-the-world are not abstractions "out there," but are specific styles and modes of expression in which Dasein exists and interprets itself. Any psychology that ignores the ground of Dasein, and pretends to separate itself from the process of time and history, destroys that very reality within which experience and meaning emerge and the only valid context within which they can be understood and explicated.

---

figure, since existence has the remarkable trait of compelling an existing individual to exist whether he wills it or not." He concludes that any rejection of the subjective ground of knowledge "has a comical presupposition, occasioned by its having forgotten, in a sort of world-historical absent-mindedness, what it means to be a human being. Not indeed, what it means to be a human being in general; for this is the sort of thing that one might even induce a speculative philosopher to agree to; but what it means that you and I and he are human beings, each one for himself." (*Concluding unscientific postscript*, p. 109.)

Thus we have seen that the natural-science model of psychology reduces man to a *tabula rasa,* devoid of meaning, so that it can, in turn, explain and interpret to man "meaning" as illusion or sublimation. It reduces man to a determined object and then "cranks" that object through the mechanical dialectic of natural science until all that is distinctly human has been obliterated and only the "biological product" remains.

Now it is one thing to use this type of reductionism to merely expose the hypocrisy of a particular culture, a particular group, or even a particular individual (e.g., to expose an "altruistic" act that is really motivated by selfishness or, in the psychoanalytic system, by "narcissism"). Still it is quite another thing to use reductionism to promulgate a psychology of nihilism and to completely destroy man's belief in meaning itself. The distinction between these two goals is so crucial that no error or ambiguity can be tolerated. Yet Binswanger asserts that Freud does confuse "the unmasking of a *particular* hypocrisy with the destruction of the meaningfulness of human existence in general."[11] Psychoanalysis "explains" any ethical or metaphysical mode of existence as merely an illusion or as a "sublimation" of frustrated biological instincts. The nihilism of such a system is clearly stated by the fact that morality can only be defined as a negation rather than an affirmation. That is, the "good" is defined only as the repression or sublimation of biological instincts to facilitate social adaptation; it can never be defined as a positive and creative act.* Binswanger even argues that the concept of sublimation itself is only another example of the confusion of reductionism. He points out that it is one thing to observe that the process of growth entails a "transition" in

*Existentialism has stressed from Heraclitus to Sartre that the creative development of human character was man's basic motive or "destiny". But psychoanalysis merely reduces this positive moral act of choice and creation to nothing more than the negative and mechanical "result of instinctual repression." (Binswanger, *op. cit.,* p. 184n. Freud and the magna charta of clinical psychiatry.)

directedness from a "lower" to a "higher" mode of existence; but a very different thing to conclude, from such an observation, that the higher mode of expression, with its own unique and original meaning, is reducible to and no more than a "derivation" of the "lower" biological mode.

Binswanger summarizes his attempt to develop general postulates for an existential anthropology by a final contrast between the self as a passive object and the self as a creative being-in-the-world. He describes Freud's view of man as a biological object under the control of the pleasure principle as "one and only one" possible mode of being-in-the-world. It is the same mode of being-in-the-world that Heraclitus noted and defined anthropologically as man's existence in the "idios-cosmos."* Examples of this private state of passive withdrawal given by Heraclitus are sleeping, dreaming, and the passive indulgence of sensory pleasure. Heraclitus challenged man to awake from this passive mode of existence, since it was but a distorted form of selfhood. In such a state, the self is unaware of its own meaning and historicity, and is merely arrested and overcome by the external or internal pressures of a particular situation. The active self, on the other hand, that is "awake" and conscious of its own self is sufficient "unto itself" and can grow and develop through encounters with other persons who share a common human awareness. It is not a self whose behavior can be controlled by these others or interpreted by them, but an autonomous self that chooses and creates its own destiny. Psychoanalysis and behaviorism reduce man to the passive "idios-cosmos"

---

*This refers to a private-world of withdrawal or "sleep" in which man abandons his self-consciousness as well as his existential freedom and responsibility. Boss describes this same passive state in terms of a numbness to the "pangs of conscience." (*Psychoanalysis and daseinsanalysis.* Trans. L. Lefebre. New York: Basic Books, 1963, p. 270.) It is also similar to the determined object state described by Sartre as "in-itself," by Buber as "it," by Heidegger as *"das Man,"* etc.

world of Heraclitus, indifferent to the fact that, for Heraclitus, this was not the real world but merely a world of illusion. Heraclitus argued that only by a free and creative act could man separate himself from this passive surrender to the "thrownness" of life, and discover the existential reality of his own authentic being-in-the-world.

Binswanger himself recognized that today man seems deaf to the challenge of Heraclitus, and preoccupied with the passive indulgence of his own "idios-cosmos" world. He recognized the fact that man in his everyday life takes his existence too lightly and that Dasein "makes light" of itself. He also recognized that the number of individuals who have found no existential base or meaning in their lives has rapidly increased, and that many have turned from a search for the meaning and substance of life to a preoccupation with the superficial problems of pleasure and adjustment. Still, Binswanger knew and pointed out to us that life is something more than the passive surrender to a biological "death instinct," or a "wise submission to the laws and mechanisms" of natural science.* He challenged psychology, as Heraclitus challenged man, to "awake" and build a new existential model of science that can encompass the full richness of human experience and behavior.

These basic themes that we have just presented in the development of an existential anthropology were the same themes that Binswanger presented in his commemorative address on Freud's eightieth birthday, to which Freud responded by saying, "I do not believe a word of it." Freud consistently and vehemently rejected any attempt to move psychology beyond a mere biological reductionism, and he emphatically declared that he would continue to reduce all human experience to his system of material determinism "even if I had another lifetime of work before me."

*Binswanger considers this latter nihilistic point of view to be the "measure" and the "center" of Freudian theory. (*Being-in-the-world*, p. 179. [Freud's conception of man in the light of anthropology.])

These, then, are the two contradictory and mutually exclusive types of anthropologies that are available to us— a "physical science" paradigm and a "human science" paradigm. Now let us examine some specific moral and social models that are explicit examples of these two types of anthropologies.

chapter 17

THE CLOSED SOCIETY: ETHICAL AND POLITICAL IMPLICATIONS OF DETERMINISM

Specific motivational assumptions lead to specific moral and social anthropologies. The mechanistic assumptions of general psychology lead to a utilitarian morality and a centralized society. The vitalistic assumptions of existential science lead to an aspiration morality* and an open society. There is considerable material on which to base these models because psychologists and philosophers invariably sketch out the moral and social implications of their basic motivational assumptions. The utilitarian ethics of Bentham and Mill, and the social systems of Bacon, Hobbes, and Skinner provide us with specific models for general psychology. So let us first outline the ethical and political implications of the natural-science conception of anthropology.

*Aspiration morality, as you will see in Chapter 18, refers to the creative development of our basic human potentials, and not to social or cultural goals with which the term "aspiration" is often associated.

MORAL MODEL

One moral philosophy has characterized the history of the "atoms and space" postulate from Democritus in ancient philosophy right down to Skinner in modern psychology. Democritus began it all with his argument that the universe was a complex machine with no purpose or design and that the only moral good was harmony or "cheerfulness." Epicurus developed this moral goal of "happiness" into the traditional moral philosophy of hedonism. There is no order in the universe since man and the world are but clusters caused by a lateral "swerve" in the otherwise vertical fall of some atoms, and by the compound collisions that followed. Even those who want to posit a god must admit that he is but an accidental cluster of atoms subject to the same mechanical laws as any other object in nature. Epicurus felt that he had liberated man from the fear of gods and death so that abstract moral and religious principles of conduct were no longer relevant. He concluded that pleasure and survival were the only legitimate guides to "moral" conduct in a universe that was made by accident and that was operated by mechanical laws. We know only that "we recognize pleasure as the first good innate in us," and that "nature leads every organism to prefer its own good to every other good."

Thus, the ethics of Democritus extends down through the history of empiricist philosophy, as well as his physics. The mechanical physics of "atoms and space" now becomes the utilitarian ethics of "pleasure and survival." The most cogent and elaborate philosophical defense for this ethics of survival has been given us by Thomas Hobbes. Hobbes argued that survival was the basic motivation in the state of nature, and that every man had an equal right to do whatever he felt was necessary to protect himself and to satisfy his needs. He meant by equality that every man had "*a right to all*,"[1] or that every man had the moral right "to do what he would, and against whom he thought fit, and to possess, use, and enjoy all what he would, or could get."[2] So the moral right of man to survive in the basic state of nature necessarily leads to the "war of all against all."[3] Man, in the state of nature, lives in "continuall feare, and danger of violent death" so that his life is "solitary, poore, nasty, brutish, and short."[4] One clearly sees that a strong centralized government with strict political controls necessarily follows from such an assumption concerning the basic nature and morality of man.

John Locke began within the same hedonist and empiricist framework, but Locke stressed a solution based on rational laws rather than on political power alone. He argued that morality was a form of objective knowledge, and could be calculated with the same precision as mathematics. He held that morality was the same type of phenomenon as mathematics and that rational laws of moral conduct could be established that would "place *morality* amongst the *sciences capable of demonstration:* wherein I doubt not but from self-evident propositions, by necessary consequences, as incontestible as those in mathematics, the measure of right and wrong might be made out, to any one that will apply himself with the same indifferency and attention to the one as he does to the other of these sciences."[5] He began his attempt to establish such rational laws of conduct from the standard moral base of hedonism: "Things then are good or evil, only in reference to pleasure or pain. That we call *good,* which is apt to cause or increase pleasure, or diminish pain in us . . . that *evil* which is apt to produce or increase any pain, or diminish any pleasure in us."[6] He then went on to establish a rational code of ethics based on man's "natural" right to private property, which he defined as "lives, liberty, and estates." He rejected Hobbes' "war of all against all," and said that in the state of nature (as he defined it) man *could* recognize and respond to a rational law of morality, because "Reason, which is that Law, teaches all Mankind, who will but consult it, that being all equal and independent, no one ought to harm another in his Life, Health, Liberty, or Possessions."[7] He did not deny that men obeyed such a law because of practical expediency and calculated hedonism, but he did defend his conviction that the rational law itself was a valid one.

His enthusiasm for a science of morals led him even to the questionable claim that the "moral revelations" of Jesus were rational as well as inspired. Such claims are not uncommon but do seem to become progressively more suspect. Locke considered Jesus a rationalist, Mill called him a utilitarian,* and Skinner has labeled him a behaviorist. We have already followed Skinner's reduction of "turning the other cheek" to primary and secondary reinforcement. Now let us see how Mill tried to transform the hedonism of Jeremy Bentham into the "golden rule" of Jesus Christ.

Bentham began his intellectual career in preparation for law, but his interests soon developed beyond the legal profession to the more general problems of moral and social reform. That reform began with his attack on the theory of "natural rights," which he rejected as nothing but meaningless rhetoric and philosophical "nonsense." He argued that such abstractions were meaningless because they were not based on a practical philosophy of sensory experience. The only valid basis for moral and social justice was the fact that man is governed by "two sovereign masters, *pain* and *pleasure.*"[8] Morality consists only in the substitution of the word "right" for pleasure and the word "wrong" for pain. Only in such an equation do "the words *ought,* and *right* and *wrong,* and others of that stamp, have

---

*"In the golden rule of Jesus of Nazareth, we read the complete spirit of the ethics of utility. To do as one would be done by, and to love one's neighbor as oneself, constitute the ideal perfection of utilitarian morality." (Mill, J. S. *Utilitarianism.* In *Collected works of John Stuart Mill.* J. M. Robson (Ed.). London: Routledge and Kegan Paul, 1969, p. 218.)

a meaning: when otherwise, they have none."[9] Moral conduct could now be measured as a function of its utility: the extent to which an act tends to "augment or diminish" pleasure. Thus the morality or pleasure of an act can be "calculated" in terms of its intensity, duration, certainty, etc. This "pleasure-pain calculus" provided us with moral values and explained the causes of our behavior as well.

Bentham describes four causes of pleasure or pain which he considers the four causes or *sanctions* of our behavior. These are physical, as in an accident caused by carelessness; political, as in a prison sentence for a crime; moral, as when help is refused someone because of his character; and religious, as when "God" condemns someone for a "sin." These sanctions represent different types of punishment; but they all control behavior by the threat of pain. They give the word "obligation" the concrete meaning of pain for disobedience, rather than the abstract meaning of responsibility or duty. Bentham insisted that morality depended only on the consequences of an act and not its motives. Bentham also was adamant in insisting that morality depended only on the quantity of pleasure involved, and not its quality. It was at this latter point that Mill began his attempts to transform both Bentham and hedonism.

John Stuart Mill was educated by his father from a very early age in what he later described as "a course of Benthamism."[10] The education was particularly relevant since his father was a close friend and colleague of Bentham, and had himself contributed significantly to the development of utilitarian philosophy. The education was also relevant since Mill spent the rest of his life trying to transform and defend the *principle of utility* proposed and promoted by Bentham and by his father. It was not an easy task from the start, and attempts to reconcile the basic conflict between pleasure and morality led only to more complex problems. But Mill could not accept Bentham's quantitative definition of pleasure and tried to give a new *qualitative* meaning to hedonism. He argued that "human beings have faculties more elevated than the animal appetites, and when once conscious of them, do not regard anything as happiness which does not include their gratification."[11] He even insisted that, given a choice, men would select a more elevated pleasure, "even though knowing it to be attended with a greater amount of discontent," and that "we are justified in ascribing to the preferred enjoyment a superiority in quality, so far outweighing quantity as to render it, in comparison, of small account."[12] Thus far Mill has only substituted the cultivated hedonism of Epicurus for the crude hedonism of Bentham. But it is the next step that produces a critical break in the argument and its defense. Now Mill no longer equates pleasure only with the sophisticated tastes of an educated man but with moral imperatives such as "altruism," "conscience," and "duty" as well. Such a generalized definition of the term *pleasure* rendered it theoretically meaningless and forced utilitarian philosophy back toward its original hedonistic base.

There was no similar attempt to broaden the meaning of hedonism and adaptation in the theories of Spencer, Darwin, and Freud. The concepts of pleasure and adjustment retained their original biological significance in these systems: morality is based only on "natural sanctions." Spencer summarized the moral philosophy for this Darwinian-Freudian model of biological man in his argument that moral laws must correspond to the laws of "natural selection" which are based on the "struggle for survival." Consequently, a pattern of behavior can be judged good or bad, within a biological system such as psychoanalysis, only to the extent that it contributes to the "natural sanctions" of hedonistic adaptation and biological survival: "Conduct is right or wrong according as its special acts, well or ill adjusted to special ends, do or do not further the general end of self-preservation."[13]

There is perfect agreement here between psychoanalysis and behaviorism, for Skinner assesses morality on the same survival basis of hedonism and adaptation. He defines the good as something that can be used as a reinforcer because it has survival value for the individual and the species: "Things are good (positively reinforcing) or bad (negatively reinforcing) presumably because of the contingencies of survival under which the species evolved." He explicitly states "that all reinforcers eventually derive their power from evolutionary selection."[14] Skinner also agrees that hedonism is characteristic of science in general, and believes that such "positive reinforcement" explains his own life and work: "I have been powerfully reinforced by many things: food, sex, music, art, and literature—and my scientific results."[15] Thus the hedonism of science has come full circle around from the sophisticated pleasures of Epicurus to the sophisticated reinforcers of Skinner.

SOCIAL MODEL

There are a number of social and political systems in the history of philosophy that were devised as models within which to develop the moral theories of empirical science. The best known of these is the *Leviathan* of Thomas Hobbes. Hobbes began from his basic assumption that individual man is motivated only by drives for pleasure and survival. Consequently a "war of all against all" was inevitable unless the destructive instincts of individual men were controlled by a powerful and sovereign state. Such control was possible only if individuals enter into a *social contract* among themselves in which each agrees to surrender his own right to govern himself to the authority of the state: "*I Authorize and give up my Right of Governing my selfe, to this Man, or to this Assembly of men, on this condition, that thou give up thy Right to him, and Authorize all his Actions in like manner.*"[16] The significant feature of the contract is that it is *among* the citizens rather than between the citizens and the state. No contract is possible with the state since *its* sovereignty is absolute and does not depend in any way on the people ruled. The will of the state *is* the will of the people, so any rebellion against the state becomes a meaningless contradiction and a return to social anarchy with its anticipated "war of all against all." It should also be made clear that the contract would hold true for *any* form of centralized government, because the citizens agree to surrender their rights "to this man, or to this assembly of men."

Nevertheless, it is a fact that Hobbes himself preferred monarchy as a social system, and that both he and Bacon were devoted monarchists in their own private lives. Hobbes shifted his loyalties to protect himself during periods of political turmoil and revolution but was able to regain his position as favorite court philosopher after the restoration of Charles II. Bacon was more active and aggressive in his personal and militant defense of monarchy. He had been supported early in his own political career by the Earl of Essex, who became his most influential friend and patron. History subsequently changed the status and fate of these two men. Essex was arrested for attempted rebellion against the rule of Elizabeth and tried for treason. Meanwhile, Bacon had advanced in politics and turned against his former friend and benefactor in the name of the Queen. He actively led the prosecution to a summary conviction and Essex was beheaded. Bacon's aggressive part in this trial coupled with his theoretical description of friendship as a means to power led to the famous conclusion that Bacon was "the wisest, brightest, meanest of mankind."*

*(Pope, A. *An essay on man.* In *Pope's Works.* J. W. Croker (Ed.) New York: Gordian Press, 1967, p. 449.) Bacon's own words (*Of wisdom for a man's self.* In *The essays of Lord Bacon.* J. Hunter (Ed.) London: Longmans, 1875, p. 98) summarized his own actions: "Wisdom for a man's self . . . is the wisdom of rats, that will be sure

Hobbes and Bacon advocated in their theories and supported in their private lives social systems based on centralized political control. Such centralized controls are necessary for any empiricist social model, because science will not wait for man "to pull himself up" by his own spiritual "boot straps." Yet Locke insisted that the necessary controls be based on the natural laws of reason that could be recognized by all men and not the arbitrary whims of a monarch. So did Bentham demand that the legal sanctions that control society be based on the pleasures of the people and not the tastes of a king. John Stuart Mill wanted to go one step further and minimize as far as possible the need for manifest political controls. Still he realized, in spite of his own arguments to the contrary, that hedonism and altruism were not synonymous in the experience of men, and that "for their own good" a general kind of systematic conditioning was necessary:

> Education and opinion, which have so vast a power over human character, should so use that power as to establish in the mind of every individual an indissolvable association between his own happiness and the good of the whole . . . so that not only he may be unable to conceive the possibility of happiness to himself, consistently with conduct opposed to the general good, but also that a direct impulse to promote the general good may be in every individual one of the habitual motives of action.[17]

---

to leave a house somewhat before it falls." Macaulay describes Bacon's actions against Essex in detail: "When it became evident that Essex was going headlong to his ruin, Bacon began to tremble for his own fortunes. What he had to fear would not indeed have been very alarming to a man of lofty character. It was not death. It was not imprisonment. It was the loss of court favor. It was the being left behind by others in the career of ambition." Nevertheless, when "the Queen looked coldly on him" Bacon decided to act against his friend and "he acted with more zeal than would have been necessary or justifiable if he had been employed against a stranger. He exerted his professional talents to shed the Earl's blood, and his literary talents to blacken the Earl's memory." (Macaulay, T. *Lord Bacon.* In *The essays of Macaulay.* New York: A. L. Burt, 1837, vol. 2, p. 174.)

And so we come to Skinner and contemporary psychology.

Skinner agrees that the historical and philosophical controversies that underlie different psychological approaches to man cannot be resolved. Yet he has "no doubt of the eventual triumph of behaviorism—not that it will eventually be proven right, but that it will provide the most direct route to a successful science of man."[18] Nor can Skinner's confidence be easily challenged for today methods of behavior modification are being widely used in all our social institutions from mental hospitals and prisons to elementary schools and kindergartens. The systematic control of man is not new as a general philosophy or as a political practice. But behaviorism as a specific psychology and as a specific technology of control *is* new. Frazier, Skinner's spokesman in *Walden Two,* realizes that this is "the first time in history that the matter was approached in an experimental way."[19] *Walden Two* is no longer a utopian fantasy written a quarter century ago, but a concrete reality that has already begun to shape our society of today and tomorrow. Consequently, we must examine in some detail the psychological model on which these contemporary changes in our social institutions are based.

Walden Two begins in the same way as any standard utopian novel. Outsiders visit a secluded society and a spokesman from the community describes it to them. His introductory remarks deal only with practical improvements that physical technology has made possible. The visitors quickly grow impatient with these details for they are not concerned with the scientific control of nature but with a social model for the scientific control of men. And gradually the outlines of that social model are presented and made clear.

First, the political structure of the government must be explained. There are four levels in the political hierarchy. The governing body is a Board of Planners composed of six members who are responsible for the operation of the community. Below the Planners are the Managers. Managers are specialists in charge of divisions such as food, health, education, labor, etc. Below the Managers are the Workers that they supervise. The final category is made up of Scientists engaged in research. The Board of Planners selects its own replacements from among the Managers. The Managers attain their positions on the basis of apprenticeship training and tested performance. There are no elections in Walden Two.

Second, the laws that control the community must be explained. Behavior is regulated by rules of conduct called the Walden Code: "Some of these, like the Ten Commandments, are rather fundamental, but many may seem trivial. Each member agrees to abide by the Code when he accepts membership. That's what he gives in return for his constitutional share in the wealth and life of the community. The Code acts as a memory aid until good behavior becomes habitual."[20] Some of the trivial rules are "Don't talk to outsiders about the affairs of the community" and "Don't gossip about the personal relations of members."[21] Here is an example of how such a rule is developed and becomes part of the Walden Code. A rule was needed to make direct expression of boredom socially acceptable in order to cut down on idle chatter. The spokesman for the community explains how it was done:

> The rule was regarded as a doubtful experiment, but it was put over quite successfully. It was announced and explained at a weekly meeting. There was a good deal of intentional joking about it. In a severe change of custom it's important to invoke a sense of humor. Each member was asked to exercise the rule at least once a day, even if it meant finding a trivial instance. Little cards appeared on the dining-room tables reading "Have you been bored today? If not, why not?" Some one complained to the Manager that the cards themselves were boring, and they were immediately taken away to prove the value of the rule. One member wrote a play called *The Man Who Bored Everybody.* The play considers

the dilemma of a man who never opens his mouth without being told that he's boring. He eventually capitalizes on his idiosyncrasy by making public appearances as the World's Greatest Bore, but the police close the show because the crowds which swarm to see him prove that boredom can't be genuine if it's that interesting. . . .

Thanks to all this publicity, a custom of expressing a lack of interest became quite commonplace and wasn't resented. The advantages to both speaker and hearer alike have been enough to keep the rule in operation.[22]

The spokesman asserts that there is nothing original in such uses of publicity and manipulation, for "Society already possesses the psychological techniques needed to obtain universal observance of a code—a code which would guarantee the success of a community or state. The difficulty is that these techniques are in the hands of the wrong people—or, rather, there aren't any right people." He means by this that most governments "won't accept the responsibility of building the sort of behavior needed for a happy state. In Walden Two we have merely created an agency to get these things done."[23] He goes on to explain the channel through which disagreement with the Code can be expressed and why there is no natural drift away from it:

As to disagreement, anyone may examine the evidence upon which a rule was introduced into the Code. He may argue against its inclusion and may present his own evidence. If the Managers refuse to change the rule, he may appeal to the Planners. But in no case must he argue about the Code with the members at large. There's a rule against that. . . .

As to any drifting away from the Code, that's prevented by the very techniques which the Managers use to gain observance in the first place. The rules are frequently brought to the attention of the members. Groups of rules are discussed from time to time in our weekly meetings. The advantages for the community are pointed out and specific applications are described. In some cases simple rules are appropriately posted.[24]

But the government, the trivial rules, and the social engineering to enforce them are not the crux of Walden Two. The foundation of the community rests upon the techniques of *behavioral engineering* applied from birth to insure complete *adaptation* and *obedience* to the essence of the Code itself:

> Let's be realistic. Each of us has interests which conflict with the interests of everybody else. That's our original sin, and it can't be helped. Now, "everybody else" we call "society." It's a powerful opponent and it always wins. Oh, here and there an individual prevails for a while and gets what he wants. Sometimes he storms the culture of a society and changes it slightly to his own advantage. But society wins in the long run, for it has the advantage of numbers and age. Many prevail against one, and men against a baby.[25]

The spokesman goes on to explain that the failure of all previous cultures to properly socialize and adjust the conduct of its citizens lies in their failure to use scientific methods: "Considering how long society has been at it, you'd expect a better job. But the campaigns have been badly planned and the victory has never been secure. The behavior of the individual has been shaped according to the revelations of 'good conduct,' never as the result of experimental study."[26] He argues that a technology of behavior based on observation and experimentation can, in fact, produce an efficient and harmonious society. He points to the *fact* of Walden Two.

The first task in the construction of Walden Two was the elimination of emotions that interfere with the development of social efficiency and harmony. It was clear that efficiency depended upon the ability to overcome emotional frustrations that would disrupt the completion of a task. Citizens had to be conditioned to *persevere* in spite of the unavoidable frustrations that would accompany their work. Training began at six months of age and the method used for the desensitization of task frustration could be termed the *Troublesome Toy*:

> Some of the toys in our air-conditioned cubicles are designed to build perseverence. A bit of a tune from a music box, or pattern of flashing lights, is arranged to follow an appropriate response—say, pulling on a ring. Later the ring must be pulled twice, later still three or five or ten times. It's possible to build up fantastically perseverative behavior without encountering frustration or rage. It may not surprise you to learn that some of our experiments miscarried; the resistance to discouragement became almost stupid or pathological. One takes some risks in work of this sort, of course. Fortunately, we were able to reverse the process and restore the children to a satisfactory level.[27]

Efficiency is not, however, the major problem in the construction of a controlled society. Harmony is even more difficult to attain because of the basic conflict of interests between individuals. A society would be "nasty, brutish, and short," unless individuals could be trained to control and delay immediate gratification of their needs. Individuals had to be conditioned to tolerate such delays in need gratification. The method used to desensitize frustrations that accompany delay of need gratification was "Subclass A3," but could be more simply termed the *Lollipop Crucifix:* "We give each child a lollipop which has been dipped in powdered sugar so that a single touch of the tongue can be detected. We tell him he may eat the lollipop later in the day, provided it hasn't already been licked. Since the child is only three or four, it is fairly diff"—one of the visitors interrupts in surprise at the early training age, but the spokesman quietly answers that "all our ethical training is completed by the age of six," and continues:

> A simple principle like putting temptation out of sight would be acquired before four. But at such an early age the problem of not licking the lollipop isn't easy. . . .
>   First of all, the children are urged to examine their own behavior while looking at the lollipops. This helps them to recognize the need for self-control. Then the lollipops are concealed, and the children are asked to notice any gain in happiness or any reduction in tension. Then a strong dis-

> traction is arranged—say, an interesting game. Later the children are reminded of the candy and encouraged to examine their reaction. The value of the distraction is generally obvious. . . . When the experiment is repeated a day or so later, the children all run with the lollipops to their lockers—a significant indication of the success of our training.[28]

But this is just the first step in developing a hierarchy of frustration tolerance. The next step is more difficult: "Concealing a tempting but forbidden object is a crude solution. For one thing, it's not always feasible. We want a sort of psychological concealment—covering up the candy by paying no attention. In a later experiment the children wear their lollipops like crucifixes for a few hours." Similar hierarchies of frustration tolerance are built up "by having the children 'take' a more and more painful shock, or drink cocoa with less and less sugar in it until a bitter concoction can be savored without a bitter face."[29]

Still, the tolerance for delay in need gratification is only the first phase in the development of a harmonious society. The real problem is to desensitize emotions of envy and jealousy that commonly accompany delay in gratification while *watching* someone else having that very need gratified. The method of desensitization used here could be termed the *Forbidden Soup:*

> A group of children arrive home after a long walk tired and hungry. They're expecting supper; they find, instead that it's time for a lesson in self-control: they must stand for five minutes in front of steaming bowls of soup. . . .
> The assignment is accepted like a problem in arithmetic. Any groaning or complaining is a wrong answer. Instead, the children begin at once to work upon themselves to avoid any unhappiness during the delay. One of them may make a joke of it. We encourage a sense of humor as a good way of not taking an annoyance seriously. The joke won't be much, according to adult standards—perhaps the child will simply pretend to empty the bowl of soup into his upturned mouth. Another may start a song with many verses. The rest join in at once, for they've learned that it's a good way to make time pass.[30]

Then the delay is made more difficult because in the next stage "we forbid all social devices. No songs, no jokes— merely silence." The spokesman explains that to avoid the danger of producing silent resentment "we follow each child carefully. If he hasn't picked up the necessary techniques, we start back a little."[31] He agrees that so far the method is similar to the other techniques of tolerance training. Now comes the final stage and the high point of behavioral engineering: "When it's time to sit down to the soup, the children count off—heads and tails. Then a coin is tossed and if it comes up heads, the 'heads' sit down and eat. The 'tails' remain standing for another five minutes."[32]

Children who successfully complete this first six-year training program are then initiated into the community at large. They can now be admitted to the society because they have been properly conditioned to assure the harmony and stability of the social structure. The *seventh* birthday of a child is a critical event and is made into an elaborate ceremony or

> 'coming out' in the main dining room. The younger children take their meals in their own building until their seventh birthday. It's quite an event when they move up. Perhaps we can catch a glimpse . . .
> As the song [*Happy Birthday to You*] was sung again and again, two silent figures moved from table to table. One of them, an older child, carried a birthday cake upon which seven candles sparkled in the dusk. She stopped at each table and allowed the children to read the inscription. The other figure was a child of seven, in her best dress, solemn as a nun, glowing with pride.[33]

Thus was Walden Two built and thus is it perpetuated.

The spokesman concludes with a moral defense of his scientific society: "I show you a community in which there is no crime and very few petty lapses, and you condemn it because none of its members have heard about, or care about, moral law. Isn't our Code enough?"[34] He asserts that only a scientific morality of hedonism and adaptation can successfully guide the development of an efficient social system. A *spiritual* morality tries "to get away from government and to allow the natural virtue of man to assert itself. What more can you ask for as an explanation of failure?"[35]

Thus we have come full circle once more. *Walden Two* completes the long progression of the "atoms and space" postulate from ancient philosophy to modern psychology. Skinner considers it "his *New Atlantis,*" and Bacon recognized only Democritus before him. The *morality* of science is based on hedonism and adaptation, and the *society* of science is based on the systematic control of men. Skinner concludes, in his autobiography, that the real danger to social development is not that the technology of behavior will be misused, but that "so called democratic principles will prevent men of good will from using it in their advance towards humane goals."[36] But it is difficult for many of us to understand the terms "good will" and "humane" in a system based on the destruction of that free and creative self which has made us human in the first place. So let us see if there is another hope for man and for society.

chapter 18

ASPIRATION MORALITY
AND THE
OPEN SOCIETY

Aspiration morality and the open society are existential alternatives to the ethical and political systems of determinism. Now let us examine the hope of these alternate moral and social "possibilities," as they are developed within the anthropology of existentialism.

MORAL MODEL

Existential science does not make the same fatal error as general psychology. It does not attempt to reduce all moral and social events to one mechanical model. Existential science recognizes two distinct types of human experience, as it recognizes two distinct types of scientific knowledge. It agrees with general psychology about the first type of human experience (i.e., pleasure and adjustment). There are no more penetrating insights concerning this type of life than the descriptions provided by Kierkegaard himself. He calls this first type of morality the stage of *either.* He means by *stage* a way of life rather than a phase

296

of development.* This first type of morality is also called the *aesthetic* stage and is comparable to the hedonism and adaptation of general psychology. Many aesthetic styles can be distinguished, and many gradations of pleasure from crude sexuality to refined cultural pleasures. Choices must be made between these rival pleasures, and immediate gratification must often be postponed in the service of long-range satisfaction. Still, the hierarchy of moral good is always determined by a calculus of pleasure and *repose* but never anything beyond itself. Kierkegaard argues that there is a vague consciousness of a higher morality even within the aesthetic stage. The failure of the aesthete (in Kierkegaard's sense of the term) to discover the meaning of these vague inclinations and to commit himself to them produces an undercurrent of despair. The smoldering energy of this despair then generates a personal crisis and a creative movement into the higher or the *ethical* stage. Now hedonism and adaptation are replaced by duty and responsibility. But this new responsibility is not directed outward toward social and moral conventions but inward toward the existential being of the self. The only duty now is to will the self "to be itself."[1] It is not to calculate shrewdly between conditioned options but to develop the self in relation to the absolute and infinite possibilities of man. The only responsibility is to encounter these metaphysical realities and to transform abstract moral principles into concrete ethical values. It is true that the *or* way of life evolves into

---

*This distinction is critical since progressive movement from one phase to another is not a function of inevitable dialectical development. Rather, individual man is confronted with a choice for which there is no rational or empirical solution and to which he must respond by an emotional *leap* into darkness. It is the same growth model provided by Bergson when he says that in theory "there is a kind of absurdity in trying to know otherwise than by intelligence," but in practice growth is possible only if "you thrust intelligence outside itself by an act of will." Bergson concludes that it is the essence of reason "to shut us up in the circle of the given," and that to create new growth "leap it must, that is, leave its own environment." (*Creative evolution,* pp. 202–4.)

complex sub-stages within a stage, but all these variations can best be understood as expressions of the same common drive toward the finite actualization of our infinite human potentials. The *or* alternative, which represents this actualization of our deeper human destiny, demands a commitment to moral and motivational processes that are more vital and more creative than hedonism and adaptation. It demands a commitment to the existential reality of freedom and love as the basis for human growth and development. Now let us approach these same two types of morality within the framework of existential science.

Bergson describes these two types of morality in terms of his basic model of biological evolution. There is the law of matter, or *pressure* morality; and the law of creation, or *aspiration* morality. Both these forms of morality must be examined in some detail. Pressure morality, or natural morality, arises from primitive patterns inherent in the original structure of human society. Children first come to recognize this natural structure in relation to the concrete authority of parents and teachers. Typical obedience at these early ages is not due to respect for teachers or parents as persons but is due only to their status of authority and control. Thus, the parents act as a proxy or symbol for a more pervasive pressure toward obedience and conformity. Children later discover that this more pervasive pressure is called *society*. It is comparable to an organism whose individual cells fall into their respective places in a rigid hierarchy and submit to systematic control for the greatest good of the whole. However, regulation of this artificial organism is not maintained by physiological processes but by psychological habits. Social morality is therefore based on a system of conditioned habits that correspond to the survival needs of the community. No one single habit exerts sufficient pressure to maintain social stability, but all the habits combine and cling together to form the pervasive network that effectively controls individual action and insures social conformity. The pressure inherent in this total network of habits is comparable to instinctual pressures in lower forms of life. Systems of habits converge to preserve human societies just as systems of instincts converge to preserve the societies of ants and bees. Thus pressure (or natural) morality is the utilitarian morality of science and general psychology. Its goal is an efficient and harmonious society based on hedonism and adaptation.

But just as the creative impetus of life thrusts up through matter, so does the creative impetus of another morality thrust up through the inertia of hedonism and adaptation. Survival morality obeys the law of matter. Creative morality breaks through that law and aspires to something more. Pressure morality is based on a natural law that preserves the internal stability of each community so that it can defend itself against all others. Aspiration morality is a leap to another stage of life and another stance for man. Now morality is no longer confined within the walls of a particular city but breaks through those walls and relates itself to all men. The natural relationship between a particular man and his particular society gives way to a spiritual relationship "between man and man"[2] in every society. The transition from one morality to another is a leap because humanity cannot be reached by widening the bounds of the city. The difference between social morality and human morality is not one of degree but one of kind. It is a breakthrough that demands an either/or decision and an existential act.

The first type of morality (pressure morality) equates the good of the individual with the good of his particular society. It is comparable to the fundamental instinct that equates the good of the anthill with the good of each individual ant. It is an ethic oriented toward survival of the system as a whole with the good of each individual, or component, determined by its relation to that whole. Such a social definition of morality permits changes within the

bounds of obedience to the code of conformity, but toler-
ates no challenge to the code itself—"there is a rule against
that." Moral progress is thus restricted to the development
of more efficient laws that better promote the established
values of hedonism and adaptation.

The morality of aspiration is different in kind because
a new relationship to humanity emerges with the crumbling
of the city walls. General psychology, by implication, defines only one type of morality that gradually changes in
relation to the increasing size of its object. Love for one's
family progresses to love for one's country and finally to
love for mankind. But existential science demands the introduction of a new type of morality to distinguish "love for
mankind" from the first two types of social relationship. This distinction is based on the fact that the first two
social patterns necessitate exclusion and hostility between
groups, while the third does not recognize the moral significance of any group but only the reality of individual
persons. It destroys all types of artificial barriers between
individuals and seeks only for that common "fire" of love
and compassion that is the basis for authentic interpersonal
communion.

The morality of existential science seeks to discover
the moral imperative that is inherent in the vital impetus of
life. Indicators point toward certain natural and human
processes that nourish and promote the development of
life in all its forms. Clues to the rudimentary beginnings of
this morality of human love and compassion are embodied
in the solicitude of a plant for its seed and the maternal love
of an animal for its young. Many *leaps* to more and more
complex stages are necessary to translate these rudimentary beginnings into existential realities, but the moral base
is inherent in the nature of life itself. The pressure morality
of hedonism and adaptation is based on the *control* of life,
but the aspiration morality of growth and creation is based

on the *nourishment* of life. The two moralities entail mutually exclusive concepts of the nature of existence and the
destiny of man.

Aspiration morality has been embodied in concrete
individuals down through our human history. Inspired
leaders from the earliest moral and religious stirrings in
man down to contemporary times have pointed us toward
these spiritual possibilities of creation and love. They embody a rejection of the *relative* morality of general psychology and point toward the *absolute* morality of infinite
possibility. The categorical distinction between these two
types of morality is made obvious by the fact that relative
morality becomes more valid as its laws become more abstract and impersonal, while absolute morality must be
embodied in the concrete example of a specific living individual. Pressure morality demands controlled obedience to
a standard law or code, while aspiration morality asks nothing. Inspired moral leaders draw the masses after them by
a process of free and spontaneous attraction rather than by
any overt or covert method of control and manipulation.
Aspiration morality is an expression of the vital impetus
that moves mankind toward higher and higher stages of
social evolution. It activates man's potential for creation
and love through processes of attraction and appeal. And
each inspired leader leaves an indelible mark on society
even though the particulars of his historical contribution
fade with time. His life has broken through the limits of
pressure morality and provided a concrete example of another moral goal and another way of life for man. This
lasting effect on society lies in the quality of the emotional
reaction that was aroused at a particular moment of historical time, and which can now be aroused again at any subsequent moment because the image of that moral leader has
been enshrined in our memory of the past and in our hope
for the future. The concrete modes of human potential

embodied in the character and lives of these men serve as beacons to light the progressive evolution of society. The lives of these men become emotional *appeals* made to the conscience of each of us by "persons who represent the best there is in humanity."[3] Pressure morality based on the control of men is patterned on instinct and habit. The power of aspiration morality flows up from the *emotional* and *metaphysical* depths of man. Only the most rigid of men has failed to feel, at some concrete moment of his life, the vital power of his own will or the saving grace of human love and compassion. It is these moments, even if they were only fleeting, that make most men recognize the authenticity of the basic emotional and metaphysical forces within them. The morality of spirit and aspiration is therefore alive in each of us and these inspired leaders merely turn us in upon ourselves to encounter and activate our own deeper human potentials.

These manifestations of aspiration or emotional morality can be given a consistent and rational defense; but it does *not* follow from this that the origin and source of such morality is in reason itself. Science and general psychology attempt to reduce all reality to rational and empirical premises. This forces them to deny all higher forms of motivation and morality, and to reduce these more complex human strivings to nothing but distorted manifestations of the aesthetic stage of hedonism and adaptation. These more complex strivings are reduced to sublimated sexual and aggressive drives in psychoanalysis, and to "neurotic if not psychotic" responses in behaviorism.[4] Bergson concludes that those who believe *passion* and *aspiration* in men can be silenced by manipulation "have never heard the voice of the one or the other very loud within themselves."[5] Now let us examine the two social models that parallel these two distinct types of morality.

SOCIAL MODEL

Pressure morality demands a closed society. The formula of operation and the code of conduct have been set, and "there is a rule" against any direct challenge to the authority in control. The primitive model is usually monarchic or oligarchic, and these two systems are indistinguishable in the rudimentary state. There is a chief, and there is a privileged class that shares in the mechanics of control. The distinction between ruler and the ruled is categorical. The authority is absolute on one side and obedience is absolute on the other. The constant comparison between human society and hymenopterous* societies is essential to the basic argument, for these societies stand at the extremes of the two principle lines of biological evolution. The differences are obvious but so are the similarities. Social life was part of the structural plan of the human species just as it was part of the structural plan of the ants and bees. These latter rudimentary societies could not rely on the "free will" of individual members and so arranged that a few should command and the rest obey. The closed society adopts this general hymenopterous pattern for its own model. A rigid hierarchy of control over rights and privileges is established, and "there is a rule" against any direct challenge to this political hierarchy. Natural (or pressure) morality and natural (or closed) societies are founded on a formula that ensures survival of the society as a whole, but at the expense of individual members of that society. The extreme form of this destruction of individuals in the name of society as a whole expresses itself in the political purges characteristic of totalitarian systems, and parallels stabbing

*An order of insects (including the bees, wasps, ants, etc.) that make up the most highly specialized and organized group, not only of insects, but of all invertebrates.

the drones to death when bees more powerful in the political hierarchy "decide" that the hive needs them no longer. A closed human society can maintain the hierarchy of power only by inculcating in each of its individual members a pressure morality that binds them in patriotic zeal to the power structure. They are *conditioned* by educational, religious and political institutions to the myth that their own individual needs are best maintained by support of the system. Nor is there any way to break down the walls of a closed society except by open rebellion against the conditioned myth, for there can be no *gradual* transition from the pressure morality of the city to the aspiration morality of humanity. The transition from the aesthetic stage to the ethical stage demands a decisive emotional revolution and so does the transition from a closed to an open society. Let us try to understand the goals of such rebellion by an examination of the open society to which aspiration morality and existential revolution lead us.

We have seen that the hierarchy of power that characterizes closed societies has its origins in instinctual and habitual patterns of survival and adaptation. The vital impetus of aspiration morality has pushed up through the weight of closed societies and begun to break down the walls of the city only in recent times. The most critical break in these walls has to do with powers and rights. Closed societies fix these powers and rights in a rigid hierarchy. The assumption is that some persons or groups are entitled to more power and rights than others. The reasons given for these claims of special privilege range all the way from religious to scientific. The only political philosophy that *in principle* challenges the natural moral and social order of a closed society, and aims in principle to transcend it, is the political philosophy of democracy.* It confers upon each

---

*Democracy is used here to describe a community based on respect for the intrinsic rights of each individual and developed within a moral context of "fraternity" or "thou." It must be contrasted to the free enterprise system in

individual citizen equal and inviolable powers and rights. No one is naive about the corruptions of democracy, but neither can anyone deny its persistent moral appeal and attraction. All those who have espoused it from Heraclitus down to Bergson are keenly aware of its potential abuses and inherent difficulties. Heraclitus recognized the personal responsibility that it demanded from each citizen when he said that only "those awake have one ordered universe in common," but "in sleep every man turns away to one of his own." Bergson recognized the same danger when he stressed that such a political philosophy demands "of all men an incorruptible fidelity to duty."[6] Such a political philosophy asks of each citizen that he respect others as he does himself and that he freely commit himself to this obligation which he holds to be absolute. Only then can the hierarchy of power and rights be destroyed and only then can each citizen be granted a direct part in the development of his own political destiny. Only through democratic processes can individual men become masters of themselves and people become sovereign over their own lives. Such is democracy in theory, and such is the goal of aspiration morality and the open society.

Closed societies based on pressure morality have as their motto "authority, hierarchy, conformity." The open society proclaims "liberty, equality, fraternity." The key to an open society and its political philosophy is the final term, fraternity. Only respect or love will reconcile the natural antagonism between liberty and equality. This essential factor of fraternity inherent in social freedom leads us to recognize the direct relationship between aspiration moral-

---

capitalist society, with which the term "democracy" is sometimes confused in our particular culture. The free enterprise system of capitalism concentrates rights and privileges in the hands of a few and then merely uses the "concept" of democracy as an illusion to maintain the established hierarchy of authoritarian power and control.

ity and the political model of democracy. An open or democratic society must be evangelical in its essence, and its motive power must be love. Criticism of the vagueness inherent in the democratic formula arises from the failure to understand its basic emotional and metaphysical character. Any precise or final definition of liberty, equality, or fraternity would be contradictory since the future must lie open to endless progress and to the creation of new conditions that will produce new possibilities that are now beyond our conceptual reach. The essence of democracy is that it represents an *ideal* or a *signpost* pointing the way toward human progress. It is a projected manifestation of the vital impetus of life and the moral aspiration of man. Psychology can reject these signposts and aspirations as superstitious *nonsense,* and attempt to build a closed society based on *the control of men.* But such attempts by psychology to abort and destroy these deeper human goals and values must be opposed by all of us. The creative impulse in man must be preserved for it is our existential guide to the development of fraternity and democracy in the world.

Pressure morality and the closed society are based on hedonism and adaptation. Aspiration morality and the open society are based on love and creation. The former stage of life can be expressed by abstract and impersonal symbols. The latter stage can be most cogently expressed through the example of the men who live it. These examples are legion, but let us choose just one that seems relevant to our particular focus on the relationship between aspiration morality and social revolution. Bergson mentions him and so have we described him briefly in our scant outline of the "flux and fire" history of philosophy—Jean-Jacques Rousseau. Bergson says that the emotional and evangelical origins of democracy can be found in the passionate soul of Rousseau. The existential significance of Rousseau is that he sought educational and political reform from the perspective of *individual* man. His philosophy be-

gins with a cry for rebellion in the name of freedom and
dignity: "Man was born free, and everywhere he is in
chains."[7] His revolution was not directed against only one
form of closed society, but against *all* forms of closed and
determined social systems. The aspiration morality at the
heart of Rousseau's political philosophy led him to bitter
personal breaks with every contemporary spokesman for
modern science and civilization, from Hume to Voltaire.
He expressed only contempt for "scientific facts," and
turned inward to discover the existential dynamics of man
and society. He embodies the spirit of the *subjective thinker*
expressed by Pascal before him and Kierkegaard after him.
He discovered his vision of man and human progress by a
passionate and personal venture into his own inner self. It
is not a philosophy based on the objective analysis of the
"person as a physical system,"[8] but on the subjective discovery of the emotional resources of the "person as an
existing individual."* It is a moral and social philosophy
based on the existential reality of freedom and of love. It
flows from that autonomous and creative inner man that
behaviorism and general psychology aim to abolish.

Rousseau claimed to be "the historian of the human
heart," and attempted to establish a utopian social model
on the aspiration morality of human compassion and fraternity. It was this passionate commitment to freedom and
love that brought him into bitter conflict with modern
science and civilization. But he forged new and original
social ideals out of the depths of his own psychological
experience that still arouse many of us. His goal was to
make men aware of their emotional resources and stir them
to challenge the institutions and systems of civilization that
threaten to completely destroy their humanity. Some argue
that man rebels only when he reaches the point where he

---

*To understand the "person as an existing individual" is the basic goal of every
  "subjective thinker" or "existentialist," regardless of his specific emphasis or his
  particular approach.

needs "more bread." But it is man's spirit and not his stomach that tells him when he has reached that point and will starve no longer. Historians disagree on the extent to which Rousseau's moral challenge did in fact stir men to political action and contribute to the storming of the Bastille and the French Revolution. Still, the dispute is only about his *relative* significance for it is fact that both his name and his political phrases were a basic part of revolutionary lore. Nor is there any doubt that he was regarded by the revolutionaries themselves as their prophet and their patron. His bust was made out of the stones of the Bastille with the *Rights of Man* inscribed around the base. Such evidence is taken as proof that Rousseau was the spiritual voice of the French Revolution and of many revolutions yet to come. Historians will continue to argue about the extent of his influence or the degree to which it was the *cult* of Rousseau rather than his political philosophy itself. Our only purpose was to provide one among many possible examples of the social and political potential inherent in the morality of aspiration.

Nor can the worst elements in any revolution be *directly* attributed to the moral aspiration that may have generated it. Rousseau can no more be directly blamed for the atrocities of the French Revolution than Gandhi can be directly blamed for the bloodshed concomitant with Indian independence, or King held directly accountable for the violence associated with the civil rights movement. They must bear the burden indirectly, for the aspiration morality that drove these men cut in its swath the brutal realities that were a part of the respective political revolutions. But the atrocities, the bloodshed, and the violence are tragic consequences of revolution, and not inherent in the moral aspiration itself. Inspired moral leaders sacrifice their lives for the cause of revolution and no one can deny that given another option they would sacrifice their lives to eliminate the brutal consequences as well.

Still, no one can protect himself from the reality of an

even more brutal fact concerning the nature of political revolution: aspiration morality often gets narrowed and forced directly into violence. It is the pain of this crucial decision concerning the means and tactics of revolution that none of us who is serious about social change can avoid. It is a terrible burden of choice that we cannot escape when confronted by destructive tyranny under extreme conditions and at critical times. But it is such a fateful decision that each one must be free to make it for himself, and each one must be his own ultimate judge.

We have contrasted the pressure morality and closed society of general psychology, with the aspiration morality and open society of existential science. The former embodies the moral and social anthropology of the "atoms and space" postulate of Democritus. The latter embodies the moral and social anthropology of the "flux and fire" postulate of Heraclitus. And today there does seem to be a new *fire* of awareness in the world, sometimes flaming openly and sometimes smoldering below the surface. It is as if mankind is trying to "awake." And no one can predict the future of his mood nor determine the exact relationship between these social forces and the moral aspirations of such men as Kierkegaard and Bergson.* But neither can anyone deny the moral authenticity that has generated this modern movement nor the critical significance of the educational and political challenges that it represents.

CONCLUSION

We have presented the basic philosophical postulates that underlie the two scientific alternatives for psychology. Now we must decide between a biology of adaptation or

*Kierkegaard was the first of the modern revolutionaries to attack the System and its institutions. The inspired voice of modern revolutionaries everywhere, Frantz Fanon, was called "Bergson" in his youth because of his constant references to the philosopher of freedom and creation.

creation; an ontology of space or time; a methodology of analysis or intuition; a morality of pressure or aspiration; and between a closed or an open society. And we must *decide,* because more data and more debate will not resolve the controversial issues that inherently separate these two approaches to psychology and man. Centuries of philosophy and science have failed to produce a rational or empirical solution because there is none. There is no "final paragraph" to complete and no "final proof" to await. The open battle today between behaviorism and existentialism attests to the perennial nature of the conflict. History has changed the names and labels of the antagonists but not the nature of the conflict itself. This type of intractable philosophical problem does not yield to systematic or scientific analysis. Nor can any *both/and* solution neutralize the conflict, because the paradoxes are absolute and the alternatives are inimical and mutually exclusive. It becomes a matter of choice. There is no escape from the burden of personal responsibility. We are confronted with an *either/or* in psychology to which each of us must respond.

Part VI

EPILOGUE

chapter 19

THE FUTURE OF HUMANISM
AND THE
FUTURE OF PSYCHOLOGY

The purpose of this work was to outline a scientific
model to guide the future development of new humanistic
approaches to psychology. The proposed model was also
intended as a means to organize and define these new approaches so that they could be defended as a legitimate
psychological enterprise. The model was based on a rapprochement between science and philosophy that situated
humanistic psychology within a meaningful body of knowledge. But it was recognized that humanistic psychology
would be "dissolved by stronger social currents" and "remembered only as a fad" unless it is grounded *now* on a
theoretical base that can sustain it. And today there is just
such a threat to the survival of humanistic psychology because it has become confused with another modern psychological movement that seems likely to be remembered in
historical perspective as no more than a social fad. Consequently, the Epilogue is an attempt to distinguish between
the future of humanistic psychology, and the future of the
new group movement that has become so popular in the
last decade.

Now we can first agree that the fate of a psychological theory rests squarely on the validity of the motivational cornerstone that supports it. The edifice that is erected may be impressive and ornate but it is only an illusion if there is a structural flaw in the cornerstone that anchors the theory to the real world. It is only a matter of time before the cornerstone splinters under the strain of existence, the foundation breaks away, and the walls come tumbling down. So it must be considered a crisis in the development of modern humanism when a significant number of professionals and laymen alike charge that there is such a crack in the cornerstone of humanistic psychology, and that no amount of cosmetic plaster can cover it. They charge that the new emperor of humanism is but a naked charlatan, and that the illusion of meaning he tries to create is a threat to the future of psychology and of man. This is a very serious charge with very serious social consequences. Anyone concerned about the future of psychology must try to understand the basic import of such criticism.

One of the most articulate critics of the new movement "caught up with the humanists" by accident at an A.P.A. convention several years ago.[1] But my own involvement in humanistic psychology was no accident. My rebellion against academic psychology began as an undergraduate student in the late 40's and has continued unabated into my present exile at a liberal Canadian university. Nor has my involvement in humanism been merely abstract and theoretical. I sought out the centers of the new movement in the early 60's and made a personal commitment to the exciting promise it seemed to hold. I worked as a psychotherapist at the Psychiatric Institute of the University of Wisconsin, the Western Behavioral Sciences Institute in La Jolla, California, and the Institute of Therapeutic Psychology in Santa Ana, California. I worked directly with those psychologists who have become most closely identified with the new group movement, such as Carl Rogers, Jack Gibb, and

Everett Shostrom. I was a very active, albeit very critical, participant in the humanistic movement for five controversial years before I came to Canada in 1968. I know in a very direct and personal way the nature of what they are doing, because I was part of the "group boom" when it began and they started doing it. Now let us try to determine if it is even worth doing at all!

There is agreement between both critic and proponent that the crux of the controversy rests squarely on the validity of the "one basic motivational assumption" of modern humanism. Critic and psychological scholar Sigmund Koch states that one basic assumption as follows: "That total psychic transparency—total self-exposure—has therapeutic and growth-releasing potential . . . that is the size of the rationale, whatever the yardage in which it is conveyed."[2] Proponent and psychological innovator Fritz Perls describes the same basic assumption: "I believe that this is the great thing to understand: *That awareness per se—by and of itself—can be curative.* Because with full awareness you become aware of this organismic self-regulation, you can let your mechanism take over without interfering, without interrupting; we can rely on the wisdom of the organism."[3] So the complexity of the controversy is simplified by agreement between both critic and proponent that the fate of the new humanism rests on the validity of its basic motivational assumption "that awareness per se—by and of itself—can be curative."

The crux of the controversy can be clearly stated but the complexity of the problem is compounded by the fact that those who have done most to promote the new group image of man spend considerable time warning about the dangers of the group process. But we soon see that they warn only about specific *tactical* dangers that they are convinced can be corrected by lists of "do's and don't's." Never do they even *mention* the possible danger inherent in the "one basic motivational assumption" itself. So is their general discussion of group theory and practice superficial and contradictory. For example, they talk about individuality and yet argue that the group and even the commune is the ideal therapeutic model. They talk about personal responsibility and yet argue that the concept of self is obsolete and must be diffused into social and even cosmic space. They chastise the "quack" who uses "gimmicks" to produce instant cures and then go on to apply their own *techniques* of "psychic stripping." They even advise the potential grouper to "be doubly cautious" if "you are sanely suspicious of your grasp on reality,"[4] but Koch notes that "to apply such a rule presupposes a remission of the condition that invites its application." And Koch further argues that even if this latter contradiction could be superficially resolved, "a committee consisting of his mother, psychiatrist, and priest could not make the necessary discrimination with accuracy."[5] Thus there is only one way to assess the value of such a confused terminology and such a contradictory psychological theory. We must dig down below the rhetoric and examine the structural cornerstone that supports it. We must examine the dynamics of the motivational process activated by group techniques.

No one denies that the encounter group phenomenon is a potent new "social invention."[6] It would not be considered such a danger to man if it were not a powerful social process. No one denies that basic personality changes do occur as a result of exposure to these group pressures and processes. Entry into the dynamics of a sensitivity group and acceptance of its norms and values *is* a decisive factor in the development of a personality. And it is precisely because these new group techniques *can* produce such basic personality changes that we must examine the implications of this modern movement so carefully. We must determine if these changes are constructive ones that will promote the evolution of man and society, or if they are but artificial digressions that confuse and block a truer course for us all. We must determine if the personality changes produced by group sensitivity techniques can best prepare man to meet the existential challenge that confronts us today.

Now we all know that every psychological approach produces its share of bizarre imitations and attracts its share of disreputable practitioners. So let us avoid any such possible distortion or contamination of our argument and examine only documented psychological theory and distinguished professional practice. But we must also recognize that boundaries are difficult to establish in this new area because a wide range of styles and moods is produced even by responsible group leaders because of their different personalities and their different approaches. Still, the overlapping patterns of professional encounter groups seem similar enough to suggest a common generic shape that encloses and defines the new group circle of humanism.* So let us base this examination of humanistic psychology on the model that is most typical of the new movement and the one that has contributed most to its modern growth and its current popularity. Let us examine the standard model for sensitivity groups and the man who did most to develop it: gestalt therapy and Fritz Perls. One advantage of this tactical approach is that no one can accuse us of attacking a straw man, because gestalt therapy is the stock model for everything on the new psychological left, from groups to drugs to modern Zen.† Another advantage is that Perls

---

*Even Rogers, whose personality and approach are much more conservative than a Perls or a Bindrim, has joined the same group movement, and stresses the same group norms and goals, e.g., "overcoming group resistance, cracking group masks," etc. (Rogers, *op. cit.*, p. 27.) It was a disappointment to many that Rogers moved toward the new group humanism in his later work rather than toward the science and philosophy of existentialism.

†Perls even considers it the model for personality changes under alpha wave stimulation, since "the alpha waves are identical with organismic self-regulation, the organism taking over and acting spontaneously instead of acting on control." (Perls, *op. cit.*, p. 20.)

himself was recognized as *the* gestalt therapist and was neither imitation nor straw man. One more advantage of a focus on gestalt therapy and Perls is that his work is so well documented that most people interested in modern psychology are familiar with it through direct exposure to scripts, tapes, or films. So let us see where Perls and modern humanism begin: Perls argues that growth occurs when the consciousness of man is overcome and the self surrenders to the healing power of the internal regulatory system of the organism. This then is the goal of sensitivity techniques and sensitivity groups—to lead the client beyond the rigid limits of his own self consciousness into the wholistic experience of organismic or cosmic consciousness. There is no reason to attack specific sensitivity techniques since there is conclusive evidence that they do accomplish the goal for which they were designed. Nor is there any reason to label these techniques as "degenerate" or "dehumanizing." The only relevant attack, if there is any legitimate grounds at all, must be on the nature of the goal itself. The only real question is whether organismic consciousness can be defended as a healing experience and a constructive process—whether it provides a meaningful and workable model for contemporary man and for social evolution. So let us assess the basic model of the new humanism in terms of the only two criteria that concern us: the value to *man* and the value to *society*.

The crux of the criticism is embedded in the image of man presented to us by the new psychological model. It offers us a modern religious faith in the healing power of the organism as a whole and at the same time tells us— much like psychoanalysis and behaviorism—that the self, character, choice, and will are obsolete and even destructive concepts: (Self) "We write the self with a lower case s. I know that many psychologists like to write the self with a capital S, as if the self would be something precious, something extraordinarily valuable. . . . The self means nothing but this thing as it is defined by *otherness.*"[7] (Character) "Once you have *character,* you have developed a rigid system. Your behavior becomes petrified, predictable, and you lose your ability to cope freely with the world with all your resources. You are predetermined just to cope with events in one way, namely, as your character prescribes it to be. So it seems a paradox when I say that the richest person, the most productive, creative person, is a person who has *no* character."[8] (Choice) "The organism does not *make decisions.* Decision is a man-made institution. The organism works always on the basis of *preference.* . . . 'Where does it want to be balanced?' Except you don't ask questions, you just respond. . . . This is again the wisdom of the organism. The organism knows all. We know very little."[9]* (Will) " *We cannot deliberately bring about changes in ourselves or in others.* This is a very decisive point: Many people dedicate their lives to actualize a concept of what they *should* be like . . . 'you should'—interferes with the healthy working of the organism."[10] Thus we see it is the reality of self, character, choice, and will that the new psychological left rejects in favor of the adaptive regulatory function of the organism: "There is only one thing that should control: the *situation.* If you understand the situation which you are in, and let the situation which you are in control your actions, then you learn how to cope with life."[11]

---

*Just try to convince this father who must decide on heart surgery for his five-year-old daughter that "decision is a man-made institution," and that "organismic preference" can spare him the anxiety and pain of human choice: "What were we to do? We experienced a state of acute worry, followed by a paralyzing indecision that lasted several days. . . . It was during these desperate days and nights that . . . I was overcome with the pain of having to make a decision, as a parent, which had potentially devastating consequences either way. If I decided on surgery, she might not survive the operation. If I decided against it, the possibility of a premature death would always haunt me. It was a terrible responsibility, being required to make a decision, a life or death decision, for someone else. This awful feeling, this overwhelming sense of responsibility . . ." (Moustakas, C. *Loneliness.* Englewood Cliffs, N.J.: Prentice-Hall, 1961, p. 1–2.)

This then is the core of the controversy and the crux of the criticism of the philosophy of the new psychological left. The sensitivity techniques and the sensitivity groups that dominate the new humanism are designed to destroy that awareness we call self consciousness and produce another kind of awareness called organismic or cosmic consciousness. But the "cure" of humanism may be just as deadly as the "bite" of behaviorism. The *organismic* response of the humanists is the same as the *conditioned* response of the behaviorists, since they both kill the *willed* response in man—the existential basis of his freedom and his dignity. Man cannot survive if the humanists cut out his heart and guts any better than if the psychoanalysts or the behaviorists do it. Yet each of us must decide for himself between these antagonistic and contradictory types of consciousness. But let us try to be as careful as possible in our use of language because all of us can agree that the stakes involved in this decision are extremely high for psychology and man during this critical period in the evolution of human society. So let us begin to clarify our language and terminology by the correction of one obvious abuse that is directly relevant to the crucial issue considered here.

The new psychological left that we have just described proudly and arrogantly calls itself existentialism: "This is why we call our approach the existential approach: We exist *as* an organism—as an organism like a clam, like an animal, and so on, and we relate to the external world just like any other organism of nature."[12] Now to call a theory that rejects the uniqueness of man, as it rejects the self, character, choice, and will "existentialism," is to tear the heart and guts out of the lion and then claim that his dead carcass still lives. It is a meaningless and even bizarre use of language and terminology. Yet I am not concerned about the logic or semantics of the problem. I am concerned only about the term *existentialism,* and I want to salvage it as a hope for the future of psychology and man. I want to stress

the fact that the new humanism is *not* existentialism because I do not want the fate of such a crucial and profound
hope to depend on the future of superficial sensitivity
games and artificial sensitivity groups. I do not want the
inner man of existentialism, that has survived the onslaught
of psychoanalysis and behaviorism, to be butchered once
more—and this time by the humanists themselves. The
basic tenet of the existential movement, regardless of its
theoretical spokesman, is to choose and will "the self that
one must be" in *defiance* of every obstacle—not, as the new
humanism preaches, "in harmony, in alignment with everything else, with medicine, with science, with the universe,
with what *is*."[13] The fundamental postulate of existentialism, from its scientific formulations by Bergson and Whitehead to its more philosophical and metaphorical expressions, is that man wills his own being out of the depths
of his own inward anxiety and pain:

> In order that our consciousness shall coincide with some-
> thing of its principle, it must detach itself from the *already-
> made* and attach itself to the *being-made*. It needs that, turning
> back on itself and twisting on itself, the faculty of *seeing*
> should be made to be one with the act of *willing*—a painful
> effort which we can make suddenly, doing violence to our
> nature, but cannot sustain for more than a few moments. In
> free action, when we contract our whole being in order to
> thrust it forward, we have the more or less clear conscious-
> ness of motives and of impelling forces, and even, at rare
> moments, of the becoming by which they are organized into
> an act.[14]

Or:

> One sees merely the whole effort of a body straining to raise
> the huge stone, to roll it and push it up a slope a hundred
> times over; one sees the face screwed up, the cheek tight
> against the stone, the shoulder bracing the clay-covered
> mass, the foot wedging it, the fresh start with arms out-
> stretched, the wholly human security of two earth-clotted
> hands. At the very end of his long effort measured by skyless

space and time without depth, the purpose is achieved. Then
Sisyphus watches the stone rush down in a few moments
towards the lower world whence he will have to push it up
again toward the summit. He goes back down to the plain.[15]

There is no way to reconcile this strain and tension of
the individual *self* and the creative *will* that is basic to the
existential concept of personality growth and development, with a calm surrender to passive faith in the wisdom
of the organism and the probity of the situation. But the
new psychological left demands that we reject any personal
commitment to our existential self, for just such a modern
faith in the organism, the group,* and even the cosmos
itself. My attempt to correct this confused use of the term
existentialism was an attempt to salvage the construct, as well
as an attempt to make a basic distinction that would eliminate the cause of the original confusion. And that basic
distinction is a plain and simple one. *Either* man chooses
existentialism with its commitment to self, character,
choice, and will; *or* man embraces modern humanism with
its faith in the absolute wisdom of organismic and cosmic
consciousness. It is only another dimension of the same
either/or decision that confronted us throughout the text
—either man makes himself or man is made by the organism and its milieu. That is exactly the size of the controversy, "whatever the yardage in which it is conveyed." And
this controversy is like all other intractable and perennial

---

*The new humanism kills individual freedom and the existential self with a su-
perficial hypocrisy that encourages deviation *after* submission to the rules of
group membership, and *within* the consensual norms of group productivity: "In
the early stages of development, the group boxes in or punishes persons who
deviate from group norms, in the later stages ... deviation is perhaps even
welcomed as a creative contribution to possible group productivity." (Gibb, J.
Humanistic elements in group growth. In *Challenges of humanistic psychology.* J.
Bugental (Ed.). New York: McGraw-Hill, 1967, p. 164.) But individual freedom
controlled by group laws is only another bizarre and even comical humanistic
contradiction.

conflicts in philosophy. There is no both/and solution because the alternatives are inimical and mutually exclusive. We are confronted with another either/or choice in psychology to which each of us must respond.

The value of this new movement to society follows directly from the assessment of its value to individual man. The new group movement talks about rebellion, and in the name of social revolution advises us to "become real, to learn to take a stand, to develop one's center, to understand the basis of existentialism: a rose is a rose is a rose."[16] But in practice sensitivity experiences do not lead to social action but to passive preoccupation with interpersonal games, communal groups, and altered states of consciousness. The contradiction between the rhetoric of revolution and the reality of adaptation is due to the contradiction between the organism and the self. The basis for any active revolution is the existential self within each individual that first *cries out,* and then forcibly demands some radical change in the system or the situation. Destroy that anxious imperative within the self by psychoanalysis, behaviorism *or* humanism and you kill existentialism and revolution at the same time. The existential stance is one of tension between the single individual and any artificially constructed experience, system, or *situation.* "The 'crowd' is the untruth,"* whether its norm is established by a common pattern of reinforcements or by a common faith in the divine wisdom of the universe. Any philosophy that seeks

*The "crowd" is the untruth "by reason of the fact that it renders the individual completely impenitent and irresponsible, or at least weakens his sense of responsibility by reducing it to a fraction." (Kierkegaard, S. *The point of view for my work as an author: A report to history.* Trans. Walter Lowrie. New York: Harper Torchbooks, 1962, p. 112.) Heidegger's equivalent of the "crowd" is "they" or "*das Man*": "Everyone is the other, and no one is himself. The '*they*' . . . is the 'nobody' to whom every Dasein has already surrendered itself in Being-among-one-another." (Heidegger, M. *Being and time.* Trans. J MacQuarrie and E. Robinson. New York: Harper & Row, 1962, pp. 165–6.)

a "balanced harmony"[†] is a philosophy of organismic adaptation but not a philosophy of existential revolution. The contradiction between an organismic theory and a self theory is irreconcilable, because the existential self rejects the "wisdom" of the organismic dogma that "there is only one thing that should control: the *situation*. If you understand the situation which you are in, and let the situation which you are in control your actions, then you learn how to cope with life."[17]

The existential self does not try to "cope" with life but struggles to *create* life in the image of its own choice and will. The adaptive life style advocated by the new humanism enables one to "cope" only within the security of those artificial groups and communes that the new movement itself has produced.[*] Such passivity breaks down under the existential pressure of the real world. Just try to convince a *coal slave* in Appalachia's poverty chain, or a *black rebel* in Rhodesia's apartheid society, to "let the situation control him," or that passive surrender to the "wisdom of his organism" can shatter the yoke of oppression, and force the political revolution that he *wills* with the sweat and blood of his own life.

Existentialism is rooted in such pain and struggle and

[†]Gestalt therapy only wants to know where the organism needs to be "balanced" (p. 319) and how to get the organism into "harmony" with everything else (p. 321).

[*]Of course, this adaptive life style also enables one to "cope" within the security of the socio-economic class that group clients and practitioners already share. But psychology's preoccupation with the pleasure and adjustment of such an insignificant proportion of the world's population must be considered irrelevant, if not immoral, against the background of human suffering in the world at large. No less a respected figure than U.N. Secretary-General Kurt Waldheim recently warned us: "The next 30 to 35 years may well be the most challenging in the history of mankind . . . for it is virtually certain that the world's population will double [to 8 billion]" and never before have "nations or the international community been faced with such expanding demand for food, shelter, employment, education, and health care." And even more ominous—the battle lines for

responds to the dread and suffering in man that is the source of authentic rebellion and revolution everywhere. The common man may not understand the philosophical language of existentialism; but he does understand the anxiety and pain in his own concrete struggle for freedom and for love—and that concrete struggle to exist is the heart and guts of the philosophy itself. Existentialism reaches out to the least among us because it is a philosophy for the one alone—and each of us is that *one!* But the new humanism seems to have abandoned those who are most in need of psychological help and social revolution: "Humanistic psychology, from whose passionate forehead the encounter group has sprung," deals only with "persons who are performing within socially acceptable parameters of legality, productivity and success," and speaks only "to those who are not sick but rather normal—normally depressed, normally dissatisfied ..."[18] I have even heard some of these new *humanists* use the same argument as a commercial tactic to get *one up on* psychiatrists who are stuck with the stereotype of "sick patient." And anyone who is naive enough to argue that these new sensitivity techniques can be adapted to serve the "sick" need only imagine the "growth-releasing potential" of two anxious and frightened patients trying to "spread-eagle" a third so that the

---

the "next 30 to 35 years" of conflict and revolution were clearly drawn at the same United Nations population conference in Bucharest where the warning itself was given. China and India joined with the developing countries of the world (making a block that represents ⅔ of the world's population) to blame "consumerism and imperialism"—not population growth—for the modern explosion of world poverty and suffering. They pledged to take no action *whatsoever* to control massive population growth *until* there is a radical redistribution of wealth between rich and poor nations." (*Newsweek* [International, September 2, 1974] New York: Newsweek, Inc.) Such an impending crisis in human history challenges psychology to do more than "neutralize" and "adjust" middle-class society by analysis, desensitization, drugs, and games. Instead, we must develop models of man, even in our work with individual clients, that can lead us to radical, creative, and effective forms of social and political change.

group can "crotch-eyeball" him. And if that imagery is not crude enough to convince you—go try it on some hospital ward.

So is it just as blatantly obvious that the new humanists do not deal with the poor. The cost of one marathon session would wreck the family budget of a working man and the cost of two would bankrupt him. And so is it obvious that these new treatment methods are available only to those who are intellectually and socially "sophisticated" enough to have *heard* of them—let alone take them seriously. The least among us intuitively understands the healing power of existential compassion and love,* but the therapeutic significance of "group-nudity," "crotch-eyeballing," and even less dramatic forms of psychic "striptease," escapes most of us. So it becomes increasingly clear as we dig below the rhetoric of the new humanism that it is in practice, as well as in principle, a shallow philosophy designed only for those who were best prepared to "cope" with life in the first place. Now I know it is true that this same criticism applies to the theory and practice of most other philosophies of psychotherapy as well. Yet we should expect much more from *humanistic* psychology than games and groups that satisfy a select few but are beyond the reach of the common man and that disregard the fundamental rights and needs of those among us who are ignorant, poor, and sick. We who are comfortable in our middle-class beds might well enjoy such chic diversions but the world at large demands a much more rugged and meaningful base on which to build its future. And one thing the

---

*"Only when the compassionate person is so related by his compassion to the sufferer that in the strictest sense he comprehends that it is his own cause which is here in question, only when he knows how to identify himself in such a way with the sufferer that when he is fighting for an explanation he is fighting for himself, renouncing all thoughtlessness, softness, and cowardice, only then does compassion acquire significance." (Kierkegaard, S. *The concept of dread*. Trans. Walter Lowrie. Princeton: Princeton University Press, 1957, p. 107.)

world does *not* need at this critical time in history is a new psychological cult that promises salvation and joy to those who will but worship the wisdom of the organism, the norms of the group, and the divinity of the cosmos.

But I realize that many new models of man will emerge now that the breakdown of traditional psychological systems has begun. And I realize that these new models may even be a necessary part of the slow transition to a more relevant and meaningful psychology. So do I realize that no amount of argument or debate will convince new group converts who have produced one of these modern psychological models that they have chosen a false god. It was not my intention to undertake that impossible task but only to explain the existential basis for rejection of sensitivity techniques and the religious fad they have produced. The real tragedy for psychology and man is not this superficial preoccupation with games and groups but the fact that it is destroying the potential of the movement to develop a more viable alternative to the sterile objectification of man that dominates psychology today. The need for some effective new antidote is so crucial because the disease that afflicts psychology is so fatal. Psychology will surely die if it does not emerge from the multitude of controversies that now besiege it as a stronger and more useful discipline. And I am convinced that humanism is our only hope for such a new beginning. So if those who call themselves humanists continue to ignore the crack in the cornerstone of their own philosophy, and simply prescribe heavier doses of group games and cosmic faith—then there is no hope for the future of psychology at all. Our quest for a new beginning will founder in the despair that waits for man at the dead end of another psychological illusion.

SOURCE NOTES

CHAPTER 1

1. Koch, S. Psychology cannot be a coherent science. *Psychology Today,* 1969, vol. 3, no. 4, pp. 14, 64, 66.
2. Koch, S. The image of man in encounter groups. *American Scholar,* 1973, vol. 42, no. 4, p. 639.
3. Jones, E. *Sigmund Freud: Life and work.* London: Hogarth Press, 1957, vol. 3, p. 495.
4. *Webster's new international dictionary.* Second edition (abridged). Springfield, Mass.: G. & C. Merriam Co., 1947, p. 484.
5. Perry, R. *The thought and character of William James: Briefer version.* New York: George Braziller, 1954, pp. 345–6.

CHAPTER 2

1. The quotations of early Greek philosophers that have been cited throughout the book are taken from two primary sources: Oates, W. *The Stoic and Epicurian philosophers.* New York: Modern Library, 1940; and Freeman, K. *Ancilla to the Pre-Socratic philosophers.* Oxford: Basil Blackwell, 1962.
2. Bacon, F. *The new organon.* New York: Liberal Arts Press, 1960, p. 57.
3. Ibid., p. 49.
4. Bacon, F. *The New Atlantis.* In *Essays, advancement of learning, New Atlantis, and other pieces.* R. F. Jones (Ed.), New York: Odyssey Press, 1937, pp. 466, 468.
5. Ibid., p. 480.
6. Hobbes, T. *Elements of philosophy.* In *The English works of Thomas Hobbes.* W. Molesworth (Ed.). vol. 1 (London: Scientia Aalen, 1839), p. 109.

7. Ibid., p. 115.
8. Hobbes, T. *Leviathan*. New York: E. P. Dutton, 1962, p. 3.
9. Ibid., p. 9.
10. Locke, J. *An essay concerning human understanding*. Oxford: The Clarendon Press, 1934, p. 286.
11. Comte, A. *The positive philosophy*, vol. 1. Trans. H. Martineau. New York: D. Appleton, 1853, pp. 1-2.
12. Ibid., p. 7.
13. Bentham, J. *An introduction to the principles of morals and legislation*. New York: Hafner, 1963, p. 1.
14. *The life and letters of Charles Darwin*. Francis Darwin (Ed.). New York: D. Appleton, 1887, vol. 2, p. 301.
15. Spencer, H. *Principles of psychology*. New York: D. Appleton, 1890, vol. 1, p. 388.
16. Spencer, H. *Principles of biology*. London: Williams & Norgate, 1898, vol. 1, p. 99.
17. Freud, S. *New introductory lectures on psychoanalysis and other works*. Trans. J. Strachey. London: Hogarth Press, 1964, p. 159.
18. Binswanger, L. *Being-in-the-world: Selected papers of Ludwig Binswanger*. Trans. Jacob Needleman. New York: Basic Books, 1963, pp. 1-2. Needleman supplies complete information about the translations and the German versions.
19. Ibid., pp. 3-4.
20. Skinner, B. F. (Untitled autobiographical essay). In Edwin G. Boring & Gardner Lindzey (Eds.), *A history of psychology in autobiography*. New York: Appleton-Century-Crofts, 1967, 5 vols., vol. 5, p. 409.
21. Skinner, B. F. *Beyond freedom and dignity*. New York: Alfred A. Knopf, 1971, p. 200.
22. Ibid, pp. 200-1.
23. Ibid, p. 201.
24. Ibid, p. 14.
25. Bacon, F. *Advancement of learning*. New York: P. F. Collier, 1902, p. 328.
26. Skinner, *Beyond freedom and dignity*, p. 20.

CHAPTER 3

1. Bergson, H. *The two sources of morality and religion*. Trans. R. Ashley Aubra & Cloudesley Brereton with the assistance of K. Horsfall Carter. New York: Holt, 1935, pp. 52-3.
2. Pascal, B. *Pensées*. Trans. H. F. Stewart. New York: Pantheon Books, 1965, p. 343.
3. Rousseau, J-J. *Discourse on the origin of inequality*. In *The social contract and discourse on the origin of inequality*. Trans. L. G. Crocker. New York: Washington Square Press, 1967, p. 177.
4. Schopenhauer, A. *The world as will and idea*. Trans. R. Haldane and J. Kemp. London: Routledge & Kegan Paul, 1957, vol. 1, p. 159.

5. Ibid., vol. 2, p. 443.
6. Ibid., vol. 2, pp. 333–4.
7. Kierkegaard, S. *Concluding unscientific postscript.* Trans. David Swenson and Walter Lowrie. Princeton: Princeton University Press, 1963, p. 165.
8. Ibid., p. 166.
9. Ibid., p. 182.
10. Ibid., p. 169.
11. Kierkegaard, S. *The sickness unto death.* In *Fear and trembling;* and *The sickness unto death.* Trans. Walter Lowrie. New York: Doubleday Anchor Books, 1954, p. 146.
12. Kierkegaard, *Fear and trembling,* p. 132.

Chapter 4

1. Kierkegaard, *Concluding unscientific postscript,* p. 165.
2. Ibid., p. 318.
3. Ibid., p. 109.
4. Heidegger, M. *Being and time.* Trans. J. MacQuarrie & E. Robinson. New York: Harper and Row, 1962, p. 32.
5. Ibid., p. 35.
6. Ibid., p. 34.
7. Ibid., p. 67.
8. Sartre, J-P. *Existentialism and humanism.* Trans. Philip Mairet. London: Methuen, 1963, p. 28.
9. Ibid., p. 28.
10. Ibid., p. 29.
11. Merleau-Ponty, M. *The structure of behavior.* Trans. A. L. Fisher. Boston: Beacon Press, 1963, p. 3.
12. Merleau-Ponty, M. *Phenomenology of perception.* Trans. Colin Smith. London: Routledge & Kegan Paul, 1962, p. viii.
13. Ibid., p. ix.
14. Merleau-Ponty, *The structure of behavior,* p. 182.
15. Marcel, G. Reflection and mystery. In vol. 1 of *The Mystery of Being.* Trans. G. S. Fraser. Chicago: Gateway Editions, 1960, pp. 260–1.
16. Marcel, G. *Being and having: An existentialist diary.* Trans. K. Farrer. New York: Harper Torchbooks, 1965, p. 155.
17. Marcel, Reflection and mystery, p. 22ff.
18. Marcel, *Being and having,* pp. 164–5.
19. Ibid., pp. 166–7.
20. Marcel, G. *Creative fidelity.* Trans. R. Rosthal. New York: Farrar, Straus, 1964, p. 153ff.
21. Ibid., p. 158ff.
22. Marcel, *Being and having,* p. 174.
23. Jaspers, K. *Way to wisdom.* Trans. C. Manheim. New Haven: Yale University Press, 1962, pp. 123–4.

24. Ibid., p. 37.
25. Jaspers, K. *Philosophy of existence.* Trans. R. Graubau. Philadelphia: University of Pennsylvania Press, 1971, p. 12.
26. Jaspers, *Way to wisdom,* p. 122.
27. Camus, A. *The myth of Sisyphus.* Trans. J. O'Brien. New York: Vintage Books, 1960, p. 91.
28. Berdyaev, N. *Slavery and freedom.* Trans. R. French. New York: Scribner's, 1944, p. 21.
29. Berdyaev, N. *Dream and reality.* Trans. K. Lampert. London: Geoffrey Bles, 1950, p. 103.
30. Ibid., p. 286.
31. Berdyaev, N. *The meaning of the creative act.* Trans. D. Lowrie. New York: Collier Books, 1962, p. 135.
32. Buber, M. *I and thou.* Trans. R. G. Smith. New York: Scribner's, 1958, p. 11.
33. Ibid., p. 34.
34. Ibid., p. 31.

CHAPTER 5

1. See Binswanger's case studies in *Existence: A new dimension of psychiatry and psychology.* Edited by R. May, E. Angel, & H. Ellenberger. New York: Basic Books, 1958, pp. 214-364; and in *Being-in-the-world: Selected papers of Ludwig Binswanger.* Trans. J. Needleman. New York: Basic Books, 1963, pp. 266–341.
2. Binswanger, L. Heidegger's analytic of existence and its meaning for psychiatry. In *Being-in-the-world,* 1963, p. 215.
3. Heidegger, *Being and time,* p. 32.
4. Binswanger, L. Heidegger's analytic of existence and its meaning for psychiatry. In *Being-in-the-world.* p. 216.
5. Ibid., p. 216.
6. Ibid., p. 284. (The case of Lola Voss. Trans. Ernest Angel.)
7. Ibid., p. 218. (Heidegger's analytic of existence and its meaning for psychiatry.)
8. Binswanger, L. Insanity as life-historical phenomenon and as mental disease: The case of Ilse. In May, Angel and Ellenberger (Eds.), *Existence,* p. 215.
9. Ibid., p. 225.
10. Binswanger, L. Existential analysis and psychotherapy. In *Progress in psychotherapy.* F. Fromm-Reichmann & J. L. Moreno (Eds.). New York: Grune & Stratton, 1956, vol. 1, p. 146.
11. Boss, M. *Psychoanalysis and daseinsanalysis.* Trans. L. Lefebre. New York: Basic Books, 1963, p. 285.
12. Ibid., p. 254.
13. Ibid., p. 271.

14. Ibid., p. 209.
15. Ibid., p. 270.
16. Ibid., p. 270.
17. Ibid., p. 270.
18. Ibid., p. 236.
19. Ibid., p. 239.
20. Ibid., p. 123.
21. Ibid., p. 240.
22. Ibid., p. 240.
23. Ibid., p. 283.

CHAPTER 6

1. *The life and letters of Charles Darwin*, vol. 2, p. 301.
2. Freud, *New introductory lectures*, p. 159.
3. See the dialogue between Binswanger and Freud, in Binswanger, *Being-in-the-world*, pp. 1–4.
4. Spencer, H. *First principles.* New York: D. Appleton, 1898, p. 407.
5. Ibid., p. 412ff.
6. Ibid., p. 442ff.
7. Ibid., p. 471ff.
8. Ibid., p. 496ff.
9, Spencer, *Principles of biology*, vol. 1, p. 99.

CHAPTER 7

1. Berdyaev, *Creative act*, pp. 134–5.
2. Bergson, H. *Creative evolution.* Trans. Arthur Mitchell. London: Macmillan, 1960, pp. 107–8.
3. Scharfstein, B. *Roots of Bergson's philosophy.* New York: Columbia University Press, 1943, contains numerous quotes from Bergson's articles in the *Anne Biologique*, 1895–1907; this quote is found on p. 75.
4. Bergson, *Creative evolution*, p. 205.
5. Ibid., p. 206.
6. Ibid., p. 384.
7. Ibid., pp. 384–5.
8. Ibid., p. xi.
9. Ibid., p. 51.
10. Ibid., p. 56.
11. Ibid., p. 58.
12. Ibid., p. 80.
13. Ibid., p. 59.

14. Ibid., p. 56.
15. Ibid., p. 58.
16. Ibid., p. 58.
17. Ibid., p. 80.
18. Ibid., p. xii.
19. Ibid., p. xiii.
20. Ibid., p. 232.
21. Ibid., p. 391.

CHAPTER 8

1. Bergson, *Creative evolution*, p. 232.
2. Berdyaev, *Creative act*, p. 135.
3. Bergson, *Creative evolution*, p. 275.
4. Ibid., p. 278.
5. Ibid., pp. 278–9.
6. Berdyaev, *Slavery and freedom*, p. 21.
7. Camus, A. *The myth of Sisyphus*. Trans. J. O'Brien. New York: Vintage Books, 1960, p. 88.
8. Ibid., p. 91.
9. Bergson, *Creative evolution*, p. 134.
10. Ibid., p. 134.
11. Ibid., p. 135.
12. Bergson, H. *Time and free will: An essay on the immediate data of consciousness.* Trans. F. L. Pogson. New York: Macmillan, 1959, p. 238.
13. Berdyaev, *Creative act*, p. 134.
14. Bergson, *Time and free will*, p. 170.
15. Ibid., p. 133.
16. Bergson, *Creative evolution*, p. 38.

CHAPTER 10

1. Kierkegaard, S. *Repetition: An essay in experimental psychology.* Trans. Walter Lowrie. New York: Harper Torchbooks, 1964, p. 33.
2. Ibid., p. 54.
3. Ibid., pp. 54–5.
4. Ibid., p. 75.
5. Ibid., p. 76.
6. Ibid., pp. 76–7.
7. Bergson, *Creative evolution*, pp. 30–1, 47–9.
8. Ibid., p. 2.
9. Ibid., p. 6.

10. Ibid., p. 8.
11. Ibid., p. 210.
12. Ibid., p. 212.
13. Kierkegaard, *Concluding unscientific postscript*, p. 373.
14. Bergson, *Creative evolution*, p. 325.

CHAPTER 11

1. Bergson, *Creative evolution*, p. 5.
2. Bergson, H. *Matter and memory*. Trans. Nancy Margaret Paul & W. Scott Palmer. London: George Allen & Unwin, 1950, p. 94.
3. Ibid., p. 95.
4. Bergson, *Creative evolution*, p. 202.
5. Ibid., p. 203.
6. Ibid., p. 204.

CHAPTER 12

1. Wundt, W. Contributions to the theory of sensory perception. In T. Shipley (Ed.). *Classics in psychology*. New York: Philosophical Library, 1961, p. 70.
2. Freud, *New introductory lectures*, p. 159.
3. Skinner, *Beyond freedom and dignity*, p. 200.

CHAPTER 13

1. Marcel, *Being and having*, p. 117–18.
2. Bergson, H. *The creative mind*. Trans. Mabelle L. Andison. New York: Philosophical Library, 1946, pp. 39–41.
3. Ibid., p. 42.
4. Skinner, B. F. *Walden two*. New York: Macmillan, 1948, p. 261.
5. Ibid., p. 262.
6. Bergson, *Creative evolution*, p. 208.
7. Bergson, H. *An introduction to metaphysics*. Trans. T. E. Hulme. New York: Liberal Arts Press, 1949, p. 23.
8. Bergson, *Creative evolution*, p. xiv.
9. Bergson, *Metaphysics*, p. 23.
10. Ibid., p. 23.
11. Ibid., p. 24.
12. Ibid., p. 53.

13. Bergson, *Creative mind,* p. 39.
14. Bergson, *Creative evolution,* p. 237.
15. Bergson, *Metaphysics,* pp. 50–1.

CHAPTER 14

1. Bergson, *Metaphysics,* p. 35.
2. Ibid., p. 35.
3. Bergson, *Creative evolution,* pp. 173–4.

CHAPTER 15

1. Binswanger, *Being-in-the-world,* p. 186. (Freud and the magna charta of clinical psychiatry.)
2. Greisinger, W. *Pathologie und Therapie der Psychischen Krankheiten,* p. 6f. In Binswanger, p. 186.
3. Ibid., p. 186.
4. Binswanger, p. 186n.
5. Ibid., p. 186.
6. Greisinger, p. 6f. In Binswanger, p. 187.
7. Ibid., p. 187.
8. Ibid., p. 187.
9. Binswanger, p. 188.
10. Greisinger, p. 9f. In Binswanger, p. 190.
11. Binswanger, pp. 193–4.
12. Freud, S. *Gesammelte Schriften,* VI, p. 223. In Binswanger, p. 194.
13. Ibid., VI, p. 223. In Binswanger, p. 195.
14. Ibid., VI, p. 253. In Binswanger, p. 195.
15. Binswanger, p. 195.
16. Ibid., p. 196.
17. Ibid., p. 197.
18. Freud, S. *Zur Auffassung der Aphasien,* p. 32. In Binswanger, p. 197.
19. Ibid., p. 89. In Binswanger, p. 197.
20. Binswanger, pp. 198–9.
21. Ibid., p. 200.
22. Freud, *Ges. Schr.,* XI, p. 223. In Binswanger, p. 200.
23. Ibid., XI, p. 222f. In Binswanger, p. 201n.
24. Ibid., VI, p. 367. In Binswanger, p. 201.
25. Ibid., XII, p. 239. In Binswanger, p. 161.
26. Ibid., XI, p. 436. In Binswanger, p. 157.
27. Ibid., XII, p. 319. In Binswanger, p. 157.

Chapter 16

1. Heidegger, M. *Kant and the problem of metaphysics.* Trans. J. Churchill. Bloomington, Ind.: Indiana University Press, 1962, p. 215.
2. Binswanger, *Being-in-the-world,* p. 167. (Freud's conception of man in the light of anthropology.)
3. Ibid., p. 168.
4. Freud, S. *Ges. Schr.,* XI, p. 222f. In Binswanger, p. 201n. (Freud and the magna charta of clinical psychiatry.)
5. Binswanger, p. 170. (Freud's conception of man in the light of anthropology.)
6. Ibid., p. 165.
7. Ibid., p. 170.
8. Ibid., p. 171.
9. Ibid., p. 171.
10. Ibid., p. 171.
11. Ibid., p. 175.

Chapter 17

1. Hobbes, T. The Citizen: Philosophical rudiments concerning government and society. In *Man and citizen.* B. Gert (Ed.). New York: Anchor Books, 1972, p. 116.
2. Ibid., p. 117.
3. Ibid., p. 118.
4. Hobbes, *Leviathan,* p. 65.
5. Locke, J. *An essay concerning human understanding.* A. C. Fraser (Ed.). New York: Dover Publications, 1959, vol. 2, p. 208.
6. Ibid., vol. 1, p. 303.
7. Locke, J. *Two treatises of government.* Peter Laslett (Ed.). London: Cambridge University Press, 1967, p. 289.
8. Bentham, J. *An introduction to the principles of morals and legislation.* J. Burns and H. Hart (Eds.). New York: Oxford University Press, 1970, p. 1.
9. Ibid., p. 4.
10. Mill, J. S. *Autobiography by John Stuart Mill.* London: Oxford University Press, 1952, p. 54.
11. Mill, J. S. *Utilitarianism.* In *Collected works of John Stuart Mill.* J. M. Robson (Ed.). London: Routledge & Kegan Paul, 1969, pp. 210–11.
12. Ibid., p. 211.
13. Spencer, H. *The principles of ethics.* New York: D. Appleton, 1898, vol. 1, p. 23.
14. Skinner, *Beyond freedom and dignity,* p. 104–5.

5 Skinner, In Boring & Lindzey (Eds.), *A history of psychology in autobiography*, p. 408.
16. Hobbes, *Leviathan*, p. 89.
17. Mill, *Utilitarianism*, p. 218.
18. Skinner, In Boring & Lindzey, p. 410.
19. Skinner, *Walden Two*, p. 105.
20. Ibid., pp. 162–3.
21. Ibid., p. 163.
22. Ibid., p. 165.
23. Ibid., p. 166.
24. Ibid., pp. 164–5.
25. Ibid., p. 104.
26. Ibid., pp. 104–5.
27. Ibid., p. 124.
28. Ibid., pp. 107–8.
29. Ibid., p. 108.
30. Ibid., p. 109.
31. Ibid., pp. 109–10.
32. Ibid., p. 110.
33. Ibid., pp. 37–9.
34. Ibid., p. 174.
35. Ibid., p. 157.
36. Skinner, In Boring & Lindzey, p. 411.

CHAPTER 18

1. Kierkegaard, S. *The sickness unto death*, p. 147.
2. This phrase is the title of one of Martin Buber's books on the nature of the I-Thou relationship. *Between man and man*. Trans. R. G. Smith. Boston: Beacon Paperbacks, 1955.
3. Bergson, *The two sources of morality and religion*, p. 75.
4. Skinner, *Beyond freedom and dignity*, p. 165.
5. Bergson, *The two sources of morality and religion*, p. 78.
6. Ibid., p. 270.
7. Rousseau, J-J. *The social contract*. In *The social contract and discourse on the origin of inequality*, p. 7.
8. Skinner, *Beyond freedom and dignity*, p. 14.

CHAPTER 19

1. Koch, The image of man in encounter groups, *American Scholar*, p. 641
2. Ibid., p. 642.

3. Perls, F. *Gestalt therapy verbatim.* Lafayette, Calif.: Real People Press, 1969, p. 16–17.
4. Shostrom, E. Group therapy: Let the buyer beware. *Psychology Today,* 1969, vol. 2, no. 12, p. 38.
5. Koch, *The image of man,* p. 640.
6. Rogers, C. The group comes of age. *Psychology Today,* 1969, vol. 3, no. 7, p. 27.
7. Perls, *Gestalt therapy verbatim,* p. 7–8.
8. Ibid., p. 7.
9. Ibid., pp. 20–22.
10. Ibid., p. 19.
11. Ibid., p. 19.
12. Ibid., p. 6.
13. Ibid., p. 16.
14. Bergson, *Creative evolution,* pp. 250–1.
15. Camus, *The myth of Sisyphus,* p. 89.
16. Perls, *Gestalt therapy verbatim,* p. 3.
17. Ibid., p. 19.
18. Shostrom, *Group therapy,* p. 39.

BIBLIOGRAPHY

The Primary Sources of Existentialism

Berdyaev, Nicolas.
The beginning and the end. Trans. R. M. French. New York: Harper Torchbooks, 1957.
The destiny of man. Trans. Natalie Duddington. New York: Harper Torchbooks, 1960.
Dream and Reality. Trans. K. Lampert. London: Geoffrey Bles, 1950.
Freedom and the spirit. Trans. O. F. Clarke. New York: Scribner's, 1935.
The meaning of the creative act. Trans. Donald A. Lowrie. New York: Collier Books, 1962.
Slavery and freedom. Trans. R. M. French. New York: Scribner's, 1944.
Solitude and society. Trans. G. Rearey. London: Geoffrey Bles, 1947.
Truth and revelation. Trans. R. M. French. London: Geoffrey Bles, 1953.

Bergson, Henri.
Creative evolution. Trans. Arthur Mitchell. London: Macmillan, 1960.
The creative mind. Trans. Mabelle L. Andison. New York: Philosophical Library, 1946.
An introduction to metaphysics. Trans. T. E. Hulme. New York: Liberal Arts Press, 1949.
Matter and memory. Trans. Nancy Margaret Paul & W. Scott Palmer. London: George Allen & Unwin, 1950.
Time and free will: An essay on the immediate data of consciousness. Trans. F. L. Pogson. New York: Macmillan, 1959.

The two sources of morality and religion. Trans. R. Ashley Aubra & Cloudesley Brereton with the assistance of K. Horsfall Carter. New York·. Holt, 1935.

Binswanger, Ludwig.
Basic forms and knowledge of human existence(Grundformen und Erkenntnis Menschlichen Daseins). Munich: Ernst Reinhardt Verlag, 1962.
The case of Lola Voss. In *Being-in-the-world. Selected papers of Ludwig Binswanger.* Trans. Jacob Needleman. N~w York: Basic Books, 1963, pp. 266–341.
Extravagance. In *Being-in-the-world. Selected papers of Ludwig Binswanger.* Trans. Jacob Needleman. New York: Basic Books, 1963, pp. 342–349.
Freud and the magna charta of clinical psychiatry. In *Being-in-the-world. Selected papers of Ludwig Binswanger.* Trans. Jacob Needleman. New York: Basic Books, 1963, pp. 182–205.
Freud's conception of man in the light of anthropology. In *Being-in-the world. Selected papers of Ludwig Binswanger.* Trans. Jacob Needleman. New York: Basic Books, 1963, pp. 149–181.
Heidegger's analytic of existence and its meaning for psychiatry. In *Being-in-the-world. Selected papers of Ludwig Binswanger.* Trans. Jacob Needleman. New York: Basic Books, 1963, pp. 206–221.
Introduction to *schizophrenie.* In *Being-in-the-world. Selected papers of Ludwig Binswanger.* Trans. Jacob Needleman. New York: Basic Books, 1963, pp. 249–265.
Existential analysis and psychotherapy. In *Progress in psychotherapy,* vol. 1. Edited by Frieda Fromm-Reichmann and J. L. Moreno. New York: Grune & Stratton, 1956, pp. 144–148.
The existential analysis school of thought. In *Existence: A new dimension of psychiatry and psychology.* Edited by R. May, E. Angel & H. Ellenberger. New York: Basic Books, 1958, pp. 191–213.
Insanity as life-historical phenomenon and as mental disease: The case of Ilse. In *Existence: A new dimension of psychiatry and psychology.* Edited by R. May, E. Angel & H. Ellenberger. New York: Basic Books, 1958, pp. 214–236.
The case of Ellen West. In *Existence: A new dimension of psychiatry and psychology.* Edited by R. May, E. Angel & H. Ellenberger. New York: Basic Books, 1958, pp. 237–364.

Boss, Medard.
The analysis of dreams. Trans. Arnold J. Pomerans. New York: Philosophical Library, 1958.

Anxiety, guilt and psychotherapeutic liberation. *Review of existential psychology and psychiatry*, vol. 2, no. 3, pp. 173–195.

'Daseinsanalysis' and psychotherapy. In J. H. Masserman & J. L. Moreno (Eds.), *Progress in psychotherapy*, vol. 2. New York: Grune & Stratton, 1957, pp. 156–161.

The fundamentals of medicine (Grundress der Medizin). Berne: Hans Huber, 1970.

Psychoanalysis and daseinsanalysis. Trans. Ludwig B. Lefebre. New York: Basic Books, 1963.

The psychopathology of dreams in schizophrenia and organic psychoses. In M. DeMartino (Ed.), *Dreams and personality dynamics*. Springfield, Ill.: C. C. Thomas, 1959, pp. 156–175.

Buber, Martin.

Between man and man. Trans. Ronald Gregor Smith. New York: Macmillan, 1965.

Eclipse of god: Studies in the relation between religion and philosophy. Trans. Maurice Friedman et. al. New York: Harper Torchbooks, 1957.

Good and evil: Two interpretations. Trans. R. G. Smith and Michael Bullock. New York: Scribner's Paperback, 1961.

I and Thou. Trans. Ronald Gregor Smith. New York: Scribner's Paperbacks, 1958.

The knowledge of man: Selected essays. Trans. Maurice Friedman & Ronald Gregor Smith. New York: Harper Torchbooks, 1964.

Pointing the way. Trans. Maurice Friedman. New York: Harper Torchbooks, 1963.

Camus, Albert.

Carnets 1935–1942. Trans. Philip Herdy. London: Hamish Hamilton, 1963.

Carnets 1942–1951. Trans. Philip Herdy. London: Hamish Hamilton, 1966.

The myth of Sisyphus, and other essays. Trans. Justin O'Brien. New York: Vintage Books, 1960.

Neither victims nor executioners. Trans. Dwight Macdonald. Chicago: World Without War Publications, 1972.

The rebel: An essay on man in revolt. Trans. Anthony Bower. New York: Vintage Books, 1956.

Resistance, rebellion and death. Trans. Justin O'Brien. New York: Vintage Books, 1974.

Heidegger, Martin.
Being and time. Trans. John Macquarrie & Edward Robinson. New York: Harper & Row, 1962.
The essence of reasons. Trans. Terrence Malick. Evanston: Northwestern University Press, 1969.
Existence and being. Trans. D. Scott, R. Hall and A. Crick. Chicago: Gateway Books, 1960.
Identity and difference. Trans. Joan Stambaugh. New York: Harper & Row, 1969.
An introduction to metaphysics. Trans. Ralph Manheim. New York· Doubleday Anchor Books, 1961.
Kant and the problem of metaphysics. Trans. James S. Churchill. Bloomington, Ind.: Indiana University Press, 1962.

Jaspers, Karl.
General psychopathology. Trans. J. Hoenig & M. Hamilton. Chicago: University of Chicago Press, 1963.
Man in the modern age. Trans. Eden & Cedar Paul. New York: Doubleday Anchor Books, 1957.
The perennial scope of philosophy. Trans. Ralph Manheim. London: Routledge & Kegan Paul, 1950.
Philosophical faith and revelation. Trans. E. B. Ashton. New York: Harper & Row, 1967.
Reason and existenz: Five lectures. Trans. William Earle. New York: Noonday Paperbacks, 1957.
The way to wisdom. Trans. Ralph Manheim. New Haven: Yale University Press, 1967.

Kierkegaard, Sören.
The concept of dread. Trans. Walter Lowrie. Princeton: Princeton University Press, 1957.
Concluding unscientific postscript. Trans. David F. Swenson & Walter Lowrie. Princeton: Princeton University Press, 1963.
Either/Or. vol. 1. Trans. David F. Swenson & Lillian Marvin Swenson; vol. 2. Trans. Walter Lowrie. New York: Doubleday Anchor Books, 1959.
Fear and trembling; and *The sickness unto death.* Trans. Walter Lowrie. New York: Doubleday Anchor Books, 1954.
The journals of Kierkegaard. Trans. A. Dru. New York: Harper Torchbooks, 1959.
Sören Kierkegaard's journals and papers. vols. 1, 2 & 3. Trans. H. Hong & E. Hong. Bloomington, Ind.: Indiana University Press, 1967–1975.

The point of view for my work as an author: A report to history. Trans. Walter Lowrie. New York: Harper Torchbooks, 1962.
Repetition: An essay in experimental psychology. Trans. Walter Lowrie. New York: Harper Torchbooks, 1964.
Stages on life's way. Trans. Walter Lowrie. New York: Schocken Books, 1967.

Marcel, Gabriel.
Being and having: An existentialist diary. Trans. Katharine Farrer. New York: Harper Torchbooks, 1965.
Creative fidelity. Trans. Robert Rosthal. New York: Farrar, Straus, 1964.
Faith and reality. Trans. René Hague. vol. 2 of *The mystery of being.* Chicago: Gateway Editions, 1960.
Metaphysical journal. Trans. Bernard Wall. Chicago: Gateway Editions, 1967.
The philosophy of existentialism. Trans. Manya Harari. New York: Citadel Press, 1961.
Reflection and mystery. Trans. G. S. Fraser. vol. 1 of *The mystery of being.* Chicago: Gateway Editions, 1960.

Merleau-Ponty, Maurice.
Phenomenology of perception. Trans. Colin Smith. New York: Humanities Press, 1962.
The primacy of perception. Trans. Arleen B. Dallery *et. al.* Evanston: Northwestern University Press, 1964.
Sense and non-sense. Trans. Hubert & Patricia Drefus. Evantson: Northwestern University Press, 1964.
Signs. Trans. Richard C. McCleary. Evanston: Northwestern University Press, 1964.
The structure of behavior. Trans. Alden L. Fisher. Boston: Beacon Press, 1963.
The visible and the invisible. Trans. Alphonso Lingis. Evanston: Northwestern University Press, 1969.

Sartre, Jean-Paul.
The age of reason. Trans. Eric Sutton. New York: Vintage Books, 1972.
Being and nothingness: An essay on phenomenological ontology. Trans. Hazel E. Barnes. New York: Washington Square Press, 1972.
The emotions: Outline of a theory. Trans. B. Frechtman. New York: Citadel Press, 1971. Outline
Existentialism and humanism. Trans. Philip Mairet. London: Methuen, 1963.

Existential psychoanalysis. Trans. Hazel E. Barnes. Chicago: Gateway Editions, 1962.

Imagination: A psychological critique. Trans. Forrest Williams. Ann Arbor: University of Michigan Press, 1972.

Search for a method. Trans. Hazel E. Barnes. New York: Vintage Books, 1968.

The transcendence of the ego: An existentialist theory of consciousness. Trans. Forrest Williams & Robert Kirkpatrick. New York: Octagon Books, 1972.

INDEX